MANAGING RESEARCH

Managing Universities and Colleges: Guides to Good Practice

Series editors:

David Warner, Principal and Chief Executive, Swansea Institute of Higher Education

David Palfreyman, Bursar and Fellow, New College, Oxford

This series has been commissioned in order to provide systematic analysis of the major areas of the management of colleges and universities, emphasizing good practice.

Current titles:
Frank Albrighton and Julia Thomas (eds): *Managing External Relations*
Allan Bolton: *Managing the Academic Unit*
Ann Edworthy: *Managing Stress*
Judith Elkin and Derek Law (eds): *Managing Information*
John M. Gledhill: *Managing Students*
Christine Humfrey: *Managing International Students*
Colleen Liston: *Managing Quality and Standards*
Patricia Partington and Caroline Stainton: *Managing Staff Development*
Harold Thomas: *Managing Financial Resources*
David Watson: *Managing Strategy*

MANAGING RESEARCH

Robert W. Bushaway

Open University Press
Maidenhead · Philadelphia

Open University Press
McGraw-Hill Education
McGraw-Hill House
Shoppenhangers Road
Maidenhead
Berkshire
England
SL6 2QL

email: enquiries@openup.co.uk
world wide web: www.openup.co.uk

and
325 Chestnut Street
Philadelphia, PA 190106, USA

First Published 2003

A catalogue record of this book is available from the British Library

ISBN 0 335 20859 2 (pb)   0 335 20860 6 (hb)

Library of Congress Cataloging-in-Publication Data

Bushaway, Robert W., 1952–
    Managing research/Robert W. Bushaway.
        p. cm. – (Managing universities and colleges)
    Includes bibliographical references and index.
    ISBN 0–335–20860–6 (hb) 0–335–20859–2 (pb)
    I. Research – Management – Great Britain. I. Title. II. Series.
    Q180.55.M3 B88 2003
    378′.00,7′2–dc21   2002035469

Typeset by RefineCatch Limited, Bungay, Suffolk
Printed in Great Britain by Bell and Bain Ltd, Glasgow

CONTENTS

SERIES EDITORS' INTRODUCTION

Post-secondary educational institutions can be viewed from a variety of different perspectives. For most of the students and staff who work in them they are centres of learning and teaching in which the participants are there by choice and consequently, by and large, work very hard. Research has always been important in some higher education institutions, but in recent years this emphasis has grown, and what for many was a great pleasure and, indeed, a treat, is becoming more of a threat and an insatiable performance indicator, which just has to be met. Maintaining the correct balance between quality research and learning/teaching, while the unit of resource, at best, holds steady, is one of the key issues facing us all. Educational institutions as work places must be positive and not negative environments.

From another aspect, post-secondary educational institutions are clearly communities, functioning to all intents and purposes like small towns and internally requiring and providing a similar range of services, while also having very specialist needs. From yet another, they are seen as external suppliers of services to industry, commerce and the professions. These 'customers' receive, *inter alia*: a continuing flow of well qualified, fresh graduates with transferable skills; part-time and short course study opportunities through which to develop existing employees; consultancy services to solve problems and help expand business; and research and development support to create new breakthroughs. It is an unwise UK educational institution which ignores this aspect, which is now given a very high priority by the UK Government.

However, educational institutions are also significant businesses in their own right. One recent study shows that higher education institutions alone are worth £35 billion a year to the UK economy.

Moreover, they create more than 562,000 full-time equivalent jobs either through direct employment or 'knock-on' effects. This is equivalent to 2.7% of the UK workforce. In addition, it has recently been realized that UK higher education is a major export industry with the added benefit of long-term financial and political returns. If the UK further education sector is also added to this equation, then the economic impact of post-secondary education is of truly startling proportions.

Whatever perspective you take, it is obvious that educational institutions require managing and, consequently, this series has been produced to facilitate that end. The editors have striven to identify authors who are distinguished practitioners in their own right and, indeed, can also write. The authors have been given the challenge of producing essentially practical handbooks, which combine appropriate theory and contextual material with many examples of good practice and guidance.

The topics chosen are of key importance to educational management and stand at the forefront of current debate. Some of these topics have never been covered in depth before and all of them are equally applicable to further as well as higher education. The editors are firmly of the belief that the UK distinction between these sectors will continue to blur and will be replaced, as in many other countries, by a continuum where the management issues are entirely common.

Since the mid-1980s, both of the editors have been involved with a management development programme for senior staff from HEIs throughout the world. Every year the participants quickly learn that we share the same problems and that similar solutions are normally applicable. Political and cultural differences may on occasion be important, but are often no more than an overlying veneer. Hence, this series will be of considerable relevance and value to post-secondary educational managers in many countries.

As mentioned earlier, the role of research in higher education has changed a lot over the last decade and a half. It is now the single most important aspect of academic life for almost everyone. Most universities in the UK crave membership of the elite Russell Group which is defined solely by research success. And even within this Group, there appears to be two categories of membership emerging. The crème de la crème live up to the soubriquet and cream off more and more of the state-derived research funds (and inevitably others), thereby leaving less and less for the rest.

At the individual level, tales of headhunting and transfer fees have proved to be not only true, but also commonplace. The series editors await with interest the next urban myth of a return to pressgangs and kidnapping. Promotion in 'old' universities is completely dependent upon research output and even those educational institutions which claim to be teaching-led, in truth, often weight research far more highly than their missions would lead the reader to expect. However, despite the occasional whinge from those whose self-assessment does not sit happily with that of their peers, the UK Research Assessment Exercise is generally reckoned to be as fair a procedure as can be achieved in an imperfect world. Consequently, many have come to understand what philosophers have known for a long time – that fair shares are not necessarily (indeed, rarely are) equal shares.

It is within this context that *Managing Research* has arrived as a comprehensive and exhaustive handbook. The series editors were so impressed by the sheer weight (literally) of the text that they implored the publishers not to demand cuts, and to risk a profit reduction by printing an over-long book rather than lose a single section. No one will be surprised that Bob Bushaway works at a Russell Group university. But it is still a little unexpected to find an author who is prepared to give so generously from 25 years of hard-earned and very successful experience. The result is a work which tempts the description 'definitive'.

PREFACE

It was with great pleasure that I accepted the invitation to write this book as a contribution to the Open University Press series on Managing Universities and Colleges, as it represents the distillation of my experience working in the sector over the past 25 years or so. When I first took up an appointment as a university administrator, one of my duties was to log research grant applications from the university's scientists and engineers in a log book and record later whether they were successful or unsuccessful. Successful grant awards were later registered against the individual principal investigator or, on rarer occasions, against a group of researchers. Apart from the financial administration associated with the resulting research grant, little else from the management viewpoint was required. If there was any intellectual property arising from the research, it was taken up by the national monopoly agency set up to exploit university commercial ideas, and if there were academic publications associated with the research, these appeared with due acknowledgements and were duly listed in the university's annual research and publications report. If contract research staff were appointed to the research grant, their names appeared with that of the principal investigator on the record for the research grant. It was a relatively simple world in which of those UK universities which pursued research to any significant degree the same group of 20 or so earned about 80 per cent of the resources for research, whether from public sources or the private sector.

It was largely a paper world in which research grants were administered and research projects performed on the basis of paper reports and balance sheets, typed without the aid of word processing and printed without laser printers. Communication took place by telephone or post and, although university research was genuinely international, it did not take place in a world of 24/7 electronic availability – an environment I have styled 'e-search'.

Since then, there has been a revolution in university-based research both in volume and in quality. Knowledge produced by research now creates the competitive advantage of national economies and our lives have been transformed by its fruits. National policy has massively increased research opportunities but at the same time has led to the increasing complexity and reorganization which an over-emphasis on 'initiatives' has produced. Public scrutiny and account-ability are obligatory through national assessments unimagined in earlier times. I was, indeed, engaged in coordinating the preparation of the University of Birmingham's Research Assessment Exercise for 2001 when I was approached to write this guide.

Most universities now seek to provide a range of services in support of research and to manage research as a 'core business' essential for their economic and intellectual survival. This guide aims to help university managers at every level in the task of creating an environment in which research will flourish. Corporate planners, senior officers, research managers, administrators, offices of research and enterprise services and chief executives of university companies, together with academic researchers themselves, should find the guide helpful in their day-to-day management of research in universities.

I could not have written this book without drawing on the input and support of all those with whom I have worked since becoming Director of Research Support in 1989 and with my present colleagues. It has been a pleasure and a privilege to have worked with some of the most eminent researchers in the UK over the years and, on occasion, I hope I and my colleagues have made some small contribution to their academic successes. I should like to thank in particular my friend and colleague Dr Pam Waddell who, as deputy director of Research and Enterprise Services, has helped me to create a professional support service for research at the University of Birmingham. Much of what follows could not have been written without the input and help of all my colleagues both past and present. Any errors, mistakes or misjudgements which appear are, of course, mine alone. I should also like to thank Meryl Haynes who, notwithstanding the benefits of modern technology, still had to make sense of a scrappy manuscript as unclear as some extinct text from a lost civilization.

R. W. Bushaway
Birmingham

LIST OF FIGURES AND TABLES

INTRODUCTION

A cursory exploration of the internet using the search phrase 'research management' reveals how extensive is the global knowledge industry and how much of that industry lies outside the world of higher education and beyond the UK. Research, it is soon revealed, is carried on worldwide by a variety of organizations, including:

- research and technology transfer companies;
- consultancy companies;
- learned societies and professional associations;
- research finance and investment services;
- clinical trials businesses;
- charitable trusts and foundations;
- private or industry-based research centres, research institutes or contract research organizations;
- independent research associations or sector-based and industry-sponsored research facilities within affiliated technology organizations;
- research parks and science centres;
- government laboratories or research agencies for both civil and defence purposes;
- research networks, regional groups and consortia and virtual research or e-search centres;
- research management specialists;
- providers of research databases, research resources, patent and intellectual property services, and test and analysis facilities for research.

One search alone produced 951 principal websites and 13 website categories.

It was not always so complicated. In the past, knowledge was advanced and disseminated by empirical means. People observed phenomena or experimented in practical ways. Knowledge was accrued, sometimes lost to be rediscovered, sometimes stored for later perusal, but mostly applied in the daily experiences of life. The management of research, as a process, has been transformed during the same period.

The aim of *Managing Research* is to provide practical help and guidance to researchers, research directors and heads of department, research managers, administrators, senior management, research support professionals and other university staff with responsibility for research in universities at the strategic or operational levels. As a compendium of information, the work is based on more than a dozen years' experience of leading a Research and Enterprise Services office in a major UK research-led university. Research is a longstanding and well-recognized function of most universities and, in one sense, the challenges encountered by university-based researchers, whether general or specific, have not changed greatly over time. But, as the context of university-based research, its funding and management, have rapidly developed in complexity since the Second World War such that, in another sense, university research has altered dramatically. It is an appropriate moment to reflect upon the management of university-based research. *Managing Research* aims to make a contribution to the developing dialogue between researchers and policy-makers and between research producers and their stakeholders.

The study is timely as higher education faces the paradox of rising public anxiety and concern in science yet declining public understanding and awareness of science, and of increasing demands for scrutiny alongside decreasing take-up of places to pursue scientific careers. Knowledge is a global commodity yet an essential ingredient for national economic prosperity and well-being. Research in higher education is in the spotlight and *Managing Research* provides illustrations on how universities are responding to this challenge.

Separate sections deal with the research context, postgraduate research, external research funding in the form of grants and contracts, managing research, supporting research and a range of perspectives on research by those engaged.

Sir Ron Dearing suggested in the UK report into higher education which bears his name that there were four main roles for research and reasons for supporting it in universities:

- To add to the sum of human knowledge and understanding.
- To inform and enhance teaching.

- To generate useful knowledge and inventions in support of wealth creation and an improved quality of life.
- To create an environment in which researchers can be encouraged and given a high level of training.

It is hoped that *Managing Research* might make a modest contribution to the encouragement of university researchers because, when all the policy-making and operational procedure-setting is done, it is the generation of original research ideas by enthusiastic and committed individuals and groups in universities which is the key to successful research. All else is peripheral.

1

THE RESEARCH CONTEXT

1.1 Background

In the past, repositories of knowledge were few – the church, the monastery, the university, a few elite libraries or collections usually sponsored by royal or noble patronage. Before the sixteenth-century printing revolution in the West, knowledge was protected by secrecy and transmitted by initiation or through learning by doing in the form of the medieval guilds and the apprenticeship system. In the seventeenth century came the so-called Scientific Revolution. The process by which knowledge was accrued accelerated across Europe through new technologies and new institutions and organizations. In England, the Royal Society was founded in 1660 as a national academy for science. Research, undertaken by individuals working mainly in universities or in private capacities, characterized the world in new and systematic ways. Few, if any, of these individuals would have regarded themselves as being managed in any way except, perhaps, through the availability of resources and the extent of their personal curiosity.

The term 'research' in English was first used in the context of a managed process of systematic investigation or enquiry during the sixteenth century. Research, driven by intellectual curiosity, had a moral purpose for thinkers such as Francis Bacon, who wrote in the *Advancement of Learning*: 'For all knowledge and wonder (which is the seed of knowledge) is an impression of pleasure in itself.' He concluded that: 'The true and lawful goal of the sciences is none other than this, that human life be endowed with new inventions and powers.' (Bacon, *Works* iv 79, quoted in Hill 1972: 88). Other contemporary usages included related terms such as 'innovation' and 'discovery' as the outcomes of a fundamental process of enquiry.

When the Royal Society of London for the Improving of Natural Knowledge (to give the Royal Society its full title) was founded in 1660 and was granted its Royal Charter two years later by Charles II as one of the first scientific societies in the world, it was recognized that research, or rather knowledge produced by the process of scientific enquiry, had implications for both the well-being of the national economy and for national security. John Evelyn, the Society's first secretary and one of its founders, recognized Britain's strategic requirement for knowledge and the important role of applying knowledge to the means of creating wealth, through agriculture, manufacture, engineering and commerce. These imperatives were not new and can be identified in earlier epochs such as those of Greece and Rome when knowledge was applied to the problems of navigation, construction, military engineering, health, human relations and society as a whole.

The 'professionalization' of knowledge as a process accelerated in the mid-nineteenth century, symbolized by two events in Britain. First, the Great Exhibition took place in 1851, demonstrating to the world the link between knowledge through research and its application for the generation of wealth. Second, in the previous year, the Royal Society received a grant from the British government of £1000 to assist scientific research directly. Until then, the funding of science had been regarded as a private venture, albeit with strategic implications for the state, as can be illustrated by the founding of the Royal Institution of Great Britain in 1799 by Sir Benjamin Thomson, Count Rumford, with Sir Joseph Banks for the dissemination of scientific knowledge. Further national scientific centres followed with the founding of the Imperial Institute in 1887 (Queen Victoria's golden jubilee year), the National Physical Laboratory in 1902 and the Imperial College of Science and Technology in 1909.

That the generation of new knowledge might result in intellectual property with a commercial value was also an old idea but it was the grant of letters patent which conferred upon the individual the exclusive right to protect and exploit an invention for a fixed period of time, in effect creating a monopoly use, which first defined in English law the principles of intellectual property rights (IPR).

Britain has one of the longest continuous histories of patent protection, with Royal letters patent dating back to the reign of Henry VII in the sixteenth century. The development of patent law became an attempt to find an appropriate balance between the public interest in preventing abuses of monopoly and the rights of the individual inventors to enjoy the commercial benefits from their inventions. Reformed in the nineteenth century, the UK Patent Office came into being in 1883.

The test of patentability remains crucial. To be successful, the patent application must demonstrate that the invention is:

- novel;
- represents an inventive advance;
- applicable (usually in the form of a device);
- not subject to exclusion;
- not a novel method or scientific 'know how', nor an aesthetic artistic creation, data nor computer software.

It was Francis Bacon who had first stated that knowledge was power: '*Nam et ipsa scientia potestas est*'. Patent protection meant, furthermore, that knowledge could turn power into wealth both for individuals and for nations. Britain's experience of industrialization in the eighteenth century arose from the combination of the advancement of knowledge and its successful application in manufacture, commerce and industry, leading to both power and wealth for the individual and the state. Embodied, for example, in the pioneers of the Lunar Society in Birmingham in the late eighteenth century, scientific knowledge was mixed directly with business acumen to produce the world's first Industrial Revolution.

In the twentieth century in Britain, especially during the First and Second World Wars, scientific knowledge was shown to lead to new discoveries on which national security and, indeed, the defence of sovereignty was dependent, requiring the full protection of the state itself in the form of the Official Secrets Act (1911). Postwar Britain witnessed, as did most of the nations which emerged from the turmoil of global war in 1945, the creation of new government institutions to develop national research strategy and the policies to encourage its growth. A process which had originated during the second half of the nineteenth century in Britain, after various national enquiries, continued during and after the First World War, and accelerated in the 1940s, 1950s and 1960s when the 'white heat of technology' forged the new postwar world in the West and in the Soviet-controlled East alike.

In Britain, the Department of Scientific and Industrial Research had been formed in 1916 during the dark days of the Great War when the UK's strategic weakness in specific areas of science was first detected. Research, it was discovered with alarm, needed to be fostered in the interests of both national prosperity and, from 1964 onwards through the newly created Ministry of Defence, for reasons of national security. Research controlled and funded by the state was made available to both government institutions and universities alike. Industrial espionage had long been practised by those seeking commercial advantage but, with the atomic age and the Cold War, the fruits of scientific research also became the potential seeds of global destruction.

Since the end of the Cold War in 1992, swords have been turned into plough shares and most nations have made considerable efforts to convert their inventiveness in defence research to commercial advantage and advanced research is now regarded worldwide as one of the major drivers for economic growth. The 'knowledge-based economy' governs national economic performance and the positions in the economic league tables of world prosperity, as well as individual wealth and productivity, by defining the ability to participate in the new economy and the extent of commercial competitiveness in companies.

Governments subject their decisions on public funding of science research to review and scrutiny from the viewpoints of both the appropriateness of expenditure and its general functions. In the UK, this process takes the form of *The Forward Look* of government-funded science, engineering and technology (SET).

The Forward Look (OST 2001b: 140) reiterates the function of government SET funding in the UK in the following terms:

> It is useful to know why R&D is being funded by the public sector. This is known as the primary purpose (pp). For SET funded by Government the primary purposes are:
>
> * ppA   General support for research –
>   all basic and applied R&D which advances knowledge plus support for postgraduate studentships.
> * ppB   Government services –
>   R&D relevant to any aspect of government service provision (all defence included here).
> * ppC   Policy support –
>   R&D which Government funds to inform policy (excluding ppB and ppD) and for monitoring developments of significance for the welfare of the population.
> * ppD   Technology support –
>   Applied R&D that advances technology underpinning the UK economy (excluding defence). The category includes strategic as well as applied research under schemes such as LINK.
> * ppE   Technology –
>   Transfer activities that encourage the exploitation of knowledge in a different place to its origin.

- ppF   Taught course awards –
  Industry awards for Masters Degrees but not for PhDs, which are included in ppA. Restructuring and redundancy costs are no longer included here.

R&D relates to ppA – ppD, while ppE and ppF cover those non-R&D activities which are included in SET. It should be noted that these boundaries are determined by the Government's primary purpose in funding the activity and not by the intentions of the researcher.

Universities are interested in all of these primary purposes and participate in delivering them either through grant-funded research projects or research contracts or through other forms of knowledge transfer such as consultancy and commercialization.

Only ppA concerns the funding of the advancement of knowledge for its own sake. Governments are not generally interested in the intrinsic value of research in universities except in so far as it either directly or indirectly delivers its primary purposes. It is important, however, to recognize that fundamental or generic research under-pins all applied research and that the latter cannot be pursued in a vacuum.

Figure 1.1 gives the amount and percentages for the UK govern-ment's spending on scientific research for 1998/99. Notwithstanding the ending of the Cold War in 1992, it is notable that one-third of the total national expenditure continues to be dedicated to defence research, which remains the largest single element of public expenditure on SET.

In the UK, government presides over a form of public resource allo-cation known as the dual support system. One stream of funding is intended to underpin university-based research through selective distribution by the funding councils' in the form of a formula-driven allocation model which takes account of research excellence. Other funding is 'won' by universities from the research councils for specific projects in a competitive bidding process of individual grant application assessed by peer review in which direct costs and a percentage figure for indirect costs are granted in each award. In addition, universities bid to a variety of other sponsors (including other government departments) for grants and contracts which fund research.

It should be noted that one-quarter of government SET expenditure in 1998/99 was accounted for by that funding which is allocated in the UK largely through the national system of research councils under the aegis of the Office of Science and Technology (OST), itself a part of the Department of Trade and Industry. The UK research councils

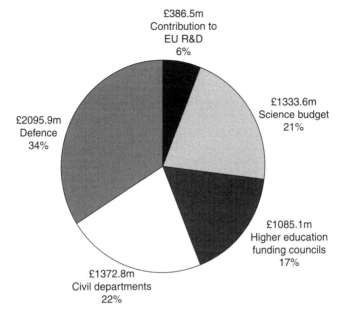

Figure 1.1   UK government-funded SET, 1998/99

are independent, non-government public bodies headed by a part-time chair drawn from the so-called user community and a full-time chief executive. Their policies and strategies are set out in the government's annual *The Forward Look* – the regular process of audit and review now carried out by the Minister for Science within the Department of Trade and Industry.

In the UK there are six research councils and a body responsible for funding research in arts and the humanities:

- Biotechnology and Biological Sciences Research Council (BBSRC)
- Economic and Social Research Council (ESRC)
- Engineering and Physical Sciences Research Council (EPSRC)
- Medical Research Council (MRC)
- Natural Environment Research Council (NERC)
- Particle Physics and Astronomy Research Council (PPARC)
- Arts and Humanities Research Board (AHRB)

The funds which the research councils expend are sometimes referred to as the 'science vote' and are largely allocated in the form of research grants to UK universities or to dedicated research council research institutions, laboratories and other facilities. The guiding principle in the UK is that government does not directly allocate funds for research but holds itself at arm's length. This is the so-called Haldane principle which requires decisions to be made, not at governmental whim, but by the scientific community, through peer review, and to the 'users' or 'beneficiaries' of scientific output who make up, in representative numbers, the policy-making and grant-awarding pools of expertise which oversee both the allocation of funds and their scrutiny. Ultimate responsibility lies with the director-general for the research councils. This structure, having its origins during the period of the Department of Scientific and Industrial Research (founded in 1916), was formalized following the UK government's major review of science in 1992 which produced the White Paper *Realising our Potential* (OST 1993). The review identified the twin imperatives for the public funding of scientific research as:

- wealth creation through economic growth; and
- improvement to the quality of life.

At the same time, discernible throughout the developed world are two noticeable trends:

- continuing audit and public scrutiny to ensure cost-effectiveness and value for money; and
- growing public interest in and government requirement for risk accountability assessment.

The UK government set up a major science network to ascertain general trends in research and the identification of future growth in world markets called Foresight. Other nations, notably Japan, had been taking advantage of a similar process for a long time. Alongside the government's annual *The Forward Look*, a comprehensive picture of the UK's science strategy was provided and a rationale for the allocation of public funds to research through the science vote and the expenditure of government departments on scientific research was given.

The move of the Office of Science and Technology to the Department of Trade and Industry in 1995 underlined the link in Britain between public expenditure on research and the importance of wealth generation, the goal being to secure competitive advantage for the UK economy by building world-class scientific knowledge and new technologies.

These arrangements are mirrored in most developed countries and follow broadly a similar pattern whereby national governments

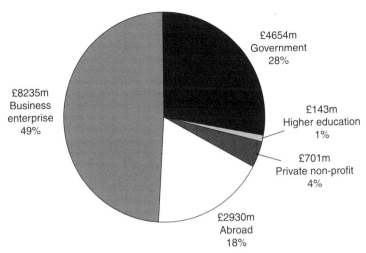

Figure 1.2   UK flow of funds for R&D – funders, 1999
Source: Office of Science and Technology (www.dti.gov.uk/ost/set-stats/fittab.htm)

decide to invest public money for the advancement of knowledge for two principal reasons:

- the creation and sustainability of national economic prosperity; and
- the well-being and quality of life of the nation's citizens.

The European Union also funds a major programme of scientific research – the Framework programme – for similar purposes, aiming to establish European competitive advantage and a specific European scientific capability.

In the individual countries of Europe, North America, Australia, New Zealand and much of the Far East, governments fund scientific research not for its intrinsic value but because it underpins society and national enterprise. However, it is not only government which funds the advancement of knowledge. Figures 1.2 and 1.3 give the flow of funds for UK R&D in 1999. As can be seen, by far the largest element of funding is provided by business enterprise (over £8.2 billion in 1999).

Not only does industry and business enterprise fund the largest proportion of research but the private sector also carries out the largest proportion of research (£11.3 billion in the UK in 1999). Industry exceeds government in the amount of research it carries out

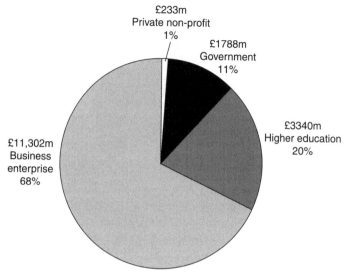

Figure 1.3 UK flow of funds for R&D – performers, 1999
Source: Office of Science and Technology (www.dti.gov.uk/ost/set-stats/polytab.htm)

in the UK. It is to be noted that higher education undertook the next largest proportion of research (£3.3 billion in 1999) whereas higher education funded directly only £143 million in the same period.

The private sector invests in its own R&D independently and collaboratively with others or through sector-based industrial research organizations, in order to develop the products and processes which support its business. Industry also has an interest in the public funding of science not only as a payer of corporate tax but also as a potential user and beneficiary of the outcomes of publicly funded scientific research, both fundamental and applied. This interest manifests itself not only through participation with government-funded research partnership schemes, which are usually pre-competitive and generic in nature, but also in involvement with policy-making through representation on public funding bodies for research, participation in consultations and reviews, partnership with research grant holders through advisory boards, and other means such as university-based industry clubs or contracts with universities.

The goal is profitability, and sectors vary in the extent of their investment in R&D. Some UK industrial sectors, such as the pharmaceutical and the aerospace industries, have a long history of involvement in research because it has been, and remains, the seed-bed of new products and processes ensuring company commercial viability and future competitive advantage. Other sectors attach less importance to R&D, preferring to 'buy in' knowledge as necessary or before it becomes too late. Industry has outsourced research for many years, and the trend in the 1980s and 1990s has been to discontinue in house R&D in many businesses under the pressure of cost-cutting for efficiency. Research has always been a difficult asset to value in the company accounts and has been equally problematic to justify in expenditure terms in the harsh environment of global competition, especially since it appeared that some national economies, like the 'Tiger' economies of the Pacific region, had successfully piggy-backed on the world's scientific advances without investing significantly in their attainment. From the perspective of the third millennium, this assessment seems less accurate, and investment in the advancement of knowledge by the state appears to be a global phenomenon. Investment, expressed as a percentage of gross domestic product (GDP) would appear to be increasing. In the United States, R&D as a percentage of GDP has risen from 2.49 per cent in 1993 to 2.63 per cent in 1999, and has increased in each of the previous years. While federal support for R&D has fallen from 0.91 per cent to 0.73 per cent in the same period, non-federal support has risen from 1.58 per cent to 1.9 per cent (see Table 1.1).

Competing in the global economy has become and will remain, in part, a matter of competing in the informed investment of public funds in the advancement of knowledge. One of the recent UK government statements on the subject *Our Competitive Future – Building the Knowledge Driven Economy* (DTI 1999), places primary importance on the role of science and technological knowledge in driving forward the nation's capacity for innovation and enterprise. In the 1980s, concern was expressed about the importance of identifying market need so that the market could identify technological requirements – market pull would drive the national economy, not technology push whereby scientific and technological advances were promoted without markets identified beforehand in which to exploit them – lava lamps and hovercraft, supersonic civil aircraft, and even nuclear power, were highlighted as examples of technology push rather than market pull, while science had not predicted the widespread consumer appetite for mobile phones, individual and family computing and personal stereo.

At the beginning of the twenty-first century, perspective has changed. The economic miracle of high-tech consumer goods and internet-based services seems to have faltered, yet national interest in the advancement of knowledge continues to grow. Two UK

Table 1.1 GDP and R&D (federally funded, non-federal and total): comparative measures of growth, 1993–99

Calendar year	GDP			R&D				R&D as a percentage of GDP		
	GDP in billions of current dollars	GDP implicit price deflator (1996=1.00)	GDP in billions of constant 1992 dollars	R&D in millions of current dollars	R&D in millions of constant 1996 dollars	Federal support for R&D in millions of constant 1996 dollars	Non-federal support for R&D in millions of constant 1996 dollars	R&D as a percentage of GDP	Federal support for R&D as a percentage of GDP	Non-federal support for R&D as a percentage of GDP
Data column	[169]	[170]	[171]	[1]	[19]	[40]	[172]	[173]	[174]	[175]
1993	6,642	0.9405	7,063	165,714	176,198	64,343	111,855	2.49	0.91	1.58
1994	7,054	0.9601	7,348	169,214	176,246	63,316	112,930	2.4	0.86	1.54
1995	7,401	0.981	7,544	183,611	187,167	64,180	122,987	2.48	0.85	1.63
1996	7,813	1	7,813	197,330	197,330	63,392	133,938	2.53	0.81	1.71
1997	8,318	1.0195	8,160	212,379	208,316	63,544	144,773	2.55	0.78	1.77
1998	8,790	1.0322	8,516	226,872	219,794	64,743	155,051	2.58	0.76	1.82
1999	9,299	1.0477	8,876	244,143	233,027	64,628	168,399	2.63	0.73	1.9

Sources: Department of Commerce, Bureau of Economic Analysis; Office of Management and Budget; and National Science Foundation/Division of Science Resources Studies tabulations (www.nsf/gov/sbe/srs/nsf01309/tables/tab5.xls)

government statements of July 2000 indicate continuing commitment to the future:

- the science and innovation White Paper *Excellence and Opportunity
  – A Science and Innovation Policy for the 21st Century* (OST 2000)
  and
- the enterprise, skills and innovation White Paper *Opportunity for
  All in a World of Change* (DfES 2000).

The messages for national governments are urgent. Nations lose out
in the global economy if they fail to harness the power of the knowledge-driven economy, and sections of their populations will be dis-
advantaged if they are excluded from the learning skills necessary
to participate in the new technology-based world of work. The thrust
of UK government policy is, therefore, to be strategic in its approach
to investment in the knowledge-base in universities which has
been undertaken through injecting new capital funds into the
refurbishment and re-equipment of the research infrastructure and to
encourage inclusiveness in the new skills and learning agenda which
has emerged.

In the 1940s and 1950s, it was the 'rise of the boffin' in defence
of national security which characterized the contribution of higher
education to the national project. Now it is the 'white-coated entre-
preneur' bringing the fruits of research to the marketplace which
is seen as the most valuable contribution for universities to make to
national well-being. In fact, the aim of university-based research has
not changed as far as most of its practitioners are concerned. The
pursuit of knowledge is a legitimate goal in its own right and the
values of academic freedom and scientific objectivity are to be
cherished by the universities.

As Francis Bacon put it: '[Knowledge is not] the couch, whereupon
to rest a searching and restless spirit; or a terrace, for a wondering and
variable mind to walk up and down with a fair prospect; or a tower of
state for a proud mind to raise itself upon; or a fort or commanding
ground, for strife and contention; or a shop for profit and sale.' The
ideas of pursuing fundamental research as an academic freedom
while at the same time recognizing entrepreneurial advantages are
not mutually exclusive in the work of an individual researcher,
research group or university in a complementary and synergistic way.
He concluded that knowledge was 'a rich storehouse, for the glory of
the creator, and the relief of man's estate . . . for the benefit and use
of life.' (Hill 1972: 94).

In 1998, in an influential report, the Organization for Economic
Cooperation and Development (OECD 1998) stated that university

research was changing, was in danger of falling into the hands of those who controlled the funds, and that the following trends were discernible:

- Government finance for research and development was declining and becoming more competitive.
- Government finance for research and development was increasingly mission orientated and contract based.
- Private industry finance for research in universities was increasing.
- There was pressure for increased economic relevance in university research.
- University research was increasingly based on cooperation and collaboration.
- University research was globalizing.
- University research was recognized as essential to the knowledge-driven economy.

The way ahead is clear. Smart companies, smart nations and smart employees will only survive in the global marketplace by producing even smarter products and processes, smarter economies and smarter skills. The way ahead is equally clear for universities as the OECD report concluded: to move away from an emphasis on generic and basic research in the pursuit of relevance in order to secure short-term and, perhaps, short-lived research contract funding would be a risky business. In fact, there is little sign in the UK that this has happened.

Figure 1.4 indicates the sources of funding for research and development in UK universities in 1998/99. Taking together grants and contracts from the UK research councils (Office of Science and Technology) and funding from the higher education funding councils, 59 per cent of funding comes from what might be termed discretionary sources, that is where the research to be undertaken is proposed by the scientific community itself. Only 7 per cent was funded by UK industry, with a further 10 per cent by government departments on a contract basis.

While it is accurate to observe that UK university research funding profiles vary enormously, to compare national figures with a representative 'civic' university, the University of Birmingham, it is evident that the pattern is similar, with 11 per cent of research funding being secured from industry. Figure 1.5 excludes the funding for research which the University receives from the Higher Education Funding Council for England (HEFCE) and, together with the total for research council grants and contracts, it exceeds 50 per cent.

Universities may be hungry to finance research, as the difference between research undertaken and research potential in Figures 1.2 and 1.3 indicate, but the rush to increase the percentage of research

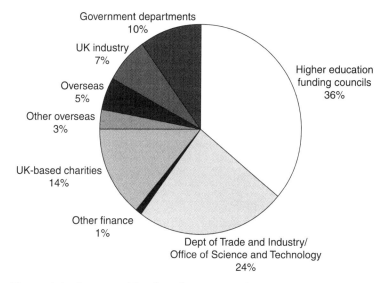

Figure 1.4 Sources of funding from research contracts in UK universities, 1998/99
Source: Higher Education Statistics Agency 1998/99 (HESA 2000)

directly funded by industry and the private sector has yet to manifest itself in the UK. Loss of the universities' autonomy, in respect of research, does not yet seem to be threatened, notwithstanding widely reported news to the contrary and some well-publicized examples of single instances.

1.2 Some definitions

So far, reference has been made to 'research', 'research and development (R&D)', 'science engineering and technology (SET)', 'advancement of knowledge', without there being a clear definition for the term 'research'. The one usually employed is the OECD Frascati definition:

> *Basic Research* is experimental or theoretical work undertaken primarily to acquire new knowledge of the underlying foundation of phenomena and observable facts, without any particular application or use in view.
> *Strategic Research* is work that has evolved from basic research and where practical applications are likely and feasible but cannot yet

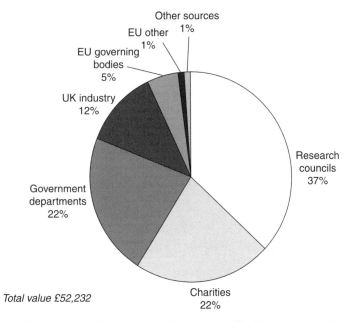

Figure 1.5 University of Birmingham externally funded research grants and contracts, 1998/99
Source: University of Birmingham Annual Finance Accounts

be specified, or where a culmination of underlying technological know-how will serve many diverse purposes (the latter is also known as *generic research*).
Applied Research is also original investigation undertaken in order to acquire new knowledge. It is, however, directed primarily towards practical aims or objectives.

The Frascati definition is used by the UK Office of Science and Technology and informs the annual *The Forward Look* of government-funded science, engineering and technology.
More generally, research in universities might also be deemed to include the following:

- Scholarship – a term introduced by Sir Ron Dearing in his report on higher education (Dearing 1997) and coupled with research.
- Applied knowledge – the use of existing knowledge in experimental development to produce new or substantially improved materials, devices, products and processes, including design and construction.

- Work of direct relevance to the needs of commerce and industry, the public sector and others, where the principles of enquiry and investigation leading to original findings occur sometimes in the form of contract research or knowledge-based consultancy.
- Invention, innovation and implementation of knowledge towards the generation of ideas, images, performances, studies, artefacts, including designs and software which then lead to new or improved insights.

It is fair to exclude from the definition of research in universities:

- Routine testing and analysis of materials, components and processes (as distinct from the development of new analytical techniques themselves).
- Development of teaching and learning materials where existing knowledge is simply synthesized.

There are four principal modes of research funding as applied to university-based research:

- *Responsive mode*. No restrictions are placed on a research theme as long as it is within the remit of the funding body. The funding body simply responds to the research proposal and usually uses peer review to assess its quality. This mode most often applies to basic research where highly innovative and speculative ideas are considered and grants are awarded.
- *Directed or managed mode*. Research proposals are called for in terms of a designated theme or programme of research, often with fixed or specific objectives and a limited duration. Guidelines are usually attached and the funding body directs or manages the research programmes, although quality and innovation remain the desirable outcomes of successful research. Peer review is still used although often in conjunction with the guidance of a programme manager and steering board. Cooperation and collaboration between researchers are usually encouraged in directed work and awards are most usually made in the form of grants.
- *Contract mode*. Research is contracted under a specific, well-defined set of conditions and requirements against a fixed timescale with measured outputs and attainments against a particular protocol or schedule of work where ownership of any resulting intellectual property will be agreed beforehand and most often the research contractor will wish to retain the intellectual property albeit on the basis of a contract negotiation where the inventor/researcher will expect to share income with the university and the present

contractor concerning the generation of original ideas during the research contract.

- *Conditional mode.* Research will be funded by a sponsor on condition that there is a more fully-developed partnership between the sponsor and the university, research group or individual researchers. Portfolio funding which recognizes the fact that a researcher or research group has already been successful in winning a number of research grants and offering further support on a continuing basis with further project-specific applications cuts down the cost of unnecessary processing of applications.

In each case, the mode is determined by the research funder or sponsor. Only research funded internally by the university from its own trading activities and investments or by that stream of funding from its government-funded allocation, the Higher Education Funding Council in the case of the UK, can be deemed to be entirely free of condition or requirement by external agencies.

1.2.1 What is a research grant?

In the general sense, a research grant is a sum of money provided by government or a public body to a university to undertake a specific programme of research in a given period of time and for a specific amount. The phrase 'grant-in-aid' is sometimes used to cover grants of public funding from one level of public authority to another with the implication of some form of structural relationship.

Grants are generally awarded in response to applications in accordance with published guidelines and are held in accordance with specified regulations applying to the nature of the grant, the grant-making authority and the recipient, including both the announcement of an award and its acceptance.

Grants are made by public bodies and, in the case of UK university-based research, by research councils, other government bodies or public funding agencies, regional and local authorities, professional or scientific associations and institutions, charitable trusts and foundations, European Framework and other European-funded research programmes, and international grant-giving bodies.

1.2.2 What is a research contract?

A research contract is a formal agreement between two or more parties which is legally binding and which prescribes a piece of research work to be carried out in accordance with the conditions of the contract.

A contract usually covers issues such as price, performance, liability, timescale, ownership of intellectual property, termination, indemnity, project management requirements, other legal requirements, with various annexes including a protocol for the research work to be carried out.

When research contracts arise from tenders it should be noted that tender documents are themselves forms of legal contract.

A research contract is a useful and necessary document which should be based on mutual trust, confidence and prior agreement because it makes clear who is responsible for what aspects of the research relationship and it should cover all areas of potential contention. Successful research usually follows the successful drawing up of research contracts in advance of the commencement of the research. Poor research usually follows on poorly drawn up research contracts.

Typical research contracts are undertaken with public or private bodies such as government departments, regional and local authorities, commercial and industrial companies of every kind.

1.3 Motivation

Having considered what is research, attention should be turned to individual and collective motivation. Why do we undertake research?

In 1997, a research project was undertaken for the Engineering and Physical Sciences Research Council (EPSRC) entitled *Research Exploitation Audit Process* (REAP) which was designed to 'achieve a better understanding of the exploitation process, and how the EPSRC, working together with the universities, can contribute to strengthening current practice' (EPSRC 1997). A three-stage methodology was adopted, including:

- The identification and interview of 15 'professorial champions' or leaders of research groups within the University of Birmingham.
- The survey of postgraduate students or associates and postdoctoral fellows who had worked within these groups.
- The completion of a detailed questionnaire by each professorial champion.

The initial interviews identified consistently two principal sources of research motivation: intellectual curiosity and stimulation, and external drivers (stakeholders).

1.3.1 Intellectual curiosity and stimulation

Whether working on pure or applied research, the principal motive identified was intellectual curiosity. Champions expressed this motivation in many different ways, for example:

- 'some questions are fascinating and you want to know the answer'
- 'the desire to understand the reason for things'
- 'to think out things that other people have not done previously'
- 'enjoyment of the pleasure and adventure of research' (EPSRC 1997)

Not, perhaps, a startling conclusion but it is nonetheless important to remind ourselves that university-based research is pursued by individuals and groups whose motivation is not the same as that of R&D teams in industry or in a research and technology organization. Nor is it the same as that of the private entrepreneurial inventor, although aspects of some or all these might be present in university research groups. University researchers rarely appear to place primary importance on financial incentives, although most would accept that this constituted a subsidiary motivation, especially in those disciplines which are more applied in nature such as engineering.

1.3.2 External drivers (stakeholders)

Most university-based research groups responded to a range of stakeholders as follows:

- *Peers*. Responsiveness to external concerns and stimuli from other research groups both national and international in areas related to their research interests.
- *Users*. Responsiveness to the contexts presented by relevant industrial sectors or other user fora such as government.
- *Beneficiaries*. Comprehension, where relevant, of the usefulness of their research to other external users or beneficiaries and wider applicability of their research findings.
- *Market*. Comprehension, where appropriate, of the commercial or innovative potential of their research, usually assisted by university-based commercialization agents.

- *Policy-makers*. Awareness of what research sponsors are prepared to fund and the wider context of government policy or the framework for public funding of university-based research.

These external drivers might determine their research priorities as in the following examples:

- – '[The researcher] works extensively with people in industry over many small and large projects which in many cases makes the decision for me.'
- – 'Research matters to me when it matters to others – say peers, the world at large, commerce and industry, other external drivers.' (EPSRC 1997)

To understand which areas of their research matter most can only be achieved, in the opinion of many university researchers, by maintaining a series of dialogues with the external world around them. This regular and systematic form of exchange of information – whether in the commercial framework of specific research contracts or consultancy, or within the customary academic framework of publications, conferences, debates and peer review – is the life-blood for their research, helping them to determine 'what knowledge is important to know', as one professorial champion put it.

1.4 The shaping of research – other factors

Alongside these powerful primary drivers, other factors begin to loom large for university researchers and can be seen to have had an increasing importance for research throughout most of the 1990s.

- *Research funders*. Of increasing importance, as an external driver, is knowledge of the cycle of research sponsorship. What is being funded? What do research funders seek to fund? Where is the funding interest? This is sometimes dismissed in cynical terms as 'the flavour of the month' or 'fashion', but most researchers in universities are increasingly aware, at a sophisticated level, of the nuances of research funding, increasingly dependent as their research progress is on achieving a flow of funding to support their chosen research fields.
- *Research and teaching*. Many researchers recognize, even if they find it difficult to articulate, a strong link between research and teaching. A continuing intellectual engagement within the specific

discipline, invigorated by the drive for research originality, enlivens and freshens teaching and provides, therefore, a secondary motivation for the able researcher.

- *External scrutiny.* The most important of these factors has been the growing requirement for external scrutiny of research performance through agreed and defined performance indicators and measurable outputs. Many factors are now in play as follows:

  - Public scrutiny of research is a requirement for most governments in their roles as custodians of the public purse. What value for money can be attached to research outputs on behalf of the tax payer? In the UK, this process takes the form of the regular Research Assessment Exercise conducted by the Higher Education Funding Council for England.
  - Universities, as employers and as global knowledge businesses, are concerned to ensure their ability to survive through the success of their researchers who are, in effect, the producers of the knowledge which makes up the universities' products and services. Many do this by scrutinizing research performance both of individuals and of groups within the university.
  - The public wishes to be assured that the outputs of university research are safe, objective and impartial, sustainable, ethical, subject to public scrutiny and made available to the public.
  - Other 'stakeholders' (business and industry, the public sector, government departments and organizations etc.) want to use the fruits of research for their purposes.
  - The academic peer group itself, who both compete and collaborate in research at a national and international level and form part of the environment of validation to which university-based research submits itself, most formally through the peer review of papers and grants.
  - Individual researchers who wish to see their professional careers flourish and prosper through rewards and promotions within and beyond the academic world.

1.5 Current research issues

The present context for research has begun to place emphasis on such issues as:

- collaborative research between disciplines;
- forms of research – the balanced portfolio;
- levels of management.

1.5.1 Collaborative research between disciplines

There is a strong tendency in universities for research to be carried out within single disciplines, although it has long been recognized that applications often require research approaches drawn from several disciplines or from the interfaces between disciplines. Partly, this tendency has arisen from the natural allegiance to disciplines fostered by those who have been responsible for the transmission of learning and teaching in those disciplines or for teaching future generations of researchers. Tony Becher (1989: 1) has argued that 'the ways in which particular groups of academics organize their professional lives are intimately related to the intellectual tasks on which they are engaged'. Disciplines emerge from the relationship between people and ideas. 'The people', he contends, 'are the practitioners in a dozen varied disciplines whose livelihood it is to work with ideas; the ideas are those which lend themselves to sustained exploration, and which form the subject matter of the disciplines in question.'

The world of university-based research itself has been wary of the polymath or 'renaissance scholar' which has, in turn, led to ever increasing research specialization on a relatively narrow basis. In a world of complex knowledge, how could any one person know a lot about more than one subject – it is argued. Over the previous two or three decades, attempts have been made to overcome the tendency to narrow specialization through establishing horizontally rather than vertically organized structures in universities, such as research centres, schools or institutions, bringing together researchers from different disciplines. In the main, such horizontal structures – beyond the narrowing confines of the traditional single discipline – have clustered around new or emerging single disciplines or relatively narrow research themes. In the 1980s in the UK, for example, the research councils actively created new centres of excellence, called Interdisciplinary Research Centres (IRCs) to foster interdisciplinary research around strategic themes such as materials, biotechnology, advanced manufacturing and so on.

Since then, other schemes have favoured interdisciplinary networks which extend beyond a single university and Interdisciplinary Research Collaborations (virtual – IRCs), based on thematic networks or transdisciplinary programmes, have been created in the UK to encourage interdisciplinary research. Other research grant schemes have been managed to encourage large collaborative programmes centred on repertoires of research ideas around single themes.

In fact, there has often been considerable confusion between the use of different terms, sometimes deployed interchangeably when referring to research based upon more than one academic discipline.

- *Interdisciplinary research* – research carried out at the interface between two or more single disciplines in a collaborative way.
- *Multidisciplinary research* – research which brings together two or more single disciplines in a collaborative way but draws down research from the core of those disciplines.
- *Transdisciplinary or cross-disciplinary research* – research which applies the findings or techniques from one or more disciplines to another.

These three forms of collaborative research are illustrated in Figure 1.6.

1.5.2 Forms of research: the balanced portfolio

Research in universities takes place in a wide variety of ways, from the work of single researchers in the tradition of the independent scholar to large multidisciplinary groups organized around a theme or programme or using large-scale specialized facilities and methodologies. Not only does the scale or organizational structure vary but the nature of the research which is being undertaken also takes many forms, resulting from the choices made by universities and researchers as to resources, facilities, priorities and requirements.

Research can be short or long term, speculative or within a range of relative predictability, grant-supported or contract-funded, well defined within a specified programme or loosely defined around a general theme. In practice, most university-based researchers carry out a multiplicity of different forms of research within a dynamic framework, needing to balance a portfolio of different forms of research during their research careers.

Incremental or innovative

The advancement of knowledge proceeds by research most usually in the form of a series of incremental steps where the answers to a set of research questions foster further research questions requiring further answers. Yet the most spectacular advances sometimes occur through innovative leaps where intuitive, or even speculative, research leads to major results. Such innovative leaps can produce progress in new and different directions or within previously dormant fields of enquiry. Research ideas, therefore, are usually formulated on incremental lines as being more likely to secure small but more predictable gains, rather than on the basis of the more speculative approach, which carries a higher risk of failure. All research should

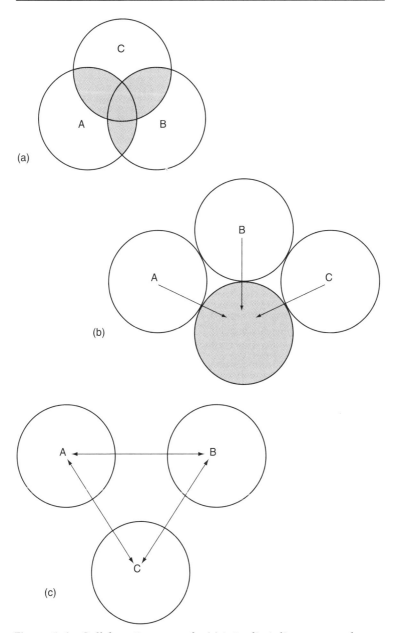

Figure 1.6 Collaborative research: (a) interdisciplinary research;
(b) multidisciplinary research; (c) trans- or cross-disciplinary research

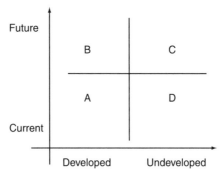

Figure 1.7 Research projects: ideas development

therefore be innovative, but the degree of innovation may be conditioned by the likelihood of securing external resources of funding, whether in responsive or directed mode and in accordance with the external funding agent's perception of innovation as a criterion for assessment.

Research, whether undertaken by individuals or groups within universities, can usually by described in terms of a matrix (see Figure 1.7).

In Figure 1.7, A usually takes the form of research ideas that are fully developed and short term, often linked to completed research programmes or previously funded research. These ideas may be thought of as *ripe fruit being harvested*. Projects of type B are usually research ideas which are fully developed but which require a much longer duration to research and which are linked to ongoing research objectives into the future. They may be thought of as *germinating seed*. Projects of type C are usually characterized as research ideas which are highly speculative, often fundamental, propositions which require much more development – they are the *seedcorn for the future*. Finally, type D projects are research ideas which are in the nature of first thoughts and have been rejected at this stage as low priorities for development – they are *dormant seed*.

As well as scale and direction, researchers must also manage their research in universities within another framework, that of the generation and development of research ideas. A second matrix can be provided to describe the generation and development of research ideas (Figure 1.8).

In Figure 1.8, A usually takes the form of near-market problem-solving often linked to consultancy or other forms of small-scale research contracts or limited research programmes. Projects of type B usually take the form of pure research to advance knowledge and are

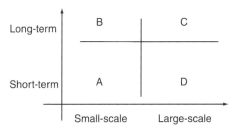

Figure 1.8   Research projects: scale and duration

often linked to small research grants from research councils, research institutions or personal grants, scholarships, fellowships, in the tradition of the single scholar. Type C projects usually take the form of 'rolling' programmes of grant support, often in directed mode, where large-scale research facilities are engaged with different researchers at different stages in their research careers – the research group or team. Such programmes can be located within the university or in partnership with others. The research may be pursued on thematic lines or be fundamental research where the scale of research facilities requires large teams pursuing 'big science'. Finally, projects of type D usually take the form of large contract-based research, often highly specific to a single user or stakeholder, where facilities are used intensively to provide specific applied research goals in a fixed period of time.

The successful researcher needs to review research ideas continuously and be able to balance them to secure a portfolio of external funding and a regular flow of research outputs – in the form of intellectual property or academic publications – in order to generate an active and dynamic research career in which the flow of research is regulated across a diverse range of projects, varied in scale and duration, and in which research ideas are constantly turned over and developed, refined or discarded.

1.5.3 Levels of research management: backing winners or winning backers

There is a difference between the successful management of research and the successful management of a research project. The latter can be accomplished within the parameters of standard project management tools and approaches, whereas the former concerns the overall environment in which research is carried out and its conduciveness to the generation of successful research ideas. One is like baking a cake, the other like holding a dinner party.

Research project management requires a clear understanding of the overall aim of a specified research project and the objectives necessary to advance the aim linked to a defined methodology, in turn mapped onto resources, facilities and timescale with review dates and other milestones, and some idea of likely outputs. Research projects need to be regularly reviewed in the form of a management group or advisory board who can identify difficulties, deal with the unexpected and reschedule resources accordingly. A research manager can organize and oversee the project, or the research group or team leader can do so, and research projects can be audited and reviewed by the head of the research team, or the head of department or centre who can, in turn, account to the university finance office, research services office, dean or pro-vice-chancellor for research, as appropriate.

The management of a successful research environment is a different matter because it involves the difficult task of managing intellectual curiosity and making choices about the allocation of resources and facilities, in support of the best research as judged by peers, external scrutiny exercises, the public, other 'stakeholders', and research performance metrics. It also means providing an environment in which successful research is promoted to a variety of audiences in order to gain further support for these research teams – a case of both 'backing winners' and 'winning backers' at the same time.

Within the university, different levels of management are responsible for different aspects of the task of maintenance of a supportive and successful research environment (Figure 1.9).

1.6 National research scrutiny exercises

All research undertaken in universities, subject only to issues of security and commercial confidentiality, should be open to public scrutiny in order not only to ensure value for money but also to assess its overall quality.

Research which is supported by external funding in the form of research grants and contracts is subject to scrutiny in the following ways:

- In responsive mode, through the mechanism of peer review both at the applications and award stage and in monitoring published outputs.
- In directed mode, through the monitoring of the specific research programme and through the regular peer review process usually undertaken by an advisory board.

Corporate responsibilities

THE UNIVERSITY Vice-Chancellor and corporate senior management team	• Corporate research mission • Corporate research strategy • Corporate research support services • Corporate research policies and operational guidance (e.g. health and safety policies, employment/contracting policies (remuneration and reward, staff development issues), ethics policies and committees, financial administration of research grants and contracts, estate issues, procurement policies and procedures for research, intellectual property policies and operational guidance) • Statutory requirements compliance • Resource allocation for research • Promotions, publicity, marketing • Capital investment programme in research facilities • Corporate sponsors and 'friend-raising' • Information and communications infrastructure • Other infrastructure (e.g. animal houses, clinical trials facilities, etc.) • Business intelligence • Market awareness • Partnership/alliance building

School or departmental responsibilities

THE SCHOOL OR DEPARTMENT Research centre or research institute: head and management team	• Unit/research centre or school research strategy • Research facilities procurement, management and maintenance • Resources allocation within school or centre budget and operational guidance • Research quality management policies • Research support (e.g. peer review, proposal approval, secretarial and technical support, appointments programme and policies) • Research environment (e.g. seminar programme, postgraduate programme, travel and conferences support, consumables and other expenses, visits and visitors, support for engagement in research culture, e.g. refereeing etc.) • Infrastructure for research/interactions, collaborations, networking and partnerships • Research prioritization • Promotion and marketing • Business intelligence • Market awareness • Partnership/alliance building

Figure 1.9   Research management   *(continued)*

Research group leader's or champion's responsibilities

RESEARCH
GROUP OR TEAM
Leader or
champion

- Group research strategy
- Research prioritization
- Utilization of research resources
- Identifying research interactions, collaboration and partnerships
- Development of research ideas
- Research environment stimulation (e.g. group seminar programmes, discussions, talks, poster presentation, encouragement to attend conferences or make visits, electronic presence through websites etc.)
- Research quality management procedures
- Daily management framework for research projects
- Leadership role in research proposals, contracts with potential external funders and sponsors
- Liaison with school/centre and corporate research support structures
- Compliance with statutory requirements
- Engagement with peer group
- Research results dissemination/exploitation
- Development of personnel
- Business intelligence
- Market awareness
- Partnership/alliance building

Individual researcher's responsibilities

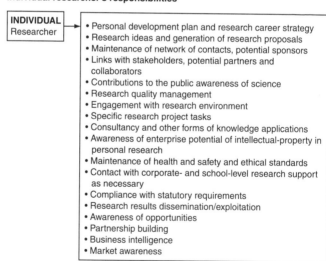

INDIVIDUAL
Researcher

- Personal development plan and research career strategy
- Research ideas and generation of research proposals
- Maintenance of network of contacts, potential sponsors
- Links with stakeholders, potential partners and collaborators
- Contributions to the public awareness of science
- Research quality management
- Engagement with research environment
- Specific research project tasks
- Consultancy and other forms of knowledge applications
- Awareness of enterprise potential of intellectual-property in personal research
- Maintenance of health and safety and ethical standards
- Contact with corporate- and school-level research support as necessary
- Compliance with statutory requirements
- Research results dissemination/exploitation
- Awareness of opportunities
- Partnership building
- Business intelligence
- Market awareness

Figure 1.9 *Continued*

- Contract research is subject to performance checking through the usual operation of contract clauses and ultimately by 'customer satisfaction'. Repeat business will follow only if the first contract was satisfactorily fulfilled. This is a market mechanism, however, rather than public scrutiny.

1.7 Peer review

The operation of peer review in the UK has from time to time been the subject of review and consultation. At its best, peer review is the most objective form of judgement, based upon submitting research to the scrutiny of academic peers – the test of all academic research. At its worst, peer review can be a form of 'old pals act', where like recognizes and rewards like on a tit-for-tat basis. Although peer review has the possibility of abuse, it remains the most favoured and most widely used form of scrutiny. Many other options have been explored but peer review continues to command respect as the fairest approach. As a human process, peer review may, at times, be flawed but it is still the preferred method throughout the research world.

1.8 Research assessment

In the 1980s and 1990s, national governments have become interested in national public scrutiny of research performance in universities, recognizing that public funding of university-based research is a major component of the national budget while, at the same time, recognizing that it is difficult to measure the public benefit arising from such expenditure.

Many different forms of audit are possible:

- self-audit;
- audit against agreed performance indicators for research;
- audit by peers of the whole institutions;
- audit by peers of single subject areas;
- audit by peers of individuals or research groups;
- audit against a standard or norm performance (normative);
- audit across a range of performance measures and subject areas (summative);
- audit to bring about overall improvement in specific subject areas (formative).

In each case, the performance measures selected are the most important factors. The difficulty in assessing research performance lies in the problem of identifying accurate objective research metrics and the balance with subjective peer judgements. At the same time, governments need to decide the extent to which the national scrutiny exercise, in whatever form it takes, is linked directly to the process by which resources for research are allocated.

Debate has raged in the UK over research performance measures and their appropriateness; in particular the value of measuring impact in the form of citation analysis has been hotly disputed. The citation of a specific publication or other form of public output is not necessarily an indication of its quality, as published work might be cited either because of its excellence or because of its notoriety. It might be a high-quality contribution to the advancement of knowledge or a low-quality example of poor work which has held back research.

The national Research Assessment Exercise (RAE) in Britain has operated in one form or another since the mid-1980s and is a compromise of different approaches. RAE's primary purpose is to produce ratings on research quality for a range of subject-based submissions by UK universities as judged by specific Units of Assessment subject panels. These ratings are applied in distributing the main grant for research to institutions. The exercise is an assessment process based on peer review and is not mechanistic.

Assessment panels use professional judgement and evidence submitted. General principles guiding RAE are: clarity, consistency, credibility, efficiency, neutrality, parity and transparency.

RAE defines research as

> original investigation undertaken in order to gain knowledge and understanding. It includes work of direct relevance to the needs of commerce and industry, as well as to the public and voluntary sectors; scholarship; the invention and generation of ideas, images, performances and artefacts including design, where these lead to new or substantially improved insights; and the use of existing knowledge in experimental development to produce new or substantially improved materials, devices, products and processes, including design and construction. It excludes routine testing and analysis of materials, components and processes e.g. for the maintenance of national standards, as distinct from the development of new analytical techniques. It also excludes the development of teaching materials that do not employ original research.
>
> (HEFCE 1999: 5)

Scholarship is defined for the RAE as the creation, development and maintenance of the intellectual infrastructure of subjects and disciplines, in forms such as dictionaries, scholarly editions, catalogues and contributions to major research databases.

(HEFCE 199: 5)

The university chooses which of its staff to submit as 'research active' for RAE purposes and provides evidence including four best publications in the given census period. Evidence is also provided on research income, postgraduate research students, research support and textual abstracts on the research environment and research plans.

The exercise currently does not collect information on volume of publications (quantity measure) or on research publications citation (impact measure) or on research income at the individual level (individual measure).

Judgements are made by Unit of Assessment panels whose membership is drawn from a process of nomination and appointment. Units of Assessment draw up, in detail, specific assessment criteria which are published in advance.

Ratings are defined as follows:

.5* Quality that equates to attainable levels of international excellence in more than half of the research activity submitted and attainable levels of national excellence in the remainder.

.5 Quality that equates to attainable levels of international excellence in up to half of the research activity submitted and to attainable levels of national excellence in virtually all of the remainder.

.4 Quality that equates to attainable levels of national excellence in virtually all of the research activity submitted, showing some evidence of international excellence.

.3a Quality that equates to attainable levels of national excellence in over two-thirds of the research activity submitted, possibly showing evidence of international excellence.

.3b Quality that equates to attainable levels of national excellence in more than half of the research activity submitted.

.2 Quality that equates to attainable levels of national excellence in up to half of the research activity submitted.

.1 Quality that equates to attainable levels of national excellence in none, or virtually none, of the research activity submitted.

Other approaches have been discussed during previous periods of consultation, especially the notion of a rolling series of subject reviews. Currently, the UK research assessment exercise is undergoing a fundamental review in consultation with universities, users and the wider academic community.

In Australia, ratings are applied to the whole institution. In other countries, more strategic approaches are adopted both to locate resources in existing centres of excellence and to develop promising areas for the future.

It is argued that a highly selective approach, resulting from the application of the ratings to resource allocation for research, concentrating research funding in fewer and fewer institutions and resulting in the difficulty of identifying and nurturing new areas of research potential is nonetheless preferable to allocating resources thinly across all research. This is especially true when the ratings from RAE might be applied to other aspects of resource allocation for research such as capital funding as a surrogate measure.

On the other hand, increasing selectivity means that research might become increasingly concentrated in fewer but larger institutions where capital investment continues to take place on a large scale or in smaller institutions that have been successful by operating in niche markets for research.

1.9 Building a research strategy

Why is it necessary to construct a research strategy?

- The external world of public and private finance for funding research in universities is now highly complex, policy driven, a balance between responsive mode and directed mode, linked directly to national scrutiny exercises and resource allocation for research, based upon large capital development programmes for research infrastructure and is highly dynamic.
- Research in universities is subject to quality measurement and project management, involves increasing numbers of contract research staff and postgraduate research students, and requires choices to be made about research areas and prioritization concerning resource allocation.
- Research in universities complies with national and international legislation and statutory requirements, policy statements on health and safety, ethical considerations and value for money, and the requirements of stakeholders, beneficiaries and other users, and research contractors.
- Successful research careers, at all levels, are based upon personal development planning, in turn linked to overall research group, departmental and corporate research strategies in which personal goal-setting for research is commensurate with corporate targets for research.

- Successful research strategies tend to lead to more successful research by increasing the focus of human and other resources on areas of actual and potential strength and can be applied by the individual researcher, the research group and/or the research institutions.
- Research strategies encourage more effective teamworking, efficient use of resources, better communication, a shared sense of purpose, clarity of vision, measurable targets and outputs, and better identification of inter- and multidisciplinary research opportunities.
- Strategy can provide an emphasis on intelligence gathering, partnership building, marketing and exploitation.

To formulate a research strategy at any level there are certain pre-requisites as follows:

- An analysis to establish the nature of the research assets possessed by the individual or the group and the competition from other universities and research providers, alongside consideration of market opportunities. This is best carried out in the form of a SWOT analysis or similar where strengths, weaknesses, opportunities and threats can be discussed.
- An understanding of the detailed costs of research undertaken by the group or individual from which a proper pricing mechanism can be identified.
- A full consideration of time available for research by the group or individual and its present distribution across current research and other commitments or a methodology to arrive at a surrogate measurement for time.
- A research funding map which plots external funding oppor-tunities.
- Understanding of 'market' and user needs.
- Personal development plans for the individual or members of the group.

Research strategy planning should be undertaken formally on an annual basis, preferably within the context of a longer-term overall strategy for the next five years, including an assessment of research projects in hand and their outputs against a continual assessment of new opportunities and challenges in a process of flexible review.

Research strategy planning at the level of the individual or group needs to be integrated with the policies and processes for research strategy planning at the higher levels of department or centre and corporate research strategy planning.

1.10 *E-search*: research in a virtual environment

The biggest single change in recent years in the research environment in universities has been the widespread availability of the internet and the World Wide Web, providing a new electronic environment in which university-based research is pursued at every level:

- local (intranet facilities);
- regional (regional networks);
- national (national networks);
- global (internet).

It is of interest to note that, in the UK, the Engineering and Physical Sciences Research Council has established a major thematic programme called *E-search* which is based on the GRID technology necessary to support scientific, business, health, learning, environmental and cultural research, providing a knowledge layer, an information layer, and a computerized data layer, similar to a basic utility such as electricity.

E-search can be characterized as research with the following contexts:

- real-time communication;
- 24/7 global environment;
- 'virtual' research collaboration;
- electronic dissemination of information;
- electronic publishing;
- marketing and promotion through websites;
- virtual international research networks;
- real-time access to research results and research resources;
- open collaboration with non-university-based stakeholders;
- rapid access to external research funding and its policies and procedures;
- sharing of datasets;
- multimedia presentation of research results.

E-search is the environment within which research is carried out; it does not mean the process of research itself.

E-search is a new phenomenon which affects all university-based researchers and which provides new challenges in both undertaking research itself and participating in the global research environment. *E-search* breaks down the walls of isolation, crumbles 'ivory towers' and broadens links between research groups, opening the possibility of access to research to the whole world.

2

POSTGRADUATE RESEARCH

2.1 Introduction: the postgraduate research student

Postgraduate research plays a unique role in university-based research. The postgraduate research student is both a *purchaser* of research services and a *provider* of research outputs. Postgraduate research is part of the process of learning whereby the student develops research skills, contributes a repertoire of research outcomes and adds to personal career achievement by accessing university research facilities and working with academic supervisors and as a part of a university research group. Simultaneously, the postgraduate research student is assigned a research project which may form part of an ongoing research programme and works alongside other research staff at graduate and postdoctoral levels as well as university researchers which, as part of a larger research programme, will contribute to the progress of the university's research and produce findings of benefit to the general advancement of knowledge within the field. Operating both as a purchaser and provider, the postgraduate research student is, therefore, in a unique position.

It is for this reason that the relationship between the postgraduate research student and the university is a complex one which requires precise regulation, guidance and a clear operational framework. The relationship between supervisor and research student is a formal one but operates best in informal circumstances. It is a longstanding relationship in the history of university-based research but has only recently begun to attract attention from research managers and university policy-makers in crucial areas such as the generation of intellectual property, the nature of the relationship between a research student and the university, the quality of the experience of

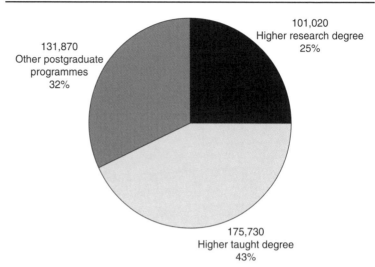

Figure 2.1 Number of postgraduate research students in the UK, 1999/2000
Source: Higher Education Statistics Agency, *Students in HE Institutions 1999/2000*

postgraduate research, the assessment process, and examination procedures. The postgraduate research student is the building-block of university-based research and the usual starting point for even the most illustrious research careers, but the experience can be traumatic and damaging unless managed well by the university as the responsible corporate entity.

In summary, postgraduate research has five main functions:

- Advancement of the careers of individual research students.
- Advancement of research as part of larger research programmes.
- Contribution to the research culture at a department, school or research centre level.
- Support for learning and teaching on undergraduate and/or masters programmes.
- Support for networking with other research centres, research sponsors, research clients and other academic staff in the university.

In the UK, roughly 5 per cent of the total number of students are postgraduate research students, whereas about 25 per cent of the postgraduate students are pursuing higher research degrees (see Figure 2.1). Opting to pursue postgraduate research was once open only to a minority of elite students who were set on a research career and for whom the period of postgraduate research was a necessary stepping stone to an academic or research-based vocation. Postgraduate researchers could expect to be employed in their future careers as researchers in:

• universities and colleges;
• government laboratories;
• government departments or facilities;
• industrial or commercial research centres;
• independent research laboratories;
• industrial or commercial operational facilities;
• other careers where postgraduate work was seen as a measure of excellence for the potential entrant.

Since the recent global expansion of higher education and the increase in public funding for the advancement of knowledge, trends in postgraduate research have included the following:

• An increasing pressure from external sponsors for postgraduate research to be completed within a fixed time – the so-called *completion rate*.
• An increasing tendency to review the purpose and future of postgraduate research in terms of relevance, employability and value for money.
• Criticism of perceived overspecialization in postgraduate research and the desire for a broader base of research training as part of the programme of postgraduate research – the so-called *industrial PhD*.
• Decline in employer demand for doctoral-level postgraduates in preference for earlier recruitment of staff to be trained within the company or employing organization.
• The identification of transferable skills as a component part of PhD research.

The most recent review of postgraduate education in the UK, the Harris Report (Harris 1996), covered both postgraduate taught and postgraduate research issues. The most significant outcome, as far as postgraduate research students were concerned, was the finding, after extensive consultation, that the UK growth in postgraduate research should be limited, in particular to ensure quality and that government funding should be linked to research funding – already distributed on a selective basis. The implication of this recommendation was that, in future, in the UK, increases in the numbers of postgraduate research students will be concentrated in higher-quality, well-equipped research departments where supervisors are active in research and where the postgraduate research student is likely to become an integral part of an existing research culture of excellence. Isolated postgraduate research, in an indifferent environment with a variable reputation, is neither conducive to good postgraduate research nor supportive of a springboard for high-calibre careers. Funding measures will be taken to ensure this outcome. The Harris Report supported a clear link between the excellence of postgraduate research and the excellence of the research environment in which the postgraduate research student pursues research.

2.2 Postgraduate research and the research environment ■

There are four integral aspects of postgraduate research which should be considered:

- *Research training* – the personal development of the individual postgraduate research student. This includes technical training but also training in transferable skills such as presentation and communication skills, research methodologies and systems, personal development, etc.
- *Research environment* – the extent to which the individual postgraduate research student becomes integrated into the research environment and the specific centre or department. This includes the research network and should involve becoming part of a wider community of researchers, national and international scholarship, within a specific field of research.
- *Research culture* – the extent to which the individual postgraduate research student can become involved in an interdisciplinary way with fellow postgraduate research students and become part of a research culture within the specific centre or department.
- *Research management* – the extent of the opportunity for the individual postgraduate research student to link in a horizontal way with other postgraduates across the university and in a vertical way within the discipline research area with the research team in the centre or department.

2.3 Changing expectation ■

In the past, postgraduate research was regarded as the natural stepping stone between a successful undergraduate degree and taking up a career in university-based research and teaching as a full-time professional academic member of staff at an institution of higher education. As such, it was open only to a small elite of outstanding students who had obtained not only the highest degree level but had been further recommended by tutors and supervisors as part of an informed network for identification of future talent. As a career option it was placed alongside similar high-level selection for careers in the civil service or the professions. In essence, the postgraduate research student was groomed for further greatness by 'sitting at the feet' of the best academic practitioners both to learn their trade and to participate in excellent research.

This model was a traditional one, dating back to the Middle Ages if not even earlier to the Classical Age. The research undertaken by the postgraduate research student was viewed as a joint enterprise between the experienced scholar and the apprentice co-worker, with the latter striving to take up the crown of laurels and repeating the process into the next generation. Other careers followed a similar model, as was the case in science, engineering and technology, commerce and industry which recruited in a similar fashion, releasing their brightest and best to undertake postgraduate research, often on a project selected jointly by the company and the student in order to advance their training in specialist areas and to undertake a specific piece of research of benefit to the company. Financial support for this process was provided by the private sector in the case of industrial awards or by a number of public bodies, in the UK typically the research councils, the British Academy together with UK charities in the medical field. The public funding of such doctoral research was regarded as functional – a national contribution to the state's training needs and part of the strategic commitment made by the country so that the brightest talents were available to industry and the private sector, government and the public sector, providing the seed-corn research and research leadership required for future national prosperity and well-being.

For the postgraduate research student undertaking research in this environment, a dilemma presented itself. Work took the form of an apprenticeship in which the research learning process inevitably became one of trial and error, and yet simultaneously the postgraduate research student was expected to produce work of the highest quality such that its contribution was immediate and significant. The result tended to be, especially in the arts, humanities and social sciences, that the postgraduate research project was regarded as a lifetime's achievement requiring considerable amounts of time and effort before thesis submission. The thesis was regarded more for its momentousness than as an example of work in progress. At the same time, the apprentice researcher was expected to demonstrate research skills which would point the way to their future abilities without these being other than indicative. The dilemma for the research student was the challenge faced by the apprentice of producing work worthy of the master during the apprenticeship.

More recently, the world of work has moved away from regarding the period of postgraduate research as a necessary prerequisite for the best in the field. Many employers have come to regard the traditional three-year intensive research degree as unnecessary, wasteful and an indulgence, and which makes little difference to the career development of the individual concerned. Only in certain sectors of industry has the importance of the postgraduate research qualification been maintained as a requirement for undertaking specific areas of research work where both the skills of the student and the research itself are of direct benefit to the economic goals of the industrial or commercial sector. For example, it has remained especially true for the pharmaceutical and biomedical industries together with certain fields in engineering, particularly aerospace and chemical engineering, that a period of postgraduate research constitutes an important feature of the careers of those employed to undertake research. Other employers have withdrawn from this process, preferring to train their own postgraduate workforce in shorter modules or 'bursts' of training using commercial courses, modules or short masters' courses available from universities or other suppliers or by training in-house.

Preference has been given to more general postgraduate research training with emphasis on personal transferable skills rather than to highly specialized research projects on narrow topics in which the skills of the researcher are inferred rather than demonstrated. Some employers have questioned the relevance of the postgraduate research doctorate for the modern requirements of the world of work, viewing it only as a personal indulgence or as an outdated constituent part of university-based research preserved and maintained for their own reasons by the universities themselves.

In the international context, as the global workforce has become a reality so the competition to undertake postgraduate research has become international and the choice for employers who wish to recruit postgraduate research students has been extensive. Multinational companies can opt for the perceived quality of postgraduate research from one country against another and can recruit accordingly. This means that the style of postgraduate research in different countries has been an issue for international comparison. While it has been difficult to assess the validity of these comparisons, it has led, in the UK, to an emphasis on applicability and on a broader base of skills training. Comparisons concerning postgraduate experience and its quality assurance have come to dominate university management.

The postgraduate research student has become not only an example of a particular university's product range and output but also a major component of its overall research capability and capacity.

Postgraduate research students are not university employees nor are they bound contractually to the university whose future has come to depend so heavily on their success. Each university now confronts postgraduate research applications with a growing concern to ensure that applicants will become assets rather than liabilities to their business endeavour. A postgraduate student who falls outside an acceptable completion rate threatens the university's position with external funders, who may withdraw support accordingly. If a research student fails to produce significant research, a negative impression of postgraduate research training available at that university will be given. On the other hand, universities must continue to recruit postgraduate research students as a significant contribution to their income through the payment of fees and as a factor in the formula funding of the research grant by national governments. Moreover, the recruitment of the best postgraduate research students is vital in order to add to the productiveness of their research teams.

Ignoring these complexities, some universities neglect the area of postgraduate research and do so at their peril. Adopting a *laissez-faire* approach is a risk to the university's continuing success in securing the financial resources necessary for its business sustainability. It is an area of the university's research business which links the resource inputs to the research base directly with the quality of its research outputs, connecting the undergraduate learning experience to postgraduate research, as the best source of supply for postgraduate recruits remains the university's undergraduate and taught masters' programmes. Postgraduate research also bridges the university's research infrastructure and its external client base in that organizations work with a university both as potential employers of postgraduate research students and as users of their research. Finally, the university's most successful ambassadors are its research graduates who, in later stages of their careers, should be able to look back upon their research experience with pride and pleasure rather than regret.

Numbers have risen steadily throughout the 1990s and early 2000s and, notwithstanding changing expectations, postgraduate research students are now drawn from a much wider range of social backgrounds and aspirations. To undertake a period of postgraduate research is no longer regarded necessarily as a stepping stone in an illustrious career but may be regarded more as a life ambition, the fulfilment of which owes as much to intellectual satisfaction as to career aspirations. Some graduate students prefer a period of postgraduate research before embarking on a career and regard it as an interesting and life-enhancing achievement similar to gaining other experience of self-fulfilment. Mature students might return to university after a period in other careers, seeking to pursue postgraduate research as an opportunity for a career break or for career redirection. Others will be seeking to refresh research skills or areas in order to make themselves of further use to their employers, while a proportion will undertake postgraduate research in the traditional mode of the stepping stone to a successful career. Postgraduate research students will be recruited from all parts of the world and many will now pursue their researches on a part-time basis or while continuing to be employed, undertaking their research externally and at some distance from the university. Some of these will be directly sponsored by their employers or supported partly by industrial funding and partly by public grants.

The difficulties faced by universities worldwide in recruiting and retaining the *best* postgraduate students is partly affected by the tempting starting salaries in many non-university careers and partly by the relatively low level of stipends available to them. Universities must institute ways of offering additional support, alongside the stipend, to postgraduate research students such as:

• scholarships and endowment programmes;
• teaching assistantships and similar paid employment;
• 'top-ups' from university income in the form of additional funds in support of stipends;
• other benefits (such as access to travel or equipment funds).

Filling postgraduate research places has not been a problem, except in some disciplines such as business and computer science, but filling them with the best students, benchmarked against international standards, is no longer a foregone conclusion. This is another incentive for the university to improve the environment for postgraduate research and to ensure the quality of the student experience.

In the UK there has been a long history of public support for postgraduate research dating back to the First World War, as the responsibility first of the Department of Scientific and Industrial Research and, more recently, of the research councils. In the past, the sponsorship of postgraduate training was available only to the universities, as the university appeared to be the best place for training to take place. The principle embodied in this approach was that training in situ by experienced researchers while carrying out larger programmes of research in which the postgraduate research student was allocated a specific research theme or project in a well-equipped milieu was preferable to non-specific research training. Before the Second World

War, fewer than 100 such studentships were funded publicly in the UK, but by 1960 this figure exceeded 2000 as the recognition increased that economic success was dependent on the generation of new knowledge and the provision of a trained research force for universities, laboratories and industry to provide the future resources for the pursuit of the advancement knowledge (Melville 1962: 67).

In the more complex postindustrial world, this simple model for postgraduate research training is being questioned with direct implications for the expectations of research students, employers, universities and governments alike. While, in the UK, the importance of postgraduate research training continues to be recognized, it is seen as one part of a more diverse whole in which the tests of value for money, applicability and suitability, relevance and appropriateness will continue to be keenly applied so that the postgraduate research experience remains of high quality and up to international standards while at the same time meeting employers' needs in all aspects as a training preparation for future careers.

During the last two decades, universities have seen a significant growth in the numbers of postgraduate research assistants, employed as contract researchers, but simultaneously registered as postgraduate research students undertaking doctoral research. Although, by this means, the university employed another source of contract research labour and the individual benefited from better pay, the arrangement can create tension, first, with postgraduate research students supported by stipends and second, with sponsors who have different sources of funding for different purposes. The relationship between the university and postgraduate research assistant undertaking doctoral research is contracted so such staff are placed in the potential conflict of interest between their contract research and their doctoral studies even where these are broadly from the same research source.

2.4 Pitfalls in postgraduate research

As with all forms of training dependent on interpersonal relationships, the principal pitfall of postgraduate research is the human framework surrounding the experience.

2.4.1 Differing perceptions

The university, through the research centre or department or school, might regard the postgraduate research student as a useful but expendable research foot soldier able and willing to carry out routine tasks, including teaching, while also bringing to the university financial benefit, and to whom the university has only the responsibility of providing research supervision. The ultimate success or failure of the postgraduate's research falls to the student alone.

The research student might regard the relationship with the university as taking the form of a contract in which the payment of fees guarantees a successful outcome and in which their work will not only be carefully guided and assisted but 'helped' to the extent that the thesis will be accepted and the degree will be awarded without difficulty.

In fact, the relationship is a reciprocal one in which the university:

- *supports* the postgraduate research student in carrying out a specific research task;
- *provides* general training and guidance;
- *places* the student in a vibrant research milieu;
- *assesses* the student's programme and performance;
- *examines* the resulting doctoral thesis.

The student, on the other hand:

- *agrees* to pursue research under personal supervision;
- *accepts* that the work must be self-generated and original;
- *contributes* to the research milieu into which the student is placed;
- *abides* by the assessment and examination process;
- *carries out* the tasks required as part of the postgraduate research.

This relationship is best set out in the form of an agreement, a concordat or other form of joint document whose precepts and conditions bind both the university and the postgraduate research student and which is signed and accepted by both at the commencement of the student's period of postgraduate research. This might be done at the point of registration and in the form of an exchange of correspondence around the student's application, but it must be a clear and definitive process resulting in an unambiguous statement of reciprocal responsibilities in the form of an agreed code of conduct.

2.4.2 Problems

If difficulties arise, these must be addressed as soon as they are identified and in relation to the original agreement, concordat or code of conduct. If difficulties are 'put off' or ignored, friction will result.

2.4.3 Standards

The postgraduate research student should accept being subject to the standards normally applied to academic and research staff and students alike as regards:

- university regulations;
- health and safety;
- ethics (for example, plagiarism);
- liability and risk;
- university codes of conduct (for example use of IT systems and services).

Equally, the university, through the research centre, school or department must provide some form of quality assessment to be assured that the postgraduate research experience is uniform in terms of treatment and expectation wherever it takes place.

Standards are best ensured through the adoption of a code of conduct for postgraduate research and by the university's graduate school.

2.4.4 Support

The postgraduate research student should be provided with a full description of the support services available during the period of their postgraduate research. A 'who does what' guide should be included in the code of conduct for postgraduate research, including details on what help is available in the following areas: finance, careers, health and safety, personal development and training, research services, intellectual property management, estates matters, technical support and welfare.

2.4.5 Communications

Frequent, systematic and regular contacts must take place so that the postgraduate research student's progress and development is monitored, documented and communicated and to ensure that the student is fully informed of progress.

2.4.6 Isolation

The most common pitfall is that the postgraduate research student becomes isolated from the research milieu and detached from the research life of the centre, department or school. This can be particularly true for those working part time, those who are registered as external postgraduates or those who may be working on themes or topics which do not form part of the mainstream research programme of the research centre, department or school.

2.4.7 Beast of burden or ship in the night?

A regular complaint of postgraduate research students is that they are 'put upon' by their departments, expected to take on more and more ancillary or related tasks, including teaching, as part of the general resource available to the head of department. What is more, they may have the perception that they are obliged to do so without the rewards, benefits or status of their academic or research colleagues. Mostly, these complaints are made when arrangements have been put in place in an ad hoc manner.

Sometimes the school or department or centre may complain that the postgraduate research student is a regular staff member who is rarely seen, passing like 'a ship in the night', and not making a general contribution.

Both these perceptions will usually be found to have arisen from a breakdown in communications or where genuine problems have not been addressed at an early stage. Regular information, access to support services, contact with the supervisor, engagement in the life of the school, department or centre, should remove these misguided perceptions. It is important to be sensitive to the signs.

- Has the postgraduate research student met their deadlines or kept appointments or carried out assigned tasks?
- Has the student been seen regularly in the school, department or centre?
- Have any personal difficulties been signalled by the student (ill health, stress, overwork, domestic difficulties, family problems and so on)?
- Has the supervisor reported any problems arising from the research or supervision?
- Does the postgraduate research student attend seminars, or other events in the research life of the school, department or centre?

2.4.8 Relationship with the sponsor

As with all sponsored research, it is important to be clear as to the nature of the relationship:

- What is the sponsor's role and expectation?
- What is the postgraduate research student's obligation to the sponsor?
- Are there regular contacts with the sponsor and have the research milestones specified in the sponsorship been met?

In brief, the sponsor is making the research possible but must not confuse the relationship with the university with that of a research contract, not least where an element of public finance is also involved.

2.5 Managing the process

The key to avoiding pitfalls is for the university to adopt the approach that postgraduate research is a *managed process*. This can be done by use of:

- postgraduate concordat or agreement;
- graduate school structure;
- quality management process;
- postgraduate research as part of an overall research strategy.

In the management of postgraduate research, it is not the case that 'one size fits all' or that one system will work for every university, nor is it necessary to sacrifice flexibility and informality for a strictly regulated regime. However, it is important to adopt a clear, systematic and uniform approach which is as simple as possible and codified in a concise way to avoid misunderstanding and the common pitfalls.

Sponsors of research are also interested to see this kind of quality assurance in order to safeguard their investment, or, in the case of public funds, to ensure that the treatment of all postgraduate research students is equitable and reasonable wherever they are located or pursue their research training.

2.6 Grant support

In the UK, the principle of postgraduate funding is that a public grant is associated with the individual and the research project not with direct support of research infrastructure in universities or centres.

The principles of the *dual support system* apply in the case of post-graduate research as with the funding of research in general. Support for the research infrastructure in universities – what used to be termed as 'the well-found laboratory' – is provided by the government through the relevant funding council (for example the Higher Education Funding Council for England in the case of English universities), by formula allocation, whereas research projects are funded in universities by external sponsors including the UK research councils where grants or contracts are awarded. The well-found laboratory concept is also thought to underpin postgraduate research where individual grants are awarded to individual postgraduate research students to carry out their researches in a particular university. Concern has been expressed in recent years as to the continuing soundness of the principle of dual support due to perceived underfunding of infrastructure costs for research both by government and external sponsors alike.

Grants for postgraduate research are allocated in the following ways:

- By competitive application – usually through individual institutions.
- By quota – a specific number allocated to eligible institutions.
- By link to research programmes – associated with larger research funding awards.
- Through industrial or other forms of external support – associated with specific industrial sectors or themes.

Sponsors, whether public, private or a combination of both, are concerned with value for money and quality of research. Perhaps unsurprisingly, these are the same characteristics which postgraduate research students expect of their research experience and training when regarding themselves as customers of universities.

In the UK, the major review of higher education carried out by Sir Ron Dearing called for a code of practice to guide institutions and inform students alike on what they can reasonably expect (Dearing 1997). The adoption of such a code of practice (encompassing the four features of the managed process outlined above) is the best way to manage changing expectations and to avoid the pitfalls which are all too familiar in postgraduate research.

2.7 Drawing up a code of conduct or practice

Drawing up a code of conduct or practice for postgraduate research should be informed by the following considerations:

- Preliminary survey of existing university administrative processes from the viewpoint of the individual postgraduate research student.
- Consultation with external sponsors (some of whom have already initiated similar codes governing postgraduate awards).
- Consultation with centres, departments and schools (where postgraduate research is carried out in the university).
- Consultation with existing university-based support services (for example finance, legal office, registry, faculty, research services and commercialization, health and safety).
- Survey of existing practice in other universities.

The code of conduct or practice will vary in form and content to suit individual institutions, and a range of model documents might be considered as a separate annex which might include examples of standard offer letters, sponsor agreements, progress evaluations and assessments, intellectual property assignments, examination arrangements and so on. Also, the university's regulations regarding postgraduate research degrees should be available as a separate document as necessary, as well as the university's official postgraduate prospectus.

All these documents form part of the postgraduate agreement and figure organizationally in the experience of individual postgraduate research students.

The code of conduct or practice should include:

- *Context*. General precepts and the aim and purpose of postgraduate research and its place in the university's mission and structure should be provided, with a statement of the reciprocal duties, responsibilities and legitimate expectations of both parties (the postgraduate research student and the university). This section might be considered as a form of service-level statement and should be clearly but concisely worded.
- *Process*. The procedures for undertaking postgraduate research should be set out and should cover each stage from initial application, acceptance, choice of subject, registration, supervision, progress and assessment, evaluation, examination, award of degree. This section might refer to the annex of documents and the university's regulations as appropriate.

- *Outcome.* This section should deal with issues affecting the outcomes of postgraduate research such as ownership of intellectual property, relationship with sponsors, code of ethics compliance, grievance procedures, appeals, legal liabilities and so on.

The code of conduct or practice should form part of the agreement between the postgraduate research student and the university at registration and should be both widely distributed and available (prospectus, website, correspondence and so on).

It might be argued that informality and flexibility are sacrificed in the act of drawing up a code of conduct or practice, but there is no reason why the relationship between the postgraduate research student and supervisor, centre or department should be adversely affected if the code is drawn up and administered in a systematic but sympathetic manner. The advantages are manifold:

- certainty and clarity;
- protection to all parties concerned;
- information and guidance to cover exigencies;
- statement of good intent and service level;
- public commitment to 'best practice' standards;
- quality control mechanism;
- a safety net;
- consistency.

A code of conduct or practice is like an umbrella: it might not always be needed but it is usually best to carry it with you.

2.8 The student–supervisor relationship

The student–supervisor relationship is at the core of the postgraduate research student experience. To be effective the relationship needs to be close, requiring trust and confidence on both sides, but its propensity to intensity can be its undoing. On the other hand, no relationship at all leads to the isolation of the postgraduate research student, a source in itself of severe problems. The university relates to each party differently as well: to the supervisor, the university is employer and has a contract of employment to define duties and responsibilities, while to the postgraduate research student the university is service provider, with defined obligations under its regulations. Both the student and supervisor are responsible adults whose relationship, while it can be given a clear framework, is a matter for personal development and exploration, but the university must ensure through its management framework that the relationship is:

- transparent;
- clear and comprehensive;
- subject to scrutiny;
- accountable;
- recorded;
- systematic, professional and methodical;
- in accordance with established policy and procedure (as represented by the code of conduct or practice, for example).

2.9 Choice of supervisor

It is a matter for the head of the research centre, department or school to ensure that all postgraduate research students are appointed a supervisor or supervisors. Postgraduate research is not effective if it is pursued in a generalized relationship to the research centre regardless of the abilities or self-reliance of the individual student. Supervisor(s) must be appointed at the outset, upon acceptance of a postgraduate research student into the research centre. This decision should not be left to a later stage, as formative work will have begun which might be difficult to shape if a supervisor has been appointed only later in the process.

The supervisor should be all of the following:

- An experienced and active researcher whose research field is close to that of the postgraduate research student's topic or who, at least, should have an interest.
- An experienced postgraduate supervisor (if this is not the case, as with first-time supervisors, a *joint* appointment with someone who has experience should be made).
- Able to cover the proposed field of enquiry (sometimes a joint appointment is necessary to cover inter- or multidisciplinary work between two or more centres or departments).
- Able and willing to take on the supervision within current commitments and workload. (While a supervisor can supervise more than one student simultaneously, a check – and even a limit – should be placed on the number of supervisions allocated to a single supervisor as specified in the code of conduct or practice.)

Supervisors and postgraduate research students should have an initial meeting to set the framework for the future, covering:

- choice of topic;
- supervision arrangements;
- evaluation;
- progress and assessment; and
- project management requirements.

Individual postgraduate applicants will have already made some assessment of the university and its research fields in choosing to make application from information supplied previously or may already know the research centre or department, having been previously an undergraduate or taught postgraduate there.

General guidance and information should be supplied on the nature of postgraduate research (induction programme, code of conduct or practice, and so on), but the most important decision is the choice of topic, which should be defined at the admission stage between the student, the supervisor and the university.

2.10 Choice of topic

Many postgraduate research students will have completed undergraduate degree programmes or taught or research master's programmes in which a major research project component will have already been undertaken. Some will have moved on to pursue further research in areas related to or developed from those initial experiences.

The choice of the general area of research is best made before admission, although the final decision on the exact nature of the topic or a precise working title and specification can take place afterwards. Making a choice should be an interactive process between the individual research student and the prospective supervisor.

It is essential to ensure that the chosen topic for research is all of the following:

- *Appropriate*. The topic complies with the requirements for the proposed period of study and research degree.
- *Manageable*. The topic is within the capability and capacity of both the research student and the prospective supervisor.
- *Feasible*. The topic can be undertaken with some confidence of success and is able to be carried out within the present state of knowledge, methodologies and facilities.
- *High quality*. The topic is likely to lead to research of the highest possible quality as measured by national and international standards of excellence.

- *Specific*. The topic is well defined and specific and is not vague or generalized.
- *Integral*. The topic is integral with the overall research plans of the centre, department or school so that the research student can benefit from the overall research strategy and milieu and will make a contribution to the general research environment without being isolated from the general direction in which research is proceeding.
- *Acceptable to stakeholders*. Where appropriate, the topic selected takes into account the needs and requirements of prospective users or beneficiaries or is in accordance with the views of the external sponsor where necessary.

2.11 Supervision

Successful supervision of postgraduate research requires a range of interpersonal skills in which clarity of communication is, perhaps, the most important. At its foundation lies the role of one-to-one contacts in the form of semi-structured meetings, the number and context of which will vary in accordance with personal choice and need and as the postgraduate research progresses but a *minimum* expectation for which should be set down in the code of conduct or practice.

Supervision means simply to oversee and consists of several components:

- Definition and agreement of tasks or goals.
- Definition of techniques and methodologies to be used.
- Comprehension of progress towards tasks or goals by evaluation.
- Identification of obstacles to tasks or goals.
- Guidance in overcoming obstacles and on research best practice and ethics.
- Support in development of skills and progress towards tasks or goals (i.e. in the form of information, training, directional guidance, provision of opportunities, identification of resources and requirements, evaluation and assessment and so on).
- Encouragement of regular seminar/poster participation and presentation of work in progress.
- Monitoring and reporting on progress.
- Advising on choice of topic, methodologies, structure of research project, form and content of work, writing up and submission.
- Providing critical judgement of research content and outcomes.
- Supporting through interaction and insistence on good practice (for example laboratory notebooks, data back-up, research practice).

For effective supervision, the following are required:

- Regular communication and contact.
- Overseeing the production of regular reports on progress, inspection of laboratory notebooks, and so on.
- Supervisory meetings (semi-structured with a record of decisions and outcomes as far as is practical).
- Integration of postgraduate research student into the centre, department or school through involvement in wider research life.

Supervision is a process of engagement between mature and responsible individuals beyond the age of majority, so the degree of formality and flexibility should be managed accordingly.

On the other hand, in most cases, the relationship will not be an equal one in that the postgraduate research student, as befits the research 'exploration', will, in one sense, be starting out on a journey with an experienced traveller as a companion. The supervisor must expect, therefore, to be:

- authoritative without being authoritarian;
- dominant without being dominating;
- formal without being formalist;
- instructive without giving instruction; and
- *laissez-aller* but not *laissez-faire*.

There is no blueprint for success in supervision. Differences in personality and temperament will always mean that the relationship between supervisor and student must evolve along lines which suit both. To continue the analogy of a journey of discovery, the research journey is that which is taken by the postgraduate research student in which the supervisor should provide the guidance necessary to avoid the pitfalls, correct the course, and help along the way.

One of the most difficult areas – and one which often causes problems – is the decision to submit the research thesis. The decision that the research is completed and written up to the best of the postgraduate research student's ability is the student's decision. A supervisor can advise, and it would be unwise for a student to insist upon submitting against the supervisor's judgement, but the decision remains the responsibility of the student alone.

If a supervisor suggests that the student's work is ready for submission, this should not be taken as indicative of success during the assessment and examination. The supervisor's view does not guarantee the outcome, and the postgraduate research student must always accept responsibility for submission. It is essential that, at this stage, communication between supervisor and student is clear and that the requisite paragraphs of the code of conduct or practice or other form of guidance documentation are explicit.

The appointment of supervisor(s) should be a matter for the head of the research centre, department or school, and it would be usual to expect the same supervisor to carry out supervisory duties for the whole of the period of research. It is not usual for the supervisor(s) to be involved in the final examination process or viva of the submitted thesis.

2.12 Student responsibilities

The student should be a positive part of the supervision and should play a full role in delivering the most suitable form and content for supervision meetings. In particular the postgraduate research student should:

- agree the most appropriate form, frequency and style of meetings with the supervisor and arrange a schedule of dates;
- raise difficulties which are being encountered rather than suffer in silence;
- attain progress goals and targets (especially the preparation of written reports and other materials);
- provide an accurate report, when requested, on progress for onward transmission (supervisor, head of centre, external sponsors as appropriate);
- decide, with the supervisor's advice, when to submit the research thesis for examination;
- understand the nature of the relationship with the supervisor and the supervisor's responsibilities.

2.13 Supervisor responsibilities

The supervisor is both mentor and critical friend to the postgraduate research student with specific responsibilities for the following:

- Regular contact and communication with the postgraduate research student:
  - guidance about how to undertake successful research;
  - research ethics and standards;
  - writing-up skills;

- research planning;
- sources, resources and methodologies;
- techniques and facilities;
- good practice in the laboratory;
- regulatory standards;
- support services available in the university;
- avoidance of plagiarism.
- Accessibility to the student.
- Guidance on completion.
- Provision of positive advice and continuing guidance on proposed work.
- Provision of training and experience opportunities in presentation, teaching and practice, and assistance with career development.
- Familiarity with a code of conduct or practice.

2.14 Quality assurance

The quality of the postgraduate research student experience must be assured from beginning to completion and beyond. The process should not be left to the chance of occasional project reviews or monitoring but should adopt an integrated quality assurance approach and be embedded throughout. This is best managed by the adoption of:

- a code of conduct or practice; and
- a graduate school framework.

Quality assurance means the process by which the total postgraduate research experience is supported by systems, mechanisms and process controls necessary to ensure that the postgraduate research student is treated with the care and attention which befits the customer or client obtaining university services.

Quality assurance should cover the following:

- marketing and promotion;
- external sponsor pricing policies;
- application and selection;
- admission and registration;
- code of conduct or practice;
- choice of topic;
- choice of supervisor;
- induction;
- supervision/methodologies and implementation;

- training;
- statutory compliance (e.g. data protection legislation, health and safety, human rights legislation, equal opportunities legislation etc);
- integration with centre or department or school;
- opportunities for presentations, demonstrations, teaching, conferences and so on;
- opportunities for research skills development;
- monitoring progress;
- guidance and information;
- project management facilities/techniques;
- dispute resolution;
- evaluation;
- writing up;
- submission;
- assessment and examination;
- career development support;
- post-degree contact;
- grievance procedures.

Standardized report forms (especially for training, supervision, progress review) can be used at every milestone and their completion should be mandatory. While the supervisor will have the key role in monitoring progress, reports should be reviewed by the head of the centre, department or school or by some other appropriate authority and be lodged with the registry or graduate school office.

Postgraduate research students should be encouraged to develop and maintain a personal development plan (PDP) with help from the supervisor and the careers centre or other authorized agency. The record of achievement should permit the recording of research and other skills attainments, research goals achieved, conferences/seminars given or attended, and other relevant information on the student's period of research and training at the university.

2.15 Postgraduate research skills and development

Development of skills takes place throughout the period of postgraduate research, both as a part of the research process itself and through the provision of an integrated programme of training and skills development courses in which there is a common element, supported by special requirements, tailored to meet the needs of the individual.

A detailed learning development programme should emerge from the student's personal development plan and should be organized around the general programme on the basis of the individual's learning profile.

Training needs will differ from student to student, but the general programme should include core skills and other common elements. The graduate school should take responsibility, with the university's other support services such as the learning and skills unit, careers centre or other training provider, for the identification with the individual student and supervisor of training needs. 'Third-party' agencies might also be used as well as any provision available from the external sponsor which, in the UK, would include the research councils. In the case of externally sponsored students, their employers should also be considered as part of the process of identifying and meeting training needs.

2.15.1 General programme

The general programme should include:

- induction – university policies and procedures;
- familiarization with the university's and the centre's, department's or school's support services and facilities;
- who does what;
- health and safety;
- public awareness and media training;
- good laboratory practice;
- equipment and facilities training;
- ethical issues;
- project management;
- quality assurance;
- presentation skills;
- intellectual property;
- the public funding of research: the national and international scene;
- papers and conferences;
- writing up.
- statutory compliance

2.15.2 School- or division-based activities

The general programme should be integrated with the delivery of school- or division-based activities and training on topics such as:

- induction;
- facilities and equipment;
- social programme;
- laboratory familiarization;
- the research strategy;
- teaching skills;
- personal development plan.
- work placements and experience (as appropriate)

In practice, the opportunity for skills development is best provided by doing research itself, but this approach should be supported by research visits, laboratory practice sessions, tutorials, help and guidance services, as deemed appropriate, at the division, centre, department or school level. Practical skills are best monitored by the supervisor and should become part of a regular and systematic review process as part of the meetings with the supervisor.

2.15.3 The research environment

The introduction to the research environment will take place in a myriad of ways and through a range of experiences. Each encounter which the postgraduate research student has will deepen their integration within the research environment and consideration should be given to each aspect of that encounter at university and division level.

- *E-search* – the website experience, the university's intranet, access to the world of *e-search*;
- newsletters and dissemination of information;
- social and cultural programme;
- departmental seminars;
- opportunities to present work in progress – posters, seminars, conferences, visits and so on;
- access to informal networking with colleagues and other postgraduate research students;
- postgraduate forum – representation in the governance of the university and centre, department or school;
- developing self-help;
- access to facilities and services;
- involvement in academic life – teaching assistants, tutorials, practicals, mentors, open days, presentation to visitors, and so on;
- public awareness of research – developing skills to popularize

research findings, communicate with the media and the wider public, disseminate in accessible language and so on;
- access to the wider world of research and *e-search* – external sponsors, opportunities, how is public funding of research organized, and so on;
- career development – Where next? What opportunities?
- work experience opportunities

Successful postgraduate research is the product of the successful development of research skills. The university and the student are partners in the learning process in which the more effective the partnership, the more effective will be the individual student's postgraduate research.

2.16 The role of the graduate school

One way to introduce the postgraduate research student to the collegiality of the research environment, ensuring the cross-connection of research students from one area to another and enabling the university's support to be consistent, is through the adoption of the graduate school structure.

The graduate school becomes an identified centre for graduate students to undertake advanced research, distinguishing them from undergraduate and other postgraduate (taught) students, and linking them together through shared training and skills development, support and guidance. The graduate school provides them with a horizontally organized 'space' in which to communicate, share issues, discuss concerns, represent views and develop a common approach to the experience of postgraduate research, beyond the possible isolation of a single discipline or narrow research area. From the university's viewpoint, the graduate school offers a way of ensuring consistency of treatment to all its graduate students by a common approach to registration, monitoring, assessment and examination, and a single framework for training and development and other support services.

The graduate school can be organized as a single, university-wide structure where postgraduate research students who are admitted to the university are registered through a single gateway and join a single, horizontally integrated school where they will mix as postgraduate students with common conditions and related concerns, operating under a single university code of conduct or practice. This model suits the smaller university or where circumstances mean that a relatively small number of postgraduate students make up the university's total postgraduate student population.

Another option, especially where a large number of postgraduate students extend across a wide range of disciplines is concerned, is to organize the graduate school on the basis of divisions – when divisions cover clusters of disciplines or research areas such as life sciences, engineering, physical sciences, social sciences, arts and humanities. If single schools recruit large numbers of postgraduate students as a subject area, then a division might conceivably be applied to a single school.

However the graduate school is organized, it is important to maintain the principle of horizontal links so that postgraduate students are able and encouraged to share experiences, learn from each other, draw on the collective resource of their cohort peers, and be subject to common standards and procedures. How far the graduate school becomes an entity within the university, with a shared identity and ethos, depends on the extent to which postgraduate research students can develop a collegiate spirit and ethos.

The advantages of the graduate school are as follows:

- Enhancement of the postgraduate environment through a shared ethos.
- Promotion to the outside world of postgraduate opportunities in order to encourage student recruitment and to attract potential external sponsors of postgraduate research.
- Collective underpinning of the postgraduate research student/ supervisor relationship and the mechanisms to engage post-graduates in the research life of the centre, department or school and the university.
- Ensure the advantages of common standards through the code of conduct or practice and quality assurance measures in a systematic manner.
- Improve the social and cultural life of postgraduate research students and their contribution to university life.
- Provide a forum of postgraduate research students to develop ownership of the research experience.
- Provide a focus for training, skills development, careers advice and the university's support services.
- Provides a focus for quality assurance procedures.

In particular, the graduate school should aim to:

- develop a core approach to training and skills learning;
- provide access to a common standard of support and facilities for postgraduate research;

- maintain and develop the university's support services in respect of postgraduate research;
- maintain the code of conduct or practice and to ensure the consistency of mechanisms and procedures covering postgraduate research;
- service the procedures applying to postgraduate research such as the admissions committee, the executive board or the postgraduate research committee and to coordinate the administrative support for the university's policies and processes as contained in the university's regulations;
- provide the university's interface to potential external sponsors and to be responsible for the coordination of sponsor management;
- manage the university's promotion and marketing of postgraduate research opportunities including their university's postgraduate prospectus;
- develop an environment whereby postgraduate research students can build a shared ethos through cultural, social and recreational programmes and the dissemination of information;
- monitor and manage the quantity assurance system applied to postgraduate research;
- promote the development of supervisory skills for academic staff and engage centres, departments and schools in their development.

The graduate school should be managed by a director with a wide experience of postgraduate research, the global market for postgraduate education, the career experience of postgraduate researchers and the needs and requirements of external sponsors of postgraduate research. The director and graduate school staff would need to work closely, through divisions if these exist, or directly with centres, departments and schools, to build an effective structure in which a vibrant postgraduate research culture and environment is encouraged.

The graduate school should be:

- a gateway not a barrier;
- a window not a wall;
- a positive agent for change not a negative source of inertia;
- a supportive network for the postgraduate researcher not a centralized bureaucracy;
- a creative fingerpost for postgraduate research not a dead hand;
- integrated with centre, department and school research environments not apart from them;

- a coordinator not a director of postgraduate affairs;
- a resource and not a filing system;
- an active advocate of best practice not a passive witness of poor practice.

The graduate school should celebrate the work of postgraduate research students, enhance advanced research to be carried out effectively by research students and see that the tension between the *customer* in receipt of university services and the *co-worker* helping to advance the university's research reputation does not threaten to overwhelm the research student but rather becomes a creative framework to inspire the production of the best research and training possible.

3

GRANT-AIDED RESEARCH

3.1 Introduction: some distinctions

The nature of a grant was defined in Chapter 1. Grant-aided research differs from contract research in three important respects. First, grant-aided research is generally undertaken on a 'best endeavours' basis and is carried out by a named *project investigator* (PI) (see section 5.13.4), whether alone or in collaboration with others. The principal investigator makes the choice of methods, facilities and approaches, although the application for grant support has usually undergone a process of peer evaluation when first submitted in which the research proposed was judged against other applications and was found to have most merit.

Second, research funded by grant leaves to the principal investigator decisions on project management even if the grant is awarded in directed mode rather than responsive mode (see Chapter 1). Research is not usually priced but is *costed* against a range of allowable direct and indirect costs and often construed in the context of the 'well-founded laboratory' or dual support where a further element of funding is secured by the allocation of resources through the public funding agency (in England, the Higher Education Funding Council for England, for example). Even where a grant is not made by a body relevant to the dual support system, grants are mostly drawn up against allowable heads of expenditure with no pricing or profitability measure.

Even in cases when the funding source requires an element of matched funding to lever the grant award or for capital grants, expenditure is agreed only against specified items on a costs basis.

Difficulties can arise with other issues such as tax (value added tax in the UK and other member states of the European Union) or with hidden costs, so it is important to specify all possible costs at the outset when the application is being prepared.

Third, the main difference between a grant and contract rests on the ownership of the results or any patentable or copyright material or knowledge. In general, research grants leave ownership of results or any patentable or copyright material (intellectual property rights – IPR) with the principal investigator and their university. There is often no need for further negotiation as this is usually stated in the conditions of grant award. Some funding agencies require there to be a clear statement of what happens next to any intellectual property (for example, how will it be exploited or commercialized?) as part of their commitment to other third parties including government that research results will be commercialized or applied by the grant holder or that the grant holder has established policy and mechanisms to allow this to happen.

More recently, some research grant funding sources have begun to blur the distinction between grants and contracts by seeking some part in the future exploitation of resulting knowledge, even owner-ship, without any attempt to move to a full pricing mechanism to reflect this fundamental change.

Some national exercises such as the UK's Transparency Exercise, have begun to demonstrate that universities struggle not to make research profitable but to break even on a *cost-plus* basis, and often make considerable losses. Not only is this a reflection of an apparent weakness of the dual support system but it is also a recognition of underfunding of research grants and contracts – a low cost/low value culture for university-based research in the UK has been permitted to develop which has introduced new pressures into the process of grant-making for research.

Figure 3.1 indicates in diagrammatic form how research ideas should be developed, targeting an appropriate research grant funder and resulting in funding coming into the centre, department or school for research projects.

Three types of body or organization provide grants for university-based research. First and foremost are the national research councils or other public organizations responsible for distributing and allo-cating public resources to university-based science, engineering and technology, or humanities and social sciences research. In the UK, this process is the responsibility of the Office of Science and Technology (OST) within the Department of Trade and Industry (DTI). An annual 'science' budget is specified through processes which now include the government's annual *The Forward Look* and also the identification of principles for funding in terms of priorities established by the

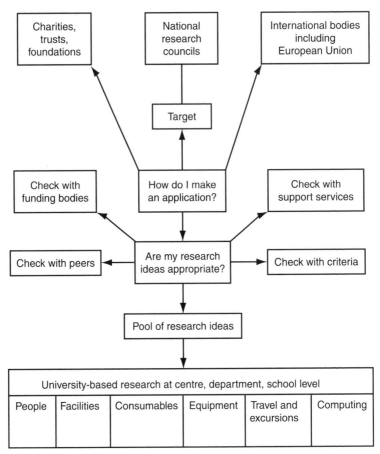

Figure 3.1 Who makes grants for university-based research?

national Foresight programme. The first Foresight exercise in Britain was completed in spring 1995 through the work of 15 sector panels (OST 1995), and since then the approach has been renewed with an emphasis being placed upon identifying new technologies and new markets in which the UK should invest its public research funds. These priorities are also applied to all forms of publicly funded research in departments of government and other public bodies and an emphasis is placed upon the integration of policy such that a common or unified direction is given to government research expenditure.

In recent years, three priorities have been discernible as far as national research council funding is concerned. First, there has been a greater emphasis placed on managed research programmes where research is directly related to *Foresight* priorities, although all research councils remain committed to maintaining a significant proportion of responsive mode funding. Elsewhere in the world this balance between managed programmes in directed mode and university-generated ideas in responsive mode is a shifting one dependent upon perceived economic need and available resources.

Second, emphasis has been placed on the need to strengthen through public schemes the collaboration between university-based research and the private sector to ensure the transference of technology and know-how from the laboratory to commercially viable applications. This process has been extended to include more socially valuable applications in such priority areas as the ageing population, personal security, citizenship and social inclusion.

Third, there has been a continuing requirement for individual research proposals to demonstrate at the outset the potential value of the research to be undertaken to a wide range of users or beneficiaries. The utilitarian function of university-based research is stressed in order to justify continuing public expenditure at a time when public resources generally for competing areas such as health, education, overseas development, and defence have meant that the OST is required to demonstrate in a continuing way the relevance and importance of public expenditure on research undertaken in the form of university-based research for the advancement of knowledge in accordance with the government's primary purposes. The twin imperatives of improvement to the quality of life and/or contribution to economic prosperity have become something of a mantra whereby individual applicants are required to identify direct benefits from their proposed research and the groups of stakeholders who would use their research findings. Grant applicants have become familiar with the process of 'friend-raising' and, while absolute quality remains the prime criterion, demonstrating applicability has also become a key factor.

By looking at the individual UK research councils and their more specific targets and priorities, it can be demonstrated that university-based research is pursued in a highly interactive way in which the dialogue between research councils and the research community represented in universities is expressed in a strategic way, impacting directly on operational policy. This dialogue has become the new framework for pursuing research goals. In part, this process has involved the research councils in engaging in a further dialogue with potential industrial, commercial or other users who are drawn into direct participation in both policy-making and the day-to-day operation of peer review as it is applied to research applications. At a higher level, the UK research community is in dialogue, via the research councils and OST, with government as each round of planning – government spending reviews – takes place, in order to seek to secure an increased allocation of resources. Such additional funding is available only if it can be argued for in order to fund new and additional research goals of perceived national importance.

3.2 Biotechnology and Biological Sciences Research Council

The Biotechnology and Biological Sciences Research Council (BBSRC) was established in 1994 by merging the former Agricultural and Food Research Council with the Biotechnology and Biological Sciences Programmes from the former Science and Engineering Research Council. The new council was given a challenging remit to sustain a wide range of interdisciplinary research and training in the burgeoning area of biosciences with a direct impact on industry, commerce and government to create wealth and improve quality of life.

The decision to create the new research council arose from the recognition of the importance of this area to both national health and economic prosperity particularly in supporting multidisciplinary research bringing together research programmes with other research councils and operating at their interface. As well as researchers in the life sciences, BBSRC has relevance for engineers, physical scientists and even social sciences. BBSRC has been particularly concerned with the interfaces between disciplines and has a responsibility for the general area of interdisciplinarity in research for the UK research councils as a whole. BBSRC manages its own research institutes and research centres as well as allocating research grants to universities and has developed a range of joint programmes with other councils. BBSRC operates in both directed and responsive mode and its managed thematic programmes have been developed in response to the priorities identified by the academic community through the Foresight programme and in consultation. The Council has taken a particular interest in the interface with business and has pioneered a number of initiatives to link university research with commercial exploitation. Publishing an annual report and maintaining a website, BBSRC has set out its strategy and operational policies and stands at an important junction between UK university-based research subject areas with a range of innovative types of grant and award.

Further information is available through its website at http://www.bbsrc.ac.uk.

3.3 Economic and Social Research Council

The Economic and Social Research Council (ESRC) was established in 1965 (as the Social Science Research Council) to support research and postgraduate training in the social sciences. Having no research institutes, all its funding is allocated to university-based research.

As with BBSRC, the Council has recognized its pivotal role in contributing to the research programmes and goals of each of the other councils and in providing multidisciplinary managed programmes relating to specific scientific or policy-relevant topics of strategic or national importance. The usual mode of operation is to identify a programme of research where priorities have been proposed by the academic community and to manage each programme through a director appointed for the purpose and a steering committee which actively encourages the generation of ideas as well as manages the programme as a whole. Responsive mode grants are also made on a standard basis and more major programmes of work are supported through the Council's regular research centre competition. Information is available through the Council's website and its thematic priorities are regularly reviewed and updated.

The ESRC has aggressively reoccupied its ground after a period in which government had doubted the relevance of social sciences research and is now a confident pioneer of new approaches and interdisciplinary centres. Further information is available through its website at http://www.esrc.ac.uk.

3.4 Engineering and Physical Sciences Research Council

The largest research council in the UK, the Engineering and Physical Sciences Research Council (EPSRC) was established in 1994, assuming responsibility for much of the original remit of the former Science and Engineering Research Council. Its responsibilities cover basic, strategic and applied research in the physical sciences and engineering together with postgraduate training, seeing its role as to proceed through partnerships and links between government, industrial and commercial enterprise and the academic sector by producing interactive and flexible programmes that meet the nation's needs.

The Council's strategic direction is managed by panels representing both academic researchers and potential beneficiaries and users.

Grants are awarded in both directed and responsive mode grouped under a range of themes, some co-terminus with individual academic disciplines and others bringing together groups in interdisciplinary programmes. The Council has a particular interest in research which draws civil benefit from defence research and has joint programmes with the Ministry of Defence (MoD) and has introduced an innovative fast-track scheme for researchers seeking support on a first-time basis. Small grants (up to £50,000) are made available without the need for panel rating. Grants are also made available for visiting fellowships, travel and a range of research fellowships, and the Council supports other non-university facilities as well. EPSRC maintains a flourishing website and enters into effective consultations with the academic community through regular 'town' meetings and in visits to the regions. Further information is available from its website at http://epsrc.ac.uk.

3.5 Medical Research Council

The Medical Research Council (MRC) supports basic, strategic and applied research in both clinical and non-clinical fields, including postgraduate research training, and is concerned with both the medical and biomedical areas. Its objective is that its funded research programmes should contribute to maintaining and improving human health. Thematic priorities are identified and research is also supported through its own research centres as well as grant funding to universities. MRC underwent a substantial restructuring in 1997, and an integrated range of research support is available beginning with large centre grants and including long-term programme grants as well as cooperative group grants, development grants, career establishment grants, innovation grants, strategic project grants, trials grants and both non-clinical and clinical research career awards. The Council is particularly effective in identifying the training requirements of every stage of a research career and has given much thought to how to bring forward the high-quality researchers of the future and the development of their careers at every stage. Further information is available from MRC's website at http://www.mrc.ac.uk.

3.6 Natural Environment Research Council

The Natural Environment Research Council (NERC) supports environmental research and training through university-based research and in its research institutes. Its themed priorities have been identified for directed mode funding in the form of managed research programmes, but the Council also retains its commitment to non-thematic or responsive mode research grants and provides core strategic funding to maintain expertise in important areas in its own institutes or centres based in universities. As with other research councils, NERC has developed special programmes to encourage interaction with industry and the private sector under its Connect scheme as well as by providing a range of fellowships appropriate for every stage of a research career by working closely with its academic community as well as stakeholders and beneficiaries. The Council disseminates information through its website at http://www.nerc.ac.uk and its annual report.

3.7 Particle Physics and Astronomy Research Council

The Particle Physics and Astronomy Research Council (PPARC) was established in 1994 from the former Science and Engineering Research Council to provide resources for basic research in particle physics and astronomy. Its academic community is a well-defined one in the UK and, although PPARC operates managed programmes of research, it also places emphasis on responsive mode funding in both non-rolling and rolling grant form. The latter reflects the particular needs of the discipline for long-term commitment in recognized centres of excellence. An industrial programme support scheme has been developed to encourage interaction with industry and a range of fellowships is available to support researchers at every stage of their careers. The Council uniquely retains fixed grant rounds (twice a year) rather than the flexible approach now adopted by most of the other councils where grants can be submitted at any time. Further information is available from its website at http://www.pparc.ac.uk.

3.8 The British Academy and the Arts and Humanities Research Board

Alongside the UK research councils, the British Academy and the Arts and Humanities Research Board (AHRB) have responsibility for the funding of research in arts and the humanities. The AHRB was established in 1998 on a three-year trial basis with a mission to cover:

- promoting and supporting excellence of research in the arts and humanities;
- improving knowledge in human culture to enhance quality of life and the creative output of the nation;
- supporting provision of highly qualified manpower in arts and humanities and preparing students for a wide range of professions and vocations, and promoting and supporting dissemination of research results to the research community and the public at large.

Both the British Academy and AHRB have relatively small amounts of public funding to allocate. The British Academy tends to support small, personal research grants, conference grants, fellowships, lectureships and professorships in special schemes and overseas exchanges, whereas the AHRB provides larger grants in responsive mode and for its own annual research centres competition. Adjudged a success in recognizing the needs of the arts and humanities in universities for support, it is probable that the AHRB will transform into a single research council for arts-based research. Further information is available from its website at http://www.ahrb.ac.uk

The shape and structure of the UK research councils, their responsibilities, remits and achievements, are reviewed from time to time, the last occasion being during the national quinquennial review of 2001 (OST/DTI 2001), and, apart from seeking some harmonizing of procedures to facilitate research grant applications, in particular to create a single route for electronic document submission and electronic processing of applications through their various stages of evaluation, the main recommendation has been to create a single arts and humanities research council following the perceived success of the experiment with the AHRB.

It would, of course, be possible to reconstruct the research councils into a variety of different groupings for subject coverage or in response to reorganization against market or technology areas, or even to create a single research council to which all applications would be made, as is the case in some other developed nations, and in particular in the United States, but the current structure has become a familiar and well tested one in the ten years or so since its creation.

3.9 The United States

The US National Science Foundation (NSF) celebrated its golden jubilee in 2000, founded as a federal organization in 1950 with a mission:

- to promote the progress of science;
- to advance the national health, prosperity and welfare;
- to secure the national defence.

This mission is carried forward in a range of activities, including:

- supporting, through grants and contracts, scientific and engineering research and programmes to strengthen scientific and engineering potential;
- graduate fellowships;
- scientific exchange;
- development of scientific methods and technologies;
- scientific federal coordination;
- scientific and technological personnel register and data on science;
- determining the federal funding distribution through US universities for the conduct of scientific and engineering research;
- international cooperation;
- applied research;
- policy formation;
- participation of women and minorities.

NSF support, in the form of grants, contracts and cooperation agreements, accounts for only 20 per cent of federal support to universities for basic research. Other federal bodies are also significant, namely:

- national institutes of health (NIH);
- Advanced Research Procurement Agency (formerly DARPA, where the D stood for 'Defence');
- national institutes of science and technology;
- other federal research and development agencies.

The key body, helping to determine national policy in the United States, is probably the NSF's National Science Board, appointed by the President, which operates with the director, deputy director and a number of assistant directors.

A cursory glance at the US structure for research grant-making to universities indicates broad similarity with the UK in:

- the use of peer review;
- the range of programmes and mechanisms;
- the distribution of funds across subjects and areas;
- the commitment to collaboration and partnership in international programmes;
- career development programmes.

3.10 Research council evaluation ▮

The most recent consideration of the current structure, remit and operational procedures of the UK research councils took place in 2001 in the *Quinquennial Review of the Grant Awarding Research Councils* in a two-stage process. The Report by the Review Team, published in November 2001 and covering 7 chapters, 5 annexes and 12 appendices, was a thoroughgoing outcome of a major consultation and evaluation exercise, involving stakeholders (OST/DTI 2001). The Review Team's overall conclusion was that, since the re-establishment of the research councils in 1994, the system was working well, particularly in the engagement of users and in the success of their mission laid down at the outset. The so-called Haldane principle was endorsed whereby decisions are made on scientific strategies without direct government involvement.

The research councils were, however, encouraged to work in closer collaboration, operating both collectively and flexibly, to meet the scientific challenges faced by accelerating and dynamic change in global knowledge. Only three major criticisms were registered:

• The lack of a clear strategic framework.
• The need to meet with stakeholders in a more collegiate fashion.
• The requirement to express more fully the principles of public service delivery.

The strategic framework should include attempts to track outcomes from public expenditure in the UK research base as well as the development of new common interfaces for the research councils at an operational level. In particular, it was recommended that more attention should be given to ensuring the quality of postgraduate training and to deliver, to a greater extent, postdoctoral research career support while at the same time giving greater consideration to the promotion of knowledge and technology transfer and exploitation. Converging operational procedures was a recurring theme as a *virtual single research council* in operational terms was recommended, making their boundaries and limits invisible to users and stakeholders and developing a spirit of 'jointery', thereby removing any obstacles to innovative scientific research at the interface between disciplines and subject areas which the current structure for research awards might unconsciously create.

One area of recommendation urged the research councils to play a specific role in science and society concerning public understanding of science, in particular, encouraging grant holders to communicate their research goals and findings to the public at large. The public understanding imperative aims to place research councils at the heart of the general agenda for modernizing government in the UK.

After such a systematic and lengthy evaluation it is, perhaps, reassuring that the overall structure of the UK research councils was found to be sound and successful and that there should be renewed general confidence in the principles determining strategy and operational procedures. That the research council structure itself might become a constraint on innovative research must clearly be guarded against so that every encouragement can be given to inter-, multi- and transdisciplinary research of the highest quality. The concept of a virtual single council is an innovative one, although it remains to be seen how this will operate in practice. Virtual one-stop shops require closer unity of purpose and vision as well as operational practice than has heretofore been the experience of research council remits and procedures. The work of the proposed Research Council's UK Strategy Group will be crucial in this respect, especially in the development, with the OST, of a 10–15 year 'rolling road map of Opportunities for Science' (OST/DTI 2001). How this will be implemented with the existing national Foresight programme and the annual *The Forward Look* is a question which will immediately present itself.

On the other hand, that the research council system has been so systematically reviewed and not found wanting must be encouraging for UK science and for university-based research alike. Together with the DTI's *Science and Innovation Strategy* (DTI 2001a), the way ahead in the UK is now signalled by a clear commitment to innovation from and exploitation of the UK's knowledge base in the quest for competitiveness for the UK economy.

As the DTI's strategy has indicated, with only 1 per cent of the world's population, the UK funds 4.5 per cent of the world's science and produces 8 per cent of the world's scientific research papers. Yet, without strategic management, the UK's strength is underexploited. Fostering partnerships between the universities and industry and commerce, developed from the relationship between research council users and stakeholders in which the focus is on innovative science of undoubted excellence and without frontiers blocking the growth of new fields of research is an important development.

3.11 Professional associations

In the UK, alongside the research councils funded through the Office of Science and Technology, a number of smaller professional bodies receive relatively small amounts of public funding to pursue support for their disciplines in terms of university research. These include the Royal Academy of Engineering (RAEng), the Royal Society and the British Academy. In the main, grants made by these bodies are provided to fund career development and training, including research chairs, senior research fellowships, secondments, awards and travel grants.

The Royal Society is the premier UK academy of science and covers the natural sciences including mathematics, engineering science, agriculture and medical research, together with the scientific aspects of archaeology, geography, experimental psychology and the history of science. Although, as we have seen in Chapter 1, the Royal Society acts as an independent body, it distributes certain types of research funding on behalf of the OST and other sponsors as well as from its own income. Most of the Royal Society's support is directed towards research at a postdoctoral level or above. The Royal Society runs a research grant scheme for awards of up to £10,000 which is particularly aimed at new members of academic staff or those moving into a new field. There is also an instrument fund, conference grants, funding for international collaborations, and a series of research fellowship schemes. In recent years the Royal Society has taken a particular interest in initiatives relating to the public understanding of science and is providing objective summary statements on the state of debate on specific science issues of concern to government and the general public.

3.12 Other schemes

Other special schemes funded through the higher education funding councils include a number of national initiatives aimed at strengthening university-based research, including capital schemes for funding equipment, refurbishment and new building programmes. Known previously as the Joint Infrastructure Fund (JIF) and in its latest form as the Science Research Investment Fund (SRIF), large capital grants of public funding are made available to universities for research support in the form of new buildings, refurbishments, equipment and support staff.

JIF was organized as a competitive scheme where submission was made by universities for specific new and additional research facilities on the basis of proposed future research projects and programmes. Requiring an element of non-government funding and commitment from the university making application, JIF had the unintended effect of increasing the problem of research infrastructures in universities rather than supporting and strengthening existing research facilities.

As the requirement also included the need to produce evidence of further 'take-up' of research funds for new research, JIF has effectively provided a further gearing to the problem of research 'overtrading' on an undercosted basis.

SRIF was *not* organized as a competition but was distributed, on a formula basis, against capital plans for further research investment, and in accordance with research measures such as size and capacity, and grant income. The requirement and methodology for future allocation of capital funds for research are currently under review.

The research councils have organized occasional research equipment initiatives where capital funds are provided against peer-reviewed applications for large items of research equipment. EPSRC has run the Strategic Equipment Initiative (SEI) and, together, the research councils funded the Joint Research Equipment Initiative (JREI) scheme. Such capital schemes arise from time to time partly in recognition of the difficulty of underfunding in universities for research which has arisen from the underfunding of the dual support system in the past, and partly in recognition of rising equipment costs and the accelerating pace of change in which new equipment and research technologies are necessary for the UK to keep pace with global developments.

Attempts to encourage links between university-based research and the private sector have led to the erection of major national initiatives as follows. First, the Teaching Company Scheme (TCS), which has operated for 30 years, is the most successful scheme for transferring technology or knowledge from the university research base to the private sector in the form of trained associates who undertake research on behalf of and within the companies or organizations who partner the specific university TCS programme, providing a bridge to university research.

Second, OST oversees through the research councils the Link initiative which was originally created as a matched funding scheme to encourage industry and the private sector to seek collaborative partnership with research and innovation in universities in order to develop their own technologies or know-how. Link schemes are organized as managed programmes usually lasting up to five years and structured around a single theme with sub-themes. Themes are drawn up in accordance with *The Forward Look* and the Foresight initiative together with consultation in the academic community. Collaborations are open to partnerships of universities and industry whose proposed projects need to be in accordance with the chosen Link theme. Awards are made to recipients of both TCS and Link scheme initiatives in the form of grants. Management of both schemes requires more project direction than would be expected in responsive mode research grant awards but in accordance with similar requirements for directed mode managed programmes.

Finally, in the UK, initiatives have been pioneered to provide funding for research where there is clear evidence of market support for the particular area. In some other developed nations such as Australia, similar attempts have been made to distribute funds to universities for research on the basis of evidence of market pull, simply by distributing the funding to industry and the private sector, allowing companies to identify their own research partners in universities to whom funding is then made available. The Faraday programme, funded through the DTI and the research councils in the UK, represents a similar attempt where public funds are allocated to consortia of universities and industry research organizations and associations to develop postgraduate training programmes where specific postgraduate research is carried out of direct benefit to the specific industrial sector. The market-pull approach is clearly attractive to government for the following reasons:

- It avoids the dangers of 'technology push' where university research is promoted and supported without hard evidence of market need being considered.
- Judgements can be made on other criteria than simple research excellence as considered by peer review.
- The link between the academic community and industry is already made and is a prerequisite.
- There is a proven 'track record' of applicability.

Such an approach has also been harnessed in the past on the basis of securing funding in the form of research contracts from industry, which can in turn provide an eligibility criterion for public grant awards. One response to the original 1993 science White Paper *Realising our Potential* was the Realising our Potential Awards Scheme (ROPAS). Funding was provided in the form of research council grant, for curiosity-driven speculative research often of a pump-priming nature, as a recognition of success, established by evidence, of the application of a particular individual's research findings in industry or of collaborative or contract research sponsored by industry.

In summary, in the UK, around £1.5 billion is allocated by the OST in the form of the science, engineering and technology (SET) budget. The largest proportion of this funding is allocated to the Engineering and Physical Science Research Council, with the Medical Research Council receiving the second highest share. The Particle Physics and Astronomy Research Council and Biotechnology and Biological

Sciences Research Council have roughly equal shares in the budget, with the Natural Environment Research Council and Economic and Social Research Council receiving the two smallest shares. In recent times, in order to create funding for new capital initiatives or for Link schemes, funding has been identified which would normally have been allocated through the research councils. For example, the UK government has decided to foster the development of entrepreneurial skill and expertise in the science base in order to accelerate the process of technology transfer and has established a scheme known as the Science Enterprise Challenge for that purpose. Proposals were invited against the criteria for the initiative in order to set up centres or institutes of science enterprise on the basis of seeking the best ideas from universities rather than prescribing the structure envisaged by government. These centres provide entrepreneurial training and support to the science base in universities to encourage better commercialization of research results and other outcomes. Some centres are organized on a regional basis and bring together a partnership of universities and other organizations.

About 40 per cent of the £1.5 billion per annum is allocated in the form of research grants to universities, with 13 per cent taking the form of postgraduate studentships and the remainder being allocated to research council institutes, international activities and subscriptions and administration. As part of the process, the government has initiated a cross-cutting review of public spending allocations, on the science base which has been boosted in recent years as a successful recipient of additional funds arising from the annual spending review process. Those funds are allocated partly through the research councils against new themes and priorities identified by them and in the form of new initiatives identified by government to stimulate development in the system of university-based research and its partnership with the private sector and other beneficiaries and stakeholders. The larger research-led universities in the UK can expect to win through competitive process by application around 40–50 per cent of their external research income in the form of research grants from the research councils, charities, trusts and foundations.

3.13 Charities, trusts and foundations

In the UK, university-based research is supported in a significant manner by grants awarded from charities, trusts and foundations which raise funds from public donations and corporate giving and whose objects include pursuit of their aims through research which, in some cases, is possible only through higher education. The policy report *Research Relationships between Higher Education Institutions and the Charitable Sector* (HEFCE 2002), followed the publication of the RAE 2001 results and highlights a range of benefits and concerns arising from this most misunderstood partnership. Recognizing that the charitable sector is a significant sponsor of university-based research, the report draws attention to:

• the need for a strategic relationship; and
• the failure of the UK's dual support system which, contrary to received wisdom, does *not* formally set out to support the relationship through the HEFCE.

Some UK charities, it should be remembered, have such substantial incomes that they are able to fund directly their own research institutes either independent from or collaborating with university-based research. In particular, the medical charitable sector and charities with single-issue objectives are major stakeholders in university research. In some research-led institutions of higher education, as much as 15–20 per cent of external research income is derived from charitable bodies. Each charity, trust or foundation is obliged by law to have guidelines and procedures together with conditions attached to grant awards available for public consultation and is required to act in a transparent and accountable fashion for the funds for which they are responsible. Many of the larger charities operate in a fashion similar to research councils, using both academic peer review and advisory boards and committees composed of representatives of the academic research community. Some smaller charities are more idiosyncratic in their operation or adopt a personal approach in which the trustees are represented through a single interface such as the secretary to the charity or the chief executive or director-general.

In the UK, many of the medical research charities are members of the Association of Medical Research Charities (AMRC) which produces an annual directory of its member charities and provides guidance and advice through the Association, but it should be noted that charities are not bound to follow AMRC's suggestions on policy and procedures, so it should not be assumed that AMRC guidance is adopted by all charities. Progress can be made in improving the prospect of successful strategic partnerships if practical steps are taken to recognize them. Key issues when making application for grant support from the charitable sector are described below.

3.13.1 Costing

Consider what expenditure cost heads for research are eligible with a particular charity, foundation or trust. These will vary from one to another and, in most cases, charities prefer not to fund unidentified indirect costs in the form of a simple percentage addition based upon the staffing costs to reflect the institution's research cost liabilities from non-attributed areas. It is usually possible to specify a far wider range of allowable direct costs than would be normal with other funders such as the research councils. In the main, charities prefer to identify all costs as directly attributable to a particular research project supported by a grant from the charity concerned which will include even relatively small items of expenditure, and it is essential to specify as many of these direct cost expenditure items as possible in order to reflect the full cost of undertaking research supported by charity grants. As indicated above, in the UK this issue is further complicated by the continuing practice of providing a small element through the funding council mechanism (as part of the dual support system) in recognition of research carried out with the charity sector. This element does not reflect the true indirect cost of operating with the sector but has provided a justification to the charities for their arguments against paying indirect costs or other administrative or central charges. In the eyes of trustees, public funding raised through charitable giving should not be directed to any expenditure items other than those which relate directly to the objectives of the particular research grant-aided project. In practice, this has resulted in an unsatisfactory position where university-based research funded by charities is more visibly loss-making, even if on a par with other forms of grant support such as research councils, and yet for major research-led universities it is an essential element of funded research, particularly in the biosciences and medical fields and the social sciences.

3.13.2 Intellectual property

Some charities are beginning to take a more aggressive stance on the ownership of intellectual property and have moved from terms and conditions for grant support towards principles more akin to the world of research contracts. It is important to distinguish between these two approaches in working with charities, trusts and foundations and to ensure that the university's policy on intellectual property is not compromised by a particular charity's attitude to funding research projects.

3.13.3 Ethical considerations

Some charities also represent industrial sectors or companies which, although not directly connected, have associations which on ethical grounds may not be acceptable to the university or to its other research sponsors. It is not always obvious in considering a particular charity solely on its name or reports whether such connections exist, and it is important to research any unfamiliar charity, trust or foundation before accepting a grant which could lead to ethical difficulties. At the same time, other charities now take a much more aggressive stance against associating their grants for research in universities which, in their view, have accepted funds for research from dubious or unacceptable sources. These ethical considerations operate in both directions and, in the UK for example, a joint protocol has been drawn up between one of the major cancer charities and the representative body for UK universities offering guidance in this complex area.

3.13.4 Corporate charity

Some charities are derived directly from industrial or commercial companies or organizations and, in some cases, confusion arises between the corporate entity and its charity. These two entities are not the same. By law, the charity must not be directly controlled by the company or commercial organization but must be managed at arm's length and in accordance with its published objectives. Where, for example, a charity, trust or foundation bears the family name of a famous company or industry, this is particularly important as there will be no connection between the two. Approaches which might be made to both by university researchers should be considered separately, and whereas the support received from the named charity will be in the form of a research grant, any support from the company will take the form either of a corporate donation to development funds (corporate giving) or of a research contract.

3.13.5 Involvement with the charitable sector

In some cases, university researchers will be involved with charities, trusts and foundations for research which directly supports their own work, either as members of boards, committees or as trustees or by setting up charitable funds in their own right. This latter circumstance is especially common in the field of medical research. It is important to recognize that such a relationship might constitute a conflict of interest and, in such cases, the independent charity, trust and foundation must be:

- transparent;
- auditable;
- accountable;
- linked directly to a specific research purpose.

Whether there is a conflict of interest or not should be checked by reference to the annual reports and accounts for such trusts and foundations and, in particular, the membership of the board of trustees. If there is any possibility of a conflict of interest, the university must ensure that its dealings with the trust are completely open and in the public domain and are above suspicion. It is likely that the ethical complexity of this position will continue to attract attention, especially from the world of the charities, trusts and foundations itself or from the Charity Commission. Charitable funding of university research has become a major enterprise and considerable funding is now made available from this source.

There are a range of publications and sources of information on research charities which should be consulted when making an application. These are as follows:

- *Association of Medical Research Charities (AMRC)*. ARMC's activities include the production of an annual handbook which gives details on almost 100 member charities (all UK based). The handbook gives summaries of each charity's objectives, types of funding available, award procedures and contact details. Individual researchers may obtain a copy from ARMC direct by email to amrc@mailbox.ulcc.ac.uk. The handbook is also available in a searchable form on the Association's website at http://www.amrc.org.uk.
- *Wisdom database (Wellcome Trust)*. The Wellcome Trust maintains an extensive web-based database as a service to the university research community which gives sources of biomedical research funding and is available at http://wisdom.wellcome.ac.uk. A fully searchable database, information is provided by subject area, type of award, name of organization and keyword, and details are included of over 100 organizations in the UK and their awards. Links are provided to the websites of the funding bodies themselves where these exist.
- *Voluntary Organizations Internet Server (VOIS)*. VOIS is a portal to

information on charities and voluntary organization at http://
www.vois.org.uk. Information is searchable by sector, keyword or
alphabetical listing of organizations.

As well as the above internet sites, regular annual publications are
available which contain useful information when considering
approaches to charities, trusts and foundations. These are as follows:

- *The Awards Almanac.* This is an international guide to career,
  research and education funds with the focus on funding for
  individuals. The Almanac lists some 1500 organizations and their
  award schemes, indexed by organization, place of study, objectives
  and subject.
- *The Directory of Grant Making Trusts.* This directory is published
  by the Charities Aid Foundation and gives information on over
  2500 organizations providing grants for a variety of purposes
  including research. Lists are searchable by subject, region and by
  organization.
- *The Henderson Top 2000 Charities.* This is the directory of UK-based
  charities listed by amount of income, subject and organization.
- *The International Foundation Directory.* Some 1500 international
  foundations and trusts as well as non-profit organizations are listed
  in the directory by country, and some 100 countries are included,
  which makes the directory particularly useful for funding for international collaboration.

3.14 General charitable funding for university-based research

Most medical charities operate in accordance with a single focus on
a particular disease or illness and therefore research is funded only
insofar as it assists progress towards curing these diseases and ill-
nesses. Their published information is clear in its guidance on who is
eligible to apply and for what subjects, so these are not listed further
here. On the other hand, some charities exist on a multidisciplinary
basis and fund university-based research through projects but in a
more general way. In the UK, these include the following: Wellcome
Trust, Leverhulme Trust, Nuffield Foundation, Joseph Rowntree
Foundation, the Sainsbury Family Charitable Trust, the Wolfson
Foundation and the National Lottery.

3.14.1 The Wellcome Trust

The largest single source of charitable funding for research in universities in the UK remains the Wellcome Trust, which has an annual budget for research which exceeds that of the Medical Research Council. The Wellcome Trust has become the largest medical research charity in the world, exercising a major influence on the organization of publicly funded research in the UK and elsewhere.

As a major donor to the government's Joint Infrastructure Fund for capital funding of new research infrastructure in universities, the Wellcome Trust has become a major policy player at government level in the UK.

3.14.2 Leverhulme Trust

The Leverhulme Trust has a total expenditure of around £20 million per annum supporting research and education. In accordance with the terms of the Trust, funding must be expended on scholarship in the broadest sense which, in practice, restricts the Trust to supporting researchers and fellowships with some elements for consumables and support staff but *not* capital equipment items. The Trust works entirely in responsive mode and does not set research priorities or fix annual budgets for different target areas, although there is a published list of exclusions. The Trust is available to fund speculative or higher risk proposals or proposals for pilot work and for research into subjects that in the Trust's judgement fall outside the general remit of other funders. Full information is available on policy and procedures in the Leverhulme Trust's annual published guide and on the internet at http://www.leverhulme.org.uk.

Grants are usually made available under the following heads:

Grants to institutions for research
- standard grants (up to 3 years);
- pilot projects (6 months – up to £15,000);
- large project grants (5 years – between £250,000 and £500,000).

Awards to individuals
- research fellowships and grants;
- emeritus fellowships;
- study abroad;
- studentships;
- special research fellowships;
- grants to institutions for academic interchange.

3.14.3 Nuffield Foundation

The Foundation allocates about £8 million per annum to UK research in the following fields:

- education and science;
- social science;
- social research and innovation;
- health;
- disability and ageing.

Information is available on their website at http://www.nuffield.org.uk.

Research is supported mainly in the form of project grants of up to £100,000. Areas of special interest include:

- child protection;
- family law and justice;
- education;
- access to justice;
- mental health.

Social sciences small grants
- undergraduate science research bursaries;
- grants for newly appointed lecturers.

Subject-specific funds
- Olive Bird Fund;
- Phoenix Fund.

3.14.4 Joseph Rowntree Foundation

The Foundation allocates about £7 million per annum to practical social sciences research and contributes to policies and practice in the fields of housing, social care and social policy.

The Foundation considers itself a partner rather than simply a funder of research and adopts a practical approach, giving the majority of support via thematic research programmes rather than to unsolicited responsive mode projects. Information is available at http://www.jrf.org.uk.

3.14.5 The Sainsbury Family Charitable Trusts

The Sainsbury Family is a generous benefactor of many research areas including education, the arts and all fields of university-based research, sport and so on. The Trust operates through individual subordinate trusts as follows:

- The Aston Trust;
- The Elizabeth Clark Charitable Trust;
- The Gatsby Charitable Foundation;
- The Headley Trust;
- The Kay Kendall Leukaemia Fund;
- The Limbrey Trust;
- The Liza Sainsbury Foundation;
- The Monument Trust.

Information is available from the Trust on all its separate charities and the principal contact officer should be consulted in advance before approaching any of these sources.

3.14.6 The Wolfson Foundation

The Foundation was founded in 1955 for the support of scientific and medical research and higher education. It should not be confused with the Wolfson Family Charitable Trust. The Foundation makes available about £10 million annually in grants to universities and publishes an annual report.

Its main focus is the support of excellence in scientific and medical laboratories in universities through its refurbishment scheme (currently operated on behalf of the Wolfson Foundation by the Royal Society). The Foundation also supports specific research fellowships and professorships in partnership with the Royal Society and others.

3.14.7 The National Lottery

National Lottery funding is not available to universities for research as a direct source but is available to third parties or through other national organizations who might pursue their objectives in partnership with universities and through university-based research. For example, funds have been made available in the past through the New Opportunities Fund (NOF) to which universities have been made eligible applicants either singly or in partnership. Equally, funding for heritage projects or for sports projects might involve grants to universities through other national organizations or third parties. It is important to check details of National Lottery funding through its website at: http://www.national-lottery.co.uk.

The National Lottery presently distributes its funds through the following bodies:

- The Community Fund;
- The Millennium Commission;
- The Sports Councils;
- The Heritage Lottery Fund;
- The Arts Councils;
- New Opportunities Fund.

Most nations have their own independent charity sector, many members of which are concerned with university-based research and are open to approaches from all interested parties. Directories of international foundations are the best source for information and the more important of these should be borne in mind when considering the possibilities of charitable support for research proposals. A particularly good source of information is the American Association for the Advancement of Science (AAAS) listing at http://www.aaas.org/international/intlinks/intbody3.htm. Other bodies and international agencies which are relevant include:

- World Bank;
- World Health Organization;
- United Nations Educational Scientific and Cultural Organization (UNESCO);
- Nato Science Programme;
- foundations such as:
  - Carnegie (United States and Scotland)
  - Ford
  - Fulbright
  - Rockefeller
  - Gulbenkian
  - Soros.

3.15 The European Union ◼

As far as the UK-based universities are concerned, the most significant source of international support for university-based research is the European Union. The EU operates through the European Commission (EC) which is in effect the administration for Europe in the manner of individual national civil services. The Commission is divided into departments with responsibilities for different activities. These are called directorates-general (DGs). Different DGs have funds of relevance to university-based research, but the most important are those operated by the Directorate-General for Science Research and Development (DG XII).

3.15.1 The Framework programme

The majority of university-based research supported by the EU is funded via the Framework programme, of which there have been five separate programmes to date. The Sixth Framework programme (FP6) is about to commence and will have a major impact on forwarding Europe's research capability and capacity through university-based research. The Framework programme is always controversial because it requires a complete consensus among EU member states. It is important to remember that the EU's interest in funding research extends only so far as, through science R&D, the overall success of the European Project is ensured in respect of the fundamental principles contained in the Treaty of Rome. The following general considerations should be borne in mind:

- All research must have relevance to EU policies such as European harmonization; European economic competitiveness; European enlargement; social or cultural aspects concerning the quality of life, the environment, employment, health and technology – in Europe and of benefit to the citizens of EU member states. There is *no* overall responsibility, requirement or desire to fund university-based research for its own sake.
- EU research is concerned to develop the Union's scientific and technical capability in order to compete with the rest of the world.
- There must be added value for Europe in the proposed research collaboration and it must be possible to demonstrate that only through EU support will it be possible to achieve these specific goals, for example by drawing together complementary expertise from different member states where the whole brings greater benefit to the European Project than simply the sum of the parts.
- All funded work must take the form of a partnership between universities, industry and commerce, private and public research organizations and must have representatives from several member states.
- Great emphasis is given to the dissemination of research findings, so close attention should be paid to stakeholders and potential beneficiaries.

- In most cases, a minimum of two partners from two EU member states or one member of one associated state is required for funding.
- It is advisable to maintain a balance between the partners rather than indicate the dominance of one member state over another. It is also important to demonstrate complementarity of expertise rather than any other artificial parameter such as geographical representation. One of the strongest myths about university research is that partnerships must include representation from less favoured regions of Europe. There is no evidence to support this view and it is more relevant to ensure that the expertise required is fully represented in the partnership.

There are many types of support available, but most operate in accordance with the award of a specific grant to the lead organization of the partnership to administer on behalf of the partnership as a whole. The terms and conditions of award are usually laid down in the form of standard European contracts which are rarely variable.

It is important to follow the guidelines for awards as closely as possible and, if difficulties are encountered, to inform the Commission at the earliest opportunity. On the other hand, and in most respects, European awards under the Framework programme operate in a similar fashion to research grants.

3.15.2 Other European funds

Other funds are made available through the European Commission which are relevant to university-based research such as structural funds (European Social Fund, European Regional Development Fund, and so on). These funds originate with other DGs and should be considered in the light of their overall responsibilities and remits. Such funding sources are *not* usually concerned with research or training for its own sake but only in so far as these make a contribution to other objectives such as creating employment, securing economic competitive advantage, achieving regional economic growth, supporting regional cultural diversity and so on. Funding is more often determined by regional policy and delivered through regional government agencies. These awards are operated in a much closer way as contracts and are not dealt with here.

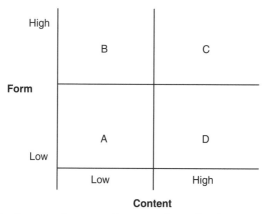

Figure 3.2   Form and content in research applications

3.16 Writing successful research grant applications

Applicants should consider carefully how to present a proposal for university-based research in the form of a grant application to any grant-giving body as categorized in the above sections.

A four-box matrix can be constructed to indicate the likely nature of applications and their outcomes (see Figure 3.2).

The boxes in Figure 3.2 correspond to:

A   Research proposals which are poor ideas and are poorly expressed *will fail.*
B   Research proposals which are poor ideas but well expressed and packaged *may succeed.*
C   Research proposals which are good ideas and are well expressed and packaged have the *best chance of success.*
D   Research proposals which are good ideas but which are poorly expressed and packaged (typically rushed) *may fail.*

It is clearly important to locate as many applications as possible in the C box in order to improve the chances of success. To do so requires:

• forethought;
• preparation;
• time;
• critical evaluation;
• review; and
• compliance with the sponsor's requirements.

Grant proposals which are hurried, poorly finished or incomplete damage the chances of a good idea succeeding in the award of a research grant, can damage the individual applicant's reputation and even adversely affect the reputation of the university as a whole.

The research grant application process starts long before a potential sponsor has been identified and the applicant is confronted by the sponsor's procedures and application forms. The application process begins with the generation of a sound research idea or proposition developed from previous work undertaken by the individual or from within the research group to which the individual belongs.

Testing the idea or research proposition should be the first stage of any successful research grant application and this is best done by formulating the idea into a brief description which can then be considered further by colleagues and peers within the research group or within the wider academic community of the university. The research might also be tested in the form of a work-in-progress paper or poster presentation or in an internal seminar from which a departmental paper might be circulated for further consideration.

As the idea is refined by interaction with colleagues and also with the external world of potential beneficiaries and users, so it must be identified as a part of the individual's research strategy or the strategy of the research group, centre or department and, through further discussion with peers or by taking the advice of the university's research support service, it should be possible to identify the best sponsor opportunity to which application for funding might be made in the most appropriate way. The research sponsor might be immediately apparent or the research proposition might require some further preparation to qualify for a relevant research grant scheme to ensure that it meets the requirements or conditions of a particular programme and will be compliant with the sponsor remit.

The more thorough the preparation, the easier will be the progress through the application process to submission and any interaction with the sponsor. The best source of support for the development of research ideas and proposals is the immediate research group to which the researcher is attached. The university's research support service can help in the process by:

- reading draft proposals and making constructive comments;
- identifying an appropriate research funder;
- providing information on the research funder's programmes and priorities;
- giving guidance on form and content of an application;
- ensuring that an application is compliant, fully and correctly costed, and in accordance with university policy and procedures.

3.17 Compliance and eligibility

All research sponsors would agree that their support is available only to research proposals of the highest quality as judged by competitive peer review. Research applications are submitted to a variety of processes by different research sponsors, but competition is usually arranged to be as open, fair and efficient as possible. The application process is always greatly assisted by the care which is taken when completing the application as well as the extent to which the idea or research proposition has been tested with the local community and potential beneficiaries *before it has been submitted to the sponsor*. It is in the sponsor's interest to encourage the most complete and finished applications and those which are of the highest quality in order to make their own selection procedures efficient and effective by not encouraging applications which might be of poor standard or non-compliant or in some other way do not meet the sponsor's requirements. Sponsors are usually prepared to discuss with potential applicants the idea or research proposition in advance of an application with a view to assessing whether it is covered by their remit.

It is not usually wise to attempt to contact the members of peer review committees or peer review panels likely to be used by the sponsor in advance of an application being made in responsive mode as this will be considered highly inappropriate behaviour. On the other hand, in many directed mode programmes, the programme coordinator will welcome discussion with the wider academic community in order to decide upon the details and priorities for the programme of research envisaged. This process is usually managed through a consultation process within a defined period of time so that full account can be taken of the suggestions which are fed back.

Most research grant sponsors set out clearly their policies and procedures applying to both directed mode and responsive mode programmes of research funding and give clear guidance on the operation of the peer review process to be used for applications. The procedure for making application is also carefully described and it must be assumed that full compliance with such guidelines is taken as a prerequisite for further consideration of an application for funding. It should not be assumed that, during the application process, departure from that guidance, however justified in the eyes of the applicant, will be accepted by the sponsor. The applicant should aim to meet explicitly the sponsor's requirements, especially in the details of format, length limits, word counts, structure and content of a research grant application. When in doubt, it is helpful to check either with a colleague who has experience of a particular sponsor or with the university's research support office or the sponsor's own programme administrators or coordinators.

3.18 Do your homework – sponsor management

Experienced applicants know well the value of 'doing your home-work' on the sponsor and the particular research programme or project scheme under which an application is to be made. It is not only a courtesy to understand the sponsor's requirements but it is also the most practical way of giving an application the best possible chance of success. By following the rules for the application to the letter, the applicant immediately places the application in a compliant state and it should be possible to identify quite clearly how the particular application fits with the particular programme or overall strategy for the chosen sponsor. This can often be accomplished only by investing sufficient time and effort in earlier stages of relationship-building and sponsor management. The larger UK research sponsors (research councils and larger research-based charities) will have their own staff who can be contacted and to whom a potential applicant might make themselves known. This can be done by making sure that opportunities given by the sponsor to communicate with or consult the academic community are pursued. Attendance at consultation meetings or in general briefing sessions is not only useful from the viewpoint of obtaining knowledge about the sponsor's research priorities and remits but also a practical way in which to meet the sponsor's staff or peer reviewers while they are in listening mode. On the other hand, the intending applicant should avoid becoming a nuisance to the potential sponsor. There is a balance to be struck between effective sponsor management and a tiresome approach to sponsor contacts.

3.19 Some general selection criteria and advice

3.19.1 Introduction

Different sponsors will make use of different criteria in different ways when considering research grant applications for their support but, even when the approach is based on peer review, it is possible to draw up a general list of the kinds of criteria that the research sponsor has in mind when inviting applications. These might be summarized as follows:

- research excellence and overall quality;
- strategic relevance;
- timeliness, promise and appropriateness;
- cost-effectiveness and value for money;
- feasibility;
- appropriateness (for example, scale and scope).

Sponsors might make use of other general criteria to do with imperatives on their funding such as:

- contribution to quality of life;
- contribution to economic prosperity;
- contribution to health;
- contribution to the sponsor's remit.

Other criteria will be drawn from the sponsor's specific stated requirements in particular programmes of research or in directed mode projects. Such criteria are always published by the sponsor in advance and should self-evidently become the blueprint for checking against by the applicant before the application is submitted. This can usefully be done by others who are not so close to the content of the research application. It is always useful to review fully a draft application before submission and to submit it to colleagues or to the research support office for a thorough check to establish the appropriateness of its form and content.

3.19.2 General tips

- Realize that you need time to prepare a bid.
- Tailor your proposal to the chosen funding body's objectives.
- Use positive language.
- Strike a balance between confidence and the danger of overstating.
- Remember that your proposal may be read by people not familiar with your research and therefore:
  - write clearly and concisely;
  - use appropriate terminology with defnitions;
  - minimize the jargon.
- Make presentation clear and professional by using:
  - diagrams and tables to aid clarity;
  - bullet points, subheadings and so on to break up dense text.
- Ensure consistency throughout your proposal.
- Link objectives to methods and to budget, timetable and outcomes.
- Follow guidelines explicitly.

- Complete application forms fully and correctly.
- Inexperienced researchers, in particular, may adopt additional strategies such as:
  - collaboration with senior colleagues (but give them an explicit role such as technical or advisory);
  - targeting schemes for new or 'first-time' principal investigators, fast-track schemes or small grant schemes;
  - building on pilot work (for example, conducted as a student project or during other research phases).

3.19.3 In advance

Do preliminary research on funding sources and their objectives by:

- reading funding body literature (guidelines, programme information, annual reports and so on);
- contacting research bodies, especially programme managers, to discuss outline ideas;
- discussing plans with experienced colleagues, especially the review panel, committee members or peer reviewers, and with the research support office;
- looking at previously successful proposals;
- ensuring that your ideas are innovative and clearly thought out by discussing with colleagues (also in other institutions);
- checking that potential users and beneficiaries have been consulted and are supportive of your proposal.

3.19.4 Title and summary

The title and the summary are the two parts which you can be sure everyone involved in considering the application will read – construct them with care and with maximum impact and clarity.

- The title should reflect the research and its relevance and have impact.
- The summary should be clear, concise, expounded in accessible language and include appropriate information.
- Do not write summaries at the end of the application process as you are running out of time.

3.19.5 Aims and objectives

- Describe the overall aim followed by specific objectives. Remember that aims and objectives, although related, are different.
- Give clear bullet points to express objectives.
- Show academic and user need benefit.
- Emphasize the contribution towards the funding body's objectives.
- Reflect the funding body's priorities in formulating the objectives for the proposal.

3.19.6 Background – context

- Focus context section in relation to aims and objectives.
- Succinct reference to literature review should be included as this:
  - demonstrates awareness of previous work in the field;
  - clearly lays the ground for proposed research;
  - identifies gaps in knowledge that you intend to claim.
- Research ideas should come across as clear and original – novel.
- Detail pilot studies – preliminary work you have conducted.
- Show that you or the research team have or have access to all the necessary expertise to carry out the project as follows:
  - even if asked for curriculum vitae, draw out relevant experience of all team members in the text;
  - institutional track record should be given;
  - existing technical support should be specified.

3.19.7 Methodology

Clearly describe and justify each stage of the project including as appropriate:

- Pilot phase.
- Sample frame – where relevant who/what is being studied.
- Sample size, with statistical justification.
- What is being done to subject/samples studied.
- Measurement/analysis techniques. (Do not assume that the reader will be familiar with techniques and records specified.)
- Justify the methodology to be used.
- Ensure the scale is appropriate to meet the objectives specified and to lead to the expected outcomes.
- Provide a clear, feasible project plan including as appropriate:

- a breakdown into tasks, who will conduct which tasks;
  - a realistic timetable which takes into account the inter-dependence of tasks and availability of people.
- Equipment.
- A graphic illustration of the timetable can add clarity (for example, a Programme Evaluation and Review Technique (PERT) or Gantt chart might be used).

3.19.8 Project management

- Show that you understand the importance of meeting objectives, timetable and budget.
- Show awareness of the critical points of your project plan where management decisions or choices may have to be made (i.e. 'milestones').
- Identify who is responsible for overall management and, if appropriate, individual parts of the project.
- Identify adviser and/or steering committee, where appropriate, and their role in project management, evaluation, outcomes.
- Explain how information will be disseminated about the project, both within the project team and with partners and/or programme managers and/or users and beneficiaries as appropriate (for example, team meetings).
- Highlight support available from within the university, for example financial management through the finance office, guidance on commercialization through the university's commercial agent, support from the university's research support office.

3.19.9 Resources

- The resources requested should be compatible with the expected outcomes and benefits and should match the scale of the research proposal.
- Give a realistic breakdown of all eligible costs and ensure that cost heads have been included for every allowable expenditure head.
- Justify all costs (including duration and grade of additional staff appointments) in relation to the completion of the project.
- Detail access to existing resources (equipment, support staff and so on.)

3.19.10 Outcomes, outputs and dissemination

Create a section on outcomes (even if not explicitly asked for) addressing:

- contribution to knowledge and implications for future research;
- benefits to users: industry, policy-makers, public services as appropriate;
- broader relevance – beneficiaries (government, commerce, society, research agency, public);
- all proposed means of dissemination: academic publications, commercial exploitation, publicity via the media, electronic means (*e-search*) through websites and the internet.

The single most important factor is to demonstrate clearly what 'big idea' is contained in the research grant application. Let the central aim shine out rather than bury it beneath the application's dense verbosity.

In summary, the sponsor's requirements in an application can be grouped in terms of four basic questions:

- Can the research be done?
- Has the research been done?
- Should the research be done and by the applicant?
- Should the research be funded by the research sponsor?

That the research is of the highest quality and is innovative must be regarded as a prerequisite of all grant-aided research.

3.20 The application process

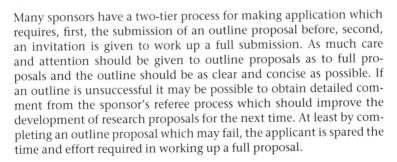

Many sponsors have a two-tier process for making application which requires, first, the submission of an outline proposal before, second, an invitation is given to work up a full submission. As much care and attention should be given to outline proposals as to full proposals and the outline should be as clear and concise as possible. If an outline is unsuccessful it may be possible to obtain detailed comment from the sponsor's referee process which should improve the development of research proposals for the next time. At least by completing an outline proposal which may fail, the applicant is spared the time and effort required in working up a full proposal.

Remember that the entire application process (whether successful or unsuccessful) can be part of a valuable learning experience and, given that the rate of success against the number of applications received by most research grant sponsors (the 'strike rate') is increasingly high, it is usual and expected for a research grant applicant to make more than one application before the first success is achieved.

The unsuccessful applicant must avoid regarding the lack of success in a particular application as a personal failure. Where a grant application does not succeed, this failure may be more a reflection of the competition for funds than the lack of excellence of the proposal. Always remember that the research sponsor, because of the number of applications, is seeking ways to say 'no' to an application rather than 'yes'.

The research applicant should regard the failure of an application as an occupational hazard and expect to make more than one application before success is achieved. It is rare for a single application to be successful at the first attempt. The aim is to make the most effective application possible, not the greatest number of applications.

3.21 Supporting the application process

Well-organized universities provide support for the process of making research grant applications through the research services office or similar body and from within schools, centres or departments. In most cases, support will also take the form of staff development programmes for training in preparation for making applications for research funding. Such university training programmes are a necessary assistance to learning the practical skills of making research grant applications and are especially valuable for new members of staff or for disseminating good practice from one research group to another as well as being particularly useful in the context of interdisciplinary research or for making larger research proposals which require coordination of more than one research group or research idea. Such support should also be featured in the university's research strategy and in strategy-setting at all levels for research. Particular attention should be focused on developing fundable research ideas. If it is clear what research sponsors consider to be the most important criteria, it is possible to respond positively to this information.

3.22 Developing grant-fundable research ideas

It is no longer possible to support the research to which universities aspire on the basis of the direct funding for research received from the government via the funding councils. Researchers need to think about their research in discrete projects which can form the basis of research grant applications. By doing this, university researchers can seek external grant funding in the knowledge that the range of sponsor opportunities can be made use of in achieving the researcher's goals and aspirations for their research. The objective is to match together:

• personal research goals;
• university aspirations and strategy for research; and
• sponsor programmes and objectives.

Having considered the personal research programme in this way, applicants should maximize their chances of success by making the best possible case for their idea or research proposition. Use the checklists set out in Figures 3.3 and 3.4.

3.23 Summary

Remember that research grant applications are not stand-alone proposals but should fit into a personal research strategy and integrate with the centre, department or school's research strategy. Applications do not emerge as isolated processes but from the context of an overall research plan and the general context of a particular field of research.

• Novel/innovative research
• Sound ideas backed by knowledge
• Well-contextualized research projects with clear direction
• Appropriate methodology
• Appropriate expertise/'track record' or access to the right 'know-how'
• Research that meets the sponsor's aims and remit
• Evidence of the value of research outputs to wider audience (including users and beneficiaries)
• Evidence that research will be well managed
• Evidence of likely research outcomes
• Value for money – appropriate scale and means

Figure 3.3   What sponsors look for

- Show thorough knowledge of research area and the key players via literature, conferences, networking
- Consider internal and external partnerships when appropriate
- Understand potential sponsors and their remit, aims and priorities (i.e. sponsor management)
- Be aware whom your research benefits in the short and long term and engage them
- Consider the application of the research idea(s) or methods to new fields and patterns and vice versa
- Choose the appropriate mode of funding (i.e. grant type, programme or scheme)
- Ensure the application sets out the best case for research proposition – check with others

Figure 3.4   How to achieve what sponsors are looking for

Chasing research grants in a haphazard way, by responding to initiatives or simply 'firing off' applications in a random fashion, is unlikely to succeed. Planning a strategy and evolving research grant applications from it which map proposals against sponsor programmes is a more systematic approach with a much greater chance of success.

Be prepared to make more than one research grant application. Sponsors agree that first-time applicants are rarely successful and that applicants need to approach sponsors with good proposals between three and seven times, depending on the different sponsor success rates, before an application will be successful.

Partly, such an outcome is the result of a process of 'getting to know you' and getting to see that there is an underlying consistency in your work, although different referees will almost certainly be involved for each application.

Partly, success rate depends upon career profile, and what evidence sponsors are prepared to make available seems to indicate that the career profile is a significant factor.

Use the opportunities made available by the sponsor:

- Attend consultation reviews and national or regional meetings and road shows.
- Make use of first-time or fast-track schemes designed for new and younger university researchers.
- Consider small grant schemes as a first step – travel grants, exchanges, collaborations, fellowships and so on.
- Make proposals realistic in terms of scale and means so that a profile for reliability and value for money can be constructed.

- Attend conferences/make presentations in the research field and ensure that external sponsors and their peer reviewers are aware of personal research development.
- Consider joint applications with a partner principal investigator with an established reputation or success rate with external sponsors.
- Make the best of experience to date, drawing out research successes in earlier career phases including undergraduate and postgraduate levels.

Much is made of success rates but, at the foundation, the only success rate that matters is the successful outcome to a research grant application, wherever it occurs and however long it takes. Until then, the most important feature of the process is to avoid becoming discouraged.

Do not regard lack of success as personal failure but as a necessary part of the research experience. Maintain morale and continue to develop good ideas and turn them into well-made research proposals which can become further research grant applications.

The hardest part of the process is the generation of ideas and research proposals. Good research will be successfully funded in the long run.

4

CONTRACT RESEARCH

4.1 Introduction: some distinctions

The nature of a contract has already been described in Chapter 1 on the research context. Contract research in universities is simply research undertaken for a third party, external to the university, where both the work to be carried out and the payment for it are specified in terms of a formal contract or other form of binding agreement. Contract research can be differentiated from grant-aided research in three important respects:

- First, research to be carried out may or may not be relevant to the programme of research being carried out by individuals or groups within the centre, department or school but, once contracted, the agreement binds the university to carry out a programme of research in accordance with a specification for the work, a required timescale and to standards which are set down. There is not usually any choice permitted as to the approach to the work and the terms and conditions, once entered into and unless separately specified, cannot be departed from or varied. Failure to complete the work or discharge the research in accordance with the agreed specification may result in penalties.
- Second, the university usually expresses the costs of contract research in terms of a single inclusive price which represents the market value of the work. Although the price, which is usually fixed, is often arrived at by first deriving the baseline of full economic costs, both direct and indirect, it is set not simply as a figure which will recover full costs alone but at a level which will generate

surpluses and will represent the premium for the research against its value in the marketplace.
- Third, contract research is usually driven solely by the third party's requirements, and research results arising from the contracted work are usually to be owned by the third party or, at least, will be covered by the contract and the conditions negotiated and agreed at the outset.

Contract research should not be confused with:

- *collaborative research*, where research is carried out in partnership between the university and the third party concerned or with other partners on a shared costs basis or with the support of public funds in the form of grant aid; or
- *sponsored research*, where research is sponsored directly by a third party in order to aid the university's research purposes, typically in the form of postgraduate research sponsorship, scholarships or fellowships, even when there may also be tangible benefits to the third party concerned.

Much confusion arises over the nature of university-based contract research partly from the apparent misunderstanding between the perceptions of universities and private or public third parties interested in university research outcomes and, partly, from the experience of operating at the crucial interface between the university and the contractor.

4.1.1 Objectives of the different parties

It should be remembered that the function and objectives of universities and other third parties (typically, commerce and industry) are not the same, although they may come together, and even overlap, in a particular research project or programme/partnership.

These differing objectives can be expressed in the following terms:

University objectives
- Teaching
- Research } academic purposes
- Knowledge and technology transfer
- Continuing education and training } advancement of knowledge

- Operates in accordance with timescales and facilities derived from the primary function of education.
- Produces surpluses and operates in accordance with academic values.
- Accountable to:
  - governing body and stakeholders (representing government and users);
  - staff (as employees);
  - students (as customers).
- Performance evaluation based on peer esteem.

Private sector objectives
- Products and processes ⎫
                          ⎬ commercial purposes
- Services   ⎭
- Informed by advances in knowledge which underpin the business.
- Operates in accordance with business production timescales.
- Makes profits.
- Accountable to:
  - shareholders;
  - customers and clients;
  - employees.
- Performance evaluation measured by competitiveness, market share and share value.

4.1.2 Motivations of the different parties

Operational motivation differs as well. For the university, contract research brings:

- Funding.
- Intellectual challenge.
- Opportunities for the application of knowledge.
- Esteem.
- Professional development for staff.
- Student/graduate opportunities.
- Opportunities to demonstrate direct contribution to economic prosperity at local, regional, national and international levels.
- Access to industrial standard know-how, practice and facilities.
- Measurable outputs relevant to national research scrutiny exercises and to other funding sources.

For the private sector, contract research brings:

- Solutions to problems.
- Technology and know-how transfer.
- Access to advanced knowledge.
- Opportunities to develop new products, processes and services.
- Profitability and increased market share.
- Access to capabilities and capacities not available within the organization.

In contract research, a contract is a document designed to make clear what is agreed between the university and the contracting third party. It should not be designed as a document which emphasizes the supremacy of one set of values or ethics over another. When contracts are clearly expressed and agreed in advance, research will proceed more effectively than when uncertainty or lack of clarity exist or issues are left unresolved.

4.2 The battle of the standards

It is wise for the university to have prepared its preferable position beforehand and even to have drawn up, with legal advice, a set of standard clauses or a range of standard contract documents covering contract research. It is to be expected that the client will also have prepared the ground beforehand and will have drawn up standard documents for use in the negotiation of contract research. Often the latter documents will be general-purpose purchase orders or other forms of purchase contract and will not have been tailored to the needs of contract research with the university. It is best to avoid the use of inappropriate documentation and to persuade the client to adopt a more specific and functional contract document.

The university's standard contract document is useful to open discussions as an indication of the university's position on contract research, but it will only rarely be acceptable without further discussion.

Contracting is best undertaken by meeting together and discussing the issues which need to be considered, setting out the programme of research, specifying deadlines, milestones or other requirements, and agreeing a fair price for the work in accordance with its market value. Once agreement on the issues has been reached, including ownership of intellectual property (to which we shall return), the draft contract can be drawn up.

This is a better method of proceeding than that in which one side 'forces' its own preferred standard or model contract on the other. The battle of the standards can be avoided by open discussion and negotiation. It is helpful to give a general indication on likely acceptable terms and areas of potential difference by exchanging standard or model contract documents in advance, but the practice is no reason for unnecessary obstruction and dogmatic insistence on one standard contract over the other or a substitute for discussion and negotiation.

4.3 The nature of research contracts

Contracts can be applied to a range of different services provided by universities, as well as research, including the following:

- Access to facilities or laboratories.
- Analysis or testing/services.
- Consultancy.
- Technology and know-how transfer.
- Product and processes service reports.
- Accommodation.
- Conferences and seminars.
- Short courses and continuing professional development (CPD).
- Service teaching.
- Design or other specialist services.
- Demonstration facilities.
- Product and processes testing and development.
- Prototyping and fabrication.
- Other specialist services.

Each of these involves the requirement for a contract document to be agreed, but these activities are not to be confused with research contracting although the underlying knowledge required for their delivery may be derived from the research function at the university. The above activities are also linked through the possibility that work in these categories was obtained by the process of competitive tendering with which universities are becoming increasingly involved.

Such activities also have in common that they are determined by the requirements of third parties or other bodies who let contracts to universities in these areas. Much of what follows, applying to research contracting, can also be applied to contracting for these activities as well. Universities undertake contract research not only with industry, commerce and the private sector but also with public authorities and government agencies such as:

- the European Union (the European Commission) and other international bodies;
- agencies of government at both national, regional and local levels (the public sector);
- departments of state;
- professional bodies and consultancies;
- the voluntary and services sector.

4.4 The third task

Many of these services are now provided systematically and routinely by universities as part of the developing role and expanding activities characterized as *third task functions*. The term 'third task' originated in Scandinavian higher education and describes all the activities in which universities engage which are directly concerned neither with teaching at degree level nor with research. In the UK, the Higher Education Funding Council for England first developed the notion that a funding stream should be created for this purpose. Known initially as third leg or stream funding, the more general term of 'outreach' has also been applied to these activities. Most universities have established platforms of outreach or outreach programmes designed to make a range of services, derived from their teaching and research, available to a wide market of clients and customers in the local, regional and national context.

Much of the practical advice and guidance which applies to drawing up contracts for research also applies where outreach activities are concerned, especially if the delivery of outreach services is dependent on a price being levied on the customer as distinct from those elements of the outreach programme which are part of the voluntary activities of the university or are designed as contributions to local community or regional development. In some cases, outreach activities attract public funding through other third-party agencies such as, in the UK, the Learning and Skills Councils or the reformed Business Link services or through the local regional development agency or other regional providers. In those cases, it is likely that a contract would be applied by the third-party agency on a surrogate basis for other customers and clients such as local communities and groups, voluntary sector organizations or small businesses. The general principles of clarity of purpose and agreed targets and deadlines apply to outreach services of this kind, and careful consideration of the basic contract document should be given in order to construct a positive framework in which the activities can be delivered efficiently and satisfactorily.

4.5 The regional context

It is not only in the UK that the importance of relationships with universities have been recognized as the foundation for regional economic development. Throughout Europe, government departments and agencies support research in universities for the purpose of economic regeneration, and in North America the role of the university in securing regional economic growth has been identified as a crucial factor in determining both the nature of economic regeneration and the likely growth path for the future. In the UK, the arrival of the Scottish Parliament and the Welsh and Northern Ireland Assemblies has highlighted the importance of regional economic development and the role of higher education. These developments have led the university into new forms of contracts and agreements with a mix of public sector bodies such as regional development agencies, national governmental organizations and institutions, private sector representative groups such as chambers of commerce or employers' organizations, semi-public institutions such as regional business support agencies or learning and skills councils and commerce and industry whose goal is to pool their resources and approaches towards mutually advantageous regional economic growth. Many models exist for such associations, but the most common is to regard the university as a storehouse of knowledge assets or knowledge capital and to seek ways of exploiting these within the region. The idea of the knowledge house or knowledge centre has become an important one for regions to the extent that, where a region has not traditionally had proximity to a university, attempts have been made to create it. Forms of association are many and varied, from limited companies to loose agreements, and will be selected according to different requirements. Where joint ventures are entered into, similar principles apply to those underpinning university contracting. The nature of joint venture agreements aimed at economic regeneration will vary from region to region but will often have certain elements in common:

- Investment in research capacity and capability in the university.
- Development of mechanisms for the exploitation of the outputs from research in the form of support for small businesses, creation of new 'spin-out' companies, partnership with larger companies, links with potential inward investors, links with venture capital sources or creation of venture capital funds to be used to develop routes to markets.

The most recent statements about English regions has been made in the government White Paper *Your Region, Your Choice: Revitalising the English Regions* published in 2002 by the Department of Transport, Local Government and the Regions and to be found at www.regions.dttr.gov.uk/governance/whitepaper/index.htm.

4.6 Drawing up a research contract

The purpose of a research contract is to agree before a research project begins on a framework for reaching a common understanding of each party's commitments and responsibilities as far as carrying out a particular research project is concerned. The contract is a legally binding document and will also provide a record of what was agreed during the negotiation stage which preceded the commencement of research.

During the project, the contract document will provide suitable mechanisms for the management of the research, its administration and any dispute resolution arrangements.

On the research project's completion, the contract document provides a record of continuing obligation placed upon each party in a reciprocal way and, as a last resort, a clear framework for litigation. It should be remembered that a contract could be held in law to exist in many forms where commitments may already have been made either orally (spoken) or verbally (written). It is important, therefore, to avoid any discussion or exchanges of correspondence which might be deemed to have formed a contract until negotiations have been formally completed and a legally binding contract has been executed.

In particular, it should be remembered that, in any contract-tendering process, all tender documents included with tender submissions are held to be formal legal documents constituting a contractual commitment in their own right. If a tender is accepted by the contractor, no further discussion or negotiation is necessary for a contract to be deemed to exist. It is, therefore, especially important to ensure that documents or exchanges made during the tendering process are accurate and in keeping with the requirements for the contract itself.

4.7 Contract issues

There are many issues surrounding the research contract which should be considered at the outset as follows:

4.7.1 Deliverables

The contract must provide a coherent, unambiguous, clear and concise account of what the research project is to involve and what is covered by the research project envisaged so that, in the worst case, an independent arbitrator could decide whether the contract had been fulfilled or not. In particular, specific 'deliverables', that is outputs from the research project at its conclusion or during its progress, must be clearly defined. If such deliverables are dependent on time or other factors, these factors must also be clearly stated so that performance can be measured against them by any objective or independent judge or by reference to a stated specification reviewed as part of the project management process.

4.7.2 Timescale

The chronology for a contract research project must be set down accurately with key dates indicated. In particular, attention should be paid to the question of start date. This might be commensurate with the date when the contract was authorized or was formally executed but it is usual to allow for an interval between contract execution and the start of the project in order to cover the inevitable negotiation period. It is not to be recommended that contracts are entered into, in a formal sense, *after* a start date has actually passed as this can create difficulties in assessing contract performance. Other keys dates must also be specified such as project review dates, output milestones, and the end date for the research project. This timescale should be clearly described and agreed in the contract from the outset.

4.7.3 Research protocol or specification

All research contracts must have contained within them or attached to them a clear project work plan expressing the aims and objectives for the research project, methodologies, resources, including personnel, facilities and equipment, and all other aspects of the practical 'carrying through' to a successful conclusion of the research. It is not possible to consider the conditions of a research contract in isolation from the research protocol or specification: to try to do so is a major error.

The contract commits the university, and the research protocol or specification describes to what the university is committed. The two must be read together.

4.7.4 Intellectual property

More is said and written about intellectual property clauses in research contracts than virtually any other aspect. The subject will be returned to later in this chapter. The ownership of foreground intellectual property developed under the project, together with rights of publication and exploitation, must be determined within the contract document. In particular, foreground intellectual property must be distinguished from background intellectual property, the latter being existing intellectual property brought to the research contract by either or both parties.

4.7.5 Risks and liabilities

Risks and liabilities must be clearly stated at the outset in the contract and there should be no hidden or obscure clauses with regard to risks and liabilities. Clauses should be mutually binding on both parties to the contract.

4.7.6 Termination

There should be termination clauses specified in the event that either party wishes to withdraw from the contract. These are sometimes referred to as sunset clauses. What happens on termination should be specified, including any retention of resources or completion of commitments or other matters as agreed beforehand. If things go wrong, the contract should be a document which can be used to settle matters expeditiously and, in particular, must provide mechanisms for dispute resolution.

4.7.7 Standard elements

The contract must refer to procedures to be followed should either party wish to modify or vary the terms and conditions of the contract. This circumstance might simply be deemed to be not permitted but, whatever the agreement, the contract is the source document describing the means to be adopted to prompt discussion on variation or modification.

   The contract should also specify the national code of law by which the contract is deemed to be interpreted or governed, whether this is English, Scottish, US or another legal system. Procedures for arbitration, in the event of irreconcilable differences, should also be specified, as these will make it easier to determine the outcome of an irretrievable breakdown and avoid long and costly legal battles.

4.8 The contract from the client's perspective

Recognizing that each party will have different perspectives on the nature of the research contract goes some way towards enlightening each party on the other's point of view. Enlightenment is essential towards a successful negotiation and research contract outcome.

The client's main objective will be to produce the appropriate research project (i.e. research which meets needs and objectives identified beforehand), on time, to budget and without any unforeseen difficulties. The client usually requires a clear timescale with defined deliverables and is likely to want to secure the following during contract negotiation:

- Ownership of intellectual property arising from the research project.
- Exclusive commercial rights to exploit arising intellectual property.
- Retention of commercial resources arising from successful exploitation of the resulting intellectual property.
- Designation of all formal intellectual property as being mutually confidential information, both during and beyond the lifetime of the research contract.

The university can begin negotiations on the basis that the client's perspective can be expected to embrace many of these points.

4.9 The contract from the university's perspective

The university will usually have engaged in contract research for two reasons. First, the university will regard contract research with the private sector or other third parties as contributing indirectly to the advancement of knowledge through the facilitation of its goals and purposes for research in general. This can take many forms, including:

- access to cutting-edge technologies available through the third party;
- special expertise;
- market application or problem-solving;

- access to premium-priced income which can be used for improving the university's facilities for research;
- enhancement of reputation through association with leading companies or other third-party organizations on a contract basis.

All of the above contribute to the expansion of the university's research base, to the enhancement of the research skills of its staff and to the generation of further research from other research sponsors who set a premium on work carried out by contract.

The second reason is more obvious and that is simply to make money in the form of surpluses based upon the price charged for individual research contracts. Some universities regard the surpluses from research contract income as 'free money' in that resources can be applied to projects or purposes of the university's choice, supplementing its income from the public sector where there are usually more constraints applied. This is, in part, an illusion in that to undertake contract research of a serious nature, facilities, expertise and marketing are required to be fully developed otherwise contract research can only be undertaken at the margin of research carried out through grant aid and usually only on a strictly marginal costs basis.

Few universities in the UK have been able to produce the model of contract research common amongst leading institutions in the United States where private sector work and the exploitation of intellectual property have led those institutions to develop as wholly independent bodies sustaining their research activities on the basis of earned income. Institutions in the UK that would aspire to such independence are aware that income from contract research can be an unstable basis for funding, vulnerable to economic boom and bust, an unbalanced portfolio of funded research making the institution vulnerable to market changes and fluctuations and leading to uncertainty in financial forecasting for those institutions. Even in the best economic conditions, the private sector in the UK probably underinvests in R&D and will cease even this level of investment when economic conditions worsen. Few institutions in the UK are able to stand the buffeting of economic change and therefore few are wholly dependent on contract research as a source of income.

There is an ethical dimension as well, as it might be argued that institutions which became more fully dependent on research contract income and commercialization might find that the university's fundamental goals and purpose expressed in its basic mission become distorted or even transformed. The university's negotiating position on research contracts must pay careful attention to the costs and price for the work to be carried out and to ownership of intellectual property and its future exploitation, not least to maintain its ethical position as an independent and objective source of research. Universities will usually strive to include in the research contract favourable terms and conditions towards the following:

- The right to publish for academic and scholarship purposes without unreasonable restriction is seen as essential to protecting the university's mission, although most contracts recognize the need to protect intellectual property through patent application as a first step before publication as not unreasonable on the part of the client.
  - Special care must be given where contract research involves the work of postgraduate research students since their future careers and, indeed, examination success are dependent on the ability to draw on their postgraduate research for the future and in the preparation of their theses.
  - Universities usually understand that premature publication could destroy the value of intellectual property by preventing the protection of the patent and simply want to protect their route to scholarship and academic publication.
- In most cases it is easy to reach a compromise which facilitates publication in accordance with normal academic practice subject to the prior written consent of the client but which may include a moratorium on publication pending applications for patent protection. Standard forms of wording can be developed to suit all circumstances and are usually found to be acceptable for most contract research.
- The university must also protect itself from any restriction on the right to use the results of the contract research project in its own future research work. A minimum requirement for such use should be for the university's own internal research purposes, but consideration might be given to the possibility of using the results with other potential clients, whereas it is extremely unlikely that a client will agree to allow the results to be used as a basis for further research with a direct competitor. Where the results of the work are likely to have characteristics for future application in fields distinct from the client's field of interest, the university should attempt to gain agreement for the use of its research results in non-competing fields in conjunction with other third parties.
- The university must seek a position on intellectual property ownership and subsequent royalty revenues arising from research undertaken by contract.
  - If ownership of intellectual property is to be transferred to the client then the university should at least ensure it has the right

to reclaim intellectual property not exploited or abandoned by the contractor in the future.

- The university should expect to retain a fair and reasonable share in financial returns if the project proves commercially successful. Clauses which give such a share to the university on a percentage basis of royalties or which specify that this matter will be negotiated at the time on a fair and reasonable basis should be included.

- Universities should not subsidize contract research from public funds. In those circumstances where a collaborative agreement is envisaged, negotiation should take place on the provision of a reasonable surplus by the university in accordance with the principle of no subsidy. This might be achieved not only through a price mechanism but also by receiving a share of royalties from exploitation in the future or from any other revenue streams obtained by the third party from the successful exploitation of resulting intellectual property. Some third parties regard this approach as unhelpful and greedy on the part of the university, but as public institutions supported by considerable amounts of public investment, it is appropriate to point out that the university can only safeguard its position and protect that part of the investment through such arrangements. When this is discussed in detail most third parties are willing to concede the validity of the argument.

4.10 Conflicts of interest

Conflicts of interest can be avoided if the university has an open policy on the declaration of interests so that likely conflicts can be identified in advance and steps taken to avoid irrevocable difficulties. The university should adopt a code of practice for ethical conduct which applies to all aspects of the university's business – teaching and learning, research and third task activities. A standard procedure can be adopted whereby staff are required on an annual basis to declare outside interests or interests likely to relate to the university's business. By self-declaration, staff should also indicate that, having considered the matter, they are confident no such outside interests exist. By adopting standards which apply in other areas of public life, embodied in a code of conduct, the university signals its intention to act in an ethical way in all matters relating to contract research.

The code should contain specific clauses designed to cover conflict of interest which ensure:

- the obligation of employees of full disclosure.
- a definition of conflict of interest, namely: personal or family links or financial involvements with any organization engaged in a financial association with the university, providing sponsorship or support, including all forms of financial involvement such as hospitality, gifts, loans or other provisions.
- personal responsibility of employees for disclosure to the lead manager as soon as they become aware of a potential conflict of interest.
- acceptance of the university's direction in the matter.

It is especially important to consider potential conflicts of interest in the area of contract research as well as in related areas such as consultancy; commercial exploitation; technology transfer; sale of goods and services; product prototyping, testing and development; provision of continuing professional development and similar services.

Any breaches of the university's code of conduct must be dealt with promptly under the terms of the code for handling cases of misconduct.

4.11 Negotiation: working together

Negotiation is simply a process for exchanging information and reaching agreement. Negotiation represents a joint effort among the university's academic staff who wish to see research carried out, its research contract staff (i.e. those responsible for the contracting process) who wish to safeguard the university's position, and the third party client who wishes to undertake a research project by contract and to protect the client's commercial interests but also to ensure that the piece of research is carried out successfully.

Negotiation is, therefore, a process which aims to achieve a specific deliverable and is not an end in itself. In most cases in UK universities, it is likely that academic staff will have made the initial contact with potential research contractors and will have developed the outlines of the specific research project around their expertise and facilities. The role of the research contract staff in the university is to determine the price for the research programme and to ensure that negotiations lead to a mutually acceptable research contract in which the university's interests are protected. The client's interests will also probably be represented by a project champion – the company's employee who makes the business case for the research to be carried out – and the company's legal, contractual or financial staff with whom the contract is to be agreed.

It is essential for all parties concerned to be clear as to the full details of projects and to understand the internal processes which must be covered by both the university and the client in order to achieve agreement on the research contract, in particular who is authorized to sign the contract. Most importantly, time must be allowed for the full details to be explored and for the negotiations to take place. Even where a standard document is found to be acceptable without modification or variation, it will still be necessary for processes of exchange of information and authorization to take place.

It is usually the best approach to bring in the university's research contract staff at as early a stage as possible. Once discussion moves from a technical level on a researcher-to-researcher basis and passes to a financial or legal level, then the research contracts officer should take over negotiations. The process of negotiation should facilitate a successful research contract which, in itself, should lead to successful research both for the academic researcher and for the client concerned.

Clients, partners and sponsors of university research will seek to draw up contracts governing the commissioning of specific research projects. Clients, partners and sponsors come not only from industry and commerce but also from the public sector, the voluntary sector, the EU and international agencies. Typically, government departments and other parts of the public sector will contract with universities for research and will seek to draw up research contracts in which many of the same principles apply. A long-held misconception by some parts of the public sector was that universities, being a part also of the public sector, could contract research on a 'knock for knock basis', that is, because public revenues had already been dedicated to higher education to provide facilities for research, research for other sections of the public sector could be undertaken on a marginal costs or even direct costs only basis. 'Knock for knock' has never been the case in reality and most public sector bodies now recognize that they must be prepared to pay the full price for university contract research if they wish to carry out such projects in universities on the same basis as private sector clients. Contracting of this kind must not be confused with public sector bodies who have the responsibility for making grants to higher education for research as part of their remit, for example the UK research councils or special initiative schemes run by other public sector or local government bodies discussed in the previous chapter. Where contracts with the public sector are to be drawn up, negotiation is usual and it is important to observe the same principles.

As has already been mentioned, contracts with the European Commission are also awarded for university-based research, and these documents, although formidable at first sight, simply reflect the basis under which the European Commission undertakes such contract research, specifying the reciprocal duties and responsibilities of all concerned.

4.12 Collaborative research

Contract research is different from collaborative research where research is undertaken in the form of partnerships between equal bodies and in which joint agreements are the most usual form of binding document. Research agreements will specify many of the same concerns as those which apply to research contracts but these will be expressed much more in terms of mutual reciprocity in which costs, risks, undertakings, research tasks and rewards will be shared. If the university seeks to develop partnerships for research, it does so in the knowledge that these will differ from work carried out in the form of research contracts.

The university requires partnerships in order to develop its overall research strategy including accessing publicly funded research collaborative schemes where third-party partnerships are a prerequisite. The university also requires partners to support its overall research strategy and to underpin its research activities supported by grant. In many cases, these partners represent the wider user community and are able to speak positively for the university's research with research councils, charities and public sector bodies responsible for determining national research policies and procedures. Research collaborations can be undertaken with the same third-party bodies as the university would undertake contract research. The categories are not mutually exclusive but it is important to differentiate between the two basic forms of contract and collaborative research even where these exist simultaneously with the same research client so that there is no confusion between work undertaken by contract and work undertaken as part of a joint agreement.

The best guide is that produced by AVRIL (AVRIL 2001).

4.13 Sponsored research

The university will seek sponsors for its research who will provide financial or other support for its own sake, in pursuit of the advancement of knowledge or for training purposes but for whom the payment for the research to be carried out is in the nature of a sponsorship agreement. This most typically applies to undergraduate projects, postgraduate research and all the varieties of studentships, fellowships, industrial placements, sponsorships and national schemes such as the integrated graduate development scheme, the Joint Research Equipment Initiative, the Faraday scheme, and post-graduate awards where partners are required. Some of the nationally funded schemes are specified in section 4.16 below, with a brief description. Even where the association with the university takes the form of a sponsorship agreement, it is important to establish clarity in dealing with the sponsor. There should be no misunderstanding as to the nature of the agreement and expectation should not be raised that the limited form of sponsorship carries with it any inherent right of access to wider research benefits. Most sponsors of university research in this form do so in order to access potential employees or to make a general contribution to the provision of skills and training or to acquire a specific research capability within proximity to the third party who might then undertake specific projects by research contract.

4.14 Strategic relationships

It is important for the university to establish strategic relationships with its major clients, partners and sponsors while recognizing that individual companies or organizations could be identified in each of these groups. Long-term and mutually beneficial relationships are the most important form of association for research which universities can establish. Strategic relationships are most often based upon an enduring capability or area of service, and some industrial sectors or commercial enterprises seek to identify exclusive agreements with a select group of university providers of research services and to form long-standing overarching agreements to define and govern such strategic relationships. Such documents usually take the form of joint agreements or even joint ventures, and it is important to ensure that such agreements describe accurately what expectations exist on each side and what services can be provided within the agreement as well as defining those which exist outside. Such overarching agreements are rarely mutually exclusive or monopolistic, that is preventing either party from contracting with or partnering competitors, and it is unlikely to be in either side's interests to restrict them in this way.

On the other hand, a *joint venture agreement* (JVA) with specific objectives in view, binding the university and its third-party partner with specific goals, is increasingly common and such, usually 'once-off', agreements need to be carefully tailored to the specific needs envisaged. Such agreements can rarely be regarded as standard even if they might draw down standard formal clauses governing certain aspects of the relationship. The research contracts officer or other university support service with responsibility for this area needs to begin discussion with a clear understanding as to the specific nature of the work to be undertaken and the goal jointly held, thereby enabling a clear distinction to be drawn between clients, partners and sponsors and the appropriate legal document to be drawn up. Attempts to 'fudge' the issues will only lead to confusion and to a generally bad relationship. It is far better to begin upon a basis of clarity so that no party has perceptions or expectations which are not understood by the other party.

4.15 Fair dealing

In the main, the principle of fair dealing is paramount in all forms of contracting. Long-term strategic relationships can rarely be fostered on badly drawn up documents or on relationships not founded in trust and confidence. Many relationships founder and research fails in circumstances of mistrust or misconception. Honouring commitments to deliver on time and to budget must be the basis for successful research contracting even if the research contract includes provision for a best endeavours approach as far as individual researchers or teams are concerned. It is not usually acceptable to clients to provide excuses for non-compliance to contract terms on the basis of the difference between the academic environment and that which prevails in the client's world. The project's specification should take into account all possibilities or circumstances likely to lead to non-delivery.

If problems are unforeseen and are of a genuine nature then early discussion towards resolution is the best approach. Fair dealing with the client remains the principle. Equally, if commercial exploitation produces revenues or royalties, the client should honour its agreement with the university to provide a share of those in return rather than expect the university to be able to identify and pursue its rights under such contracts. Fair dealing is a mutually reciprocal principle.

4.16 Government and public sector research contracts

Most governments need to inform their operational policies and procedures by research, some part of which will be carried out in universities. Public sector contracts with universities represent an area of research activity which is of growing importance to universities.

UK government departments, for example, allocate a total of approximately £3.3 million to R&D (excluding the science, engineering and technology funding). Of this, by far the largest proportion, around £2.2 billion, is spent by the Ministry of Defence. The purpose of this research by government departments is to enable the achievement of their policy objectives. The research tends to be strategic or applied in nature and much of it is conducted by the departments or their agencies through their own laboratories and other facilities. Most departments will contract external expertise (including academic expertise from universities if appropriate) to conduct research on their behalf. Much of this work is contracted and takes the form of research contracting in a similar way to that in the private sector. Such research is usually allocated on the basis of competitive tendering following a public announcement and is carried out in accordance with EU directives. Such announcements usually give the aims and objectives set by the particular government department together with the timescale for the project, leaving those tendering to propose the working method and necessary resources. The best tender – not necessarily defined as the lowest-priced tender – will be selected on the basis of best value for money against the objectives. Tender procedures are usually applied even if there is a programme director acting on behalf of the department or agency.

Universities wishing to take a share of this work are required to monitor government announcements in order to identify emerging priorities and themes which might take the form of future contract tenders. Information is available in the context of *e-search* (through the internet) as well as via printed information and advertisements in the relevant journals and press. The European Commission also advertises contract tenders in this way through *e-search* and official European journals. Having identified the appropriate contact point or 'desk holder' responsible for the particular field of enquiry within an appropriate government department, it is possible for academic researchers to discuss their expertise and to gain an understanding of the likely themes and priorities which will arise.

It is important to attend tender information days (where these take place) and to obtain tender information packs in order to comprehend fully the nature of the particular government contract being let. In most cases, government departments follow a similar pattern in that the UK *The Forward Look* process will set out, at three levels, details of the likely research to be undertaken. At the first level, a general mission statement will be given which sets out policy objectives and ties to them research themes and priorities. At the next level,

The Forward Look will include details of themes and priorities being pursued or those which have a place in the present strategic plan for the department itself. These themes and priorities are usually generalized but will give a clear indication of the direction of the research required by the particular department. At the third level, individual projects will be described and future requirements itemized so that it is possible to determine likely tenders in the coming year. This information can be enhanced by discussion with the appropriate desk holder and through close review of official sources of information.

By consulting the department's website and the relevant section in the latest edition of *The Forward Look* it is possible to establish the current research priorities for each UK department and to identify the source of further information.

As an example, the UK Department of Trade and Industry (DTI) is selected. Improving the excellence of UK science through research is essential to the DTI's aim, not least because it houses the Office of Science and Technology (OST) through which the research councils and similar bodies are funded. The DTI is also responsible for the Foresight programme and makes a major contribution to *The Forward Look*. Furthermore, the DTI is responsible for the cross-cutting review of science being undertaken by government in 2002 and for the allocation of the science, engineering and technology (SET) budget. More significant for wealth creation is the DTI's support for UK companies to increase their competitiveness, especially in the circumstances of the global economy. Innovation is one of the major ways that competitiveness is achieved, and the DTI promotes innovation through its innovation unit and through its support of research innovation in the development of new products and processes. The DTI is also concerned to develop links between universities and UK industry and commerce in order to ensure that the latest and most innovative techniques and technologies are available to Britain's companies. Operating through a number of industrial sectors or activities, the DTI provides specific assistance to particular sectors of industry and to technology transfer and training accordingly. The DTI also provides themed support through schemes such as the Management Best Practice Programme, Biotechnology Means Business, the Environment and Business Initiative, the Information Society Initiative and the Focus Technical Programme.

More important to universities in the UK has been the long-standing support for the Link scheme described below.

4.16.1 Link scheme

The Link scheme is the UK government's principal mechanism for supporting collaborative research between UK industry and the science and engineering base. The scheme provides up to 50 per cent of eligible costs towards a specific research project. The Link scheme is organized under thematic programmes with a programme manager and a limited timescale but themes are sufficiently broad to enable the development of a variety of different research projects. Further details are available on the Link web page at www.dti.gov.uk/ost/LINK/LINKhome.htm.

4.16.2 The Smart scheme

Grants are provided through the DTI to small companies for conducting or commissioning feasibility studies in innovative technology or for development of new products or processes involving a significant technological advance. Such projects might be undertaken in partnership with university researchers or may even take the form of a university spin-out company.

4.16.3 The Teaching Company Scheme (TCS)

The former Teaching Company Scheme – now known simply as TCS – has provided major support for partnerships between industry and universities in which technology is transferred and embedded in a particular company by use of trained personnel referred to as Teaching Company Associates. Graduates work with a particular company alongside its workforce but supervised by an academic researcher around a single project to introduce or improve, through technology transfer, products, services or processes. Public funding in excess of 50 per cent of the cost of the project is available depending on the size of company, although the company's contribution is based upon a real financial contribution rather than an in-kind contribution, as is the case with Link.

4.16.4 Postgraduate Training Partnerships

Postgraduate Training Partnerships (PTPs) are a joint initiative between the DTI and Engineering and Physical Sciences Research Council, managed through TCS. PTPs take the form of research and technology organizations and universities working together to provide industry-orientated training for research postgraduates jointly supervised by university staff.

The example of the DTI will serve to illustrate one government department's approach to carrying out research to deliver its core mission. In the case of the DTI, the relationship between university and industry is central to that mission and its schemes are much more directly applicable, but in the case of other government departments the potential for contract research is equally as strong, for example, the Department of Health and the NHS expend annually in excess of £55 million on commissioning external research balancing the Department's own centrally developed strategic framework for priority-setting with regional implementation.

Government can only operate through the development of policy objectives and their implementation and much of the process requires university-based research to inform, shape and direct its objectives and priorities. Appendix 1 at the end of this book gives the *e-search* details for each UK government department or agency for information.

In all cases, such work allocated to universities through the tender process requires the drafting of a formal research contract. In many cases government departments will use standard contract forms which are difficult to modify or vary, but in some cases it is possible to develop separate documents which reflect the mutual interests of both parties. Government is usually concerned only to ensure the implementation of its policy objectives and is not concerned to undermine the university's interests in academic freedom or freedom to publish or in its commercial desire to protect and exploit intellectual property. It was standard at one time for intellectual property rights to be vested automatically in the Crown or in the Secretary of State as far as government contracts were concerned, but this has been relaxed in recent times with the recognition that universities are better placed to identify more immediate partnerships for exploitation for work developed under government contract. As far as work contracted with the Ministry of Defence is concerned, contracts are usually governed by a higher imperative for national security which needs to be carefully considered before entering into agreements for such work. Research contract work requiring the highest level of security usually carries with it the most constraints and the most implications for the ethos of university-based research.

Government departments can also collaborate with universities in partnerships of equal value and shared costs as well as sponsoring research in ways familiar to industry in the private sector. As with private sector contracting, it is important to recognize clearly the different forms of relationship and to provide for them accordingly with the appropriate documentation, whether contract agreement or sponsorship agreement.

4.17 Research costing and pricing: general issues

The costing and pricing of research is a controversial issue and is much misunderstood. Whether contract research or grant-aided research, it is important, if not fundamental, for a university to know how to cost and price its research, as with all its products and services. The university must adopt mechanisms to provide accurate costing and pricing to protect the university from underselling its research or from unconsciously subsidizing contract work from public funds.

The two terms 'costing' and 'pricing' are not mutually interchangeable. Cost means the total expenditure – both direct and indirect – attributable to a specific and defined activity, in this case, the research project. Price means the commercial value in the marketplace for a specifically defined product, service or process, in this case the research project. Price must include, as a minimum, the total full economic cost of the research, otherwise a particular research project will not be fully funded.

Cost, in the UK, is complicated by the working of the dual support system as far as grant-aided research is concerned in that research grant-giving bodies will set attributable costs in the knowledge of dual support, often adding a fixed percentage for indirect costs, that is those items of expenditure which are difficult to attribute directly to the research project. This practice has complicated matters by misleading university clients into accepting the cost of research for only the total of attributable direct costs and an arbitrary fixed addition – usually expressed as a percentage of salary costs – for indirect costs, rather than to be persuaded of a price determined by market value.

The result has been the development of a low-cost, low-value culture with which universities collude in a bizarre cartel and where research grant funders and clients together keep research pricing low in the misguided belief that the dual support system covers every other cost where these are non-attributable to research projects. The net result of 20 or more years of this culture has been to lead research universities to 'overtrade', while the research infrastructure has been eroded over successive years as research failed to meet its costs or, in general, to command premium prices.

There are some simple principles which must be applied:

- identify all attributable costs;
- calculate/devise a mechanism for assessing indirect costs;
- know the market value; and
- determine the price.

Understand the marketplace and develop a premium price based upon value which exceeds the total of attributable costs and indirect costs.

Since the 1980s, in the UK, there have been numerous enquiries conducted into the costing and pricing of university-based research. The direction of policy has been towards ensuring universities recover the full economic cost of research.

Beginning with the report published by the Committee of Vice-Chancellors and Principals (CVCP), in 1988, *Costing of Research and Projects in the UK Universities* (Hanham Report), it has been recognized that the true value of university-based research is rarely recovered in the price charged to customers and clients.

The higher education funding councils commissioned accountants KPMG to produce, in October 1996, a report entitled *Management Information for Decision Making: Costing Guidelines for Higher Education Institutions* (KPMG 1996).

In August 1998, CVCP revisited Hanham and produced a 'Hanham II' entitled *Costing, Pricing and Valuing Research and Other Projects: Report and Recommendations to Universities* (1998). The principles of differentiation between cost and price were endorsed and the notion of value was introduced, suggesting that universities should act under government contracting, in essence establishing the principle that universities should be able to make surpluses from their contract research and recover full costs from all forms of research.

The Joint Costing and Pricing Steering Group (JCPSG) had been established in July 1997, consisting of representatives of universities, relevant users of research and government departments. Among its output have been the highly useful *Pricing Tool Kit for the Higher Education Sector*, *Pricing Strategies for Universities* and the *Transparent Approach to Costing: Guidance Manual*. More recently, it has undertaken the government-requested Treasury-inspired *Transparency Review of Research* (JCPSG 1999). The report and other documents can be consulted at JCPSG's website at: www.jcpsg.ac.uk.

At one level, the *Transparency Review* has been an exercise in attributing costs to the correct activity cost pools. At another level, the exercise has been to demonstrate that research has been consistently underpriced to all research funders in the UK and that, in a highly competitive field, universities have operated collectively – and, probably, unconsciously – to maintain a low-price, low-value cartel in the UK. At a more sophisticated level, *Transparency* has been about language, the application of different accounting terms to the world of higher education, on the basic principle that everything can and should be costed and attributed while, at the same time, attempting to convince HM Treasury that the world is far more complex and that, through the operation of the law of unintended consequences, apparently benign principles of dual support have undermined attempts to adopt more robust methodologies with external clients.

As was shown by earlier work, research funders have simply not accepted the rules proposed by Hanham, and universities have not won the argument about true costs and value for research to the customer. A rather fluid debate has been allowed to congeal since 1988 whereby the focus has been on direct and indirect costs, in particular the level of the latter. If a new beginning is to take place, the sector and its funders must move the debate on to price and value, and accept accurate cost methodologies as a fair presumption, as aimed at by annual transparency returns. Comparative value for research will, of course, be novel territory for most university research negotiations in the UK.

Most universities in the UK now use or are moving to methodologies for costing and pricing derived from the general principles of activity-based costing (ABC) but will have different approaches to cost allocation and apportion and to identifying relevant cost drivers. Whatever level of detail is chosen (and it is advised that accuracy is achieved which gives a fair estimate of costs rather than seeks to cost every driver down to a detailed level), by using the transparent approach to costing (TRAC) methodology recommended by JCPSG, institutions can identify the full economic cost of all research contracts.

Full costs, though, as Hanham originally demonstrated, do not necessarily equate to price or value. Activity-based costing should not lead institutions away from identifying market value and fixing a price accordingly which the customer will be prepared to pay. It is not just accounting principles but a change in the whole pricing culture for research which is required by universities in the UK. By moving away from an insistence on the focus on direct and indirect costs, a dialogue can at last be commenced with the research funders to establish a proper price/value culture.

4.18 Costing a research project

To begin at the beginning, all research projects (whether externally or internally funded) should be properly costed at the outset under the following headings:

- *Staff costs.* An estimate should be made of the total staff time required for the envelope of research work specified by the research contract specification. The estimate should include the total costs of additional staff (academic and non-academic) to be appointed to the research contract as well as existing staff (academic and non-academic) directly engaged on the research contract, whether for the whole or only part of their time. The estimation process must include consideration of the *level and types* of staff required, together with some idea of likely prior experience, so that costings can reflect the appropriate staff salary range and level of seniority, duration of association with the research contract, and the additional costs associated with the employees.

  In many ways, the element of staff costs is the most difficult to estimate as it requires the researcher or research team to be able to work out what level of their input is going to be necessary to complete the task – the estimate can only be based upon experience, present expenditure and further progress against the specification. This can never be an exact process, but it must always err on the side of overestimating rather than underestimating staff effort required.
- *Other recurrent costs.* Full consideration must be given in advance to all other likely expenditure heads, namely:
  - travel and expenses;
  - computing and information technology (C&IT) costs;
  - specialist services;
  - laboratory costs;
  - equipment and related costs;
  - consumables (for example chemicals or materials, office stationery);
  - software licences and running costs;
  - survey, interviewing or related expenditure;
  - energy costs and facilities for dedicated equipment;
  - specialist or related information and publications;
  - consultancy and other fees-based services;
  - recruitment costs;
  - marketing costs.
- *Capital equipment costs.* Dedicated equipment for the project plus its additional costs (for example, installation, insurance)

must be considered carefully in the context of the related costs
of:
- research funder's allowable items;
- procurement principles;
- university health and safety;
- university estates' requirements;
- university insurance and procurement procedures.
* *Other capital items.*
  - Building costs, etc.

Most universities now have access to, or use in their accounting
procedures, computer-based costing software or other tools to make
the process simpler, but it still requires close consideration and often
some discussion to ensure that all items have been identified for
costing.

4.19 Collaboration and partnerships

As we have noted, collaboration and partnerships with other agencies
or third parties are not the same as contract research. Such arrangements are usually described and defined by joint venture agreements
or other such documents, and these relationships are often of a more
strategic nature and operate for longer than contract research. Aims
and objectives in such arrangements tend to be more aspirational
than contractual even where activities to be undertaken jointly are
described.

In such cases, the full economic cost must be calculated and
the arrangements applying to the recovery of these costs should be
specified. Are they to be shared? Is each party to cover its own costs?
Are applications for funds to other agencies envisaged? Are there
intended/expected revenue streams and, if so, how are these to be
applied? and so on.

Resist any temptation to argue that costs are or can be:

* absorbed
* marginal
* 'lost', or
* ignored.

Collaborative or partnership research projects and associations
differ from university to university but have common features
such as:

- Genuine involvement of all parties in shared or common goals and tasks.
- Real benefit to all parties from the results, outputs or other tangible products arising from the collaboration or partnership.
- Eligibility, in general, for joint approach to other funding schemes and initiatives designed to promote and support such collaborations and partnerships whether in the UK or in Europe.
- Shared contributions being made by all parties and joint arrangements for the dissemination and exploitation of resulting intellectual property.
- Understanding of the assets brought by each party to the collaboration or partnership.
- Shared approach to the full economic costs of activities undertaken through the collaboration or partnership.

The main defining feature of collaborative or partnership research is the mutually beneficial nature of the relationships.

Of course, within a wider collaboration or partnership agreement, contract research can still take place and for that purpose the contractual agreement can be used. It is important to allow for this possibility in any collaboration or partnership so that, if need arises, there is no misunderstanding at that point.

4.20 Sponsored research agreements

Sponsored research is work funded by an external funder, in whole or in part, where there is no intrinsic benefit to the sponsor or, at least, where there is little or no direct value from the research to the sponsor.

Typically, sponsored research might involve research which is at the basic, generic or precompetitive stage which the university was already pursuing and for which sponsorship was sought. Sometimes, work might be undertaken in a final year undergraduate project, a master's programme or as postgraduate research.

The defining aspect in such research is academic: the generation of new knowledge for its own sake or in the form of academic output of teaching and learning programmes. The work is of sole benefit to the university or its students, postgraduates and researchers and concerns the advancement of knowledge in the general interests of scientific or other research goals.

Such sponsorship which might be gained is made available in a philanthropic spirit by the sponsor or because of the sponsor's particular commitment to research endeavour for its own sake. Usually, such sponsorship might simply be acknowledged (unless the sponsor wished to remain anonymous) in any published or other public output.

Where support for postgraduate research is envisaged, it is important to identify its true nature. If there is direct value for the external funder or it involves specific public partnership scheme funding, such a studentship is contractual. It should be clearly recognized that a funded postgraduate research studentship (for example Co-operative Awards in Science and Engineering – CASE – or other forms of industrial support) should not be regarded as a cheaper substitute for contract research.

4.21 Intellectual property management

This is not the place to explore in detail the intricacies of intellectual property law or management but merely to emphasize its overwhelming importance.

Intellectual property rights (IPR) attach to knowledge which arises from research or invention and which can be commercialized in accordance with patent, copyright or design right law (including trade names/and service marks). It might be suggested that a commercial value can be attached to *all* knowledge, in that it is possible to make profits from its utilization in a multiplicity of forms such as developments, consultancy or dissemination. Intellectual property rights, however, are only those which can be recognized by reference to law as those which can be protected by patent, copyright or design right.

Knowledge can be made to work to commercial advantage, but only *inventions* can be protected as IPR.

There is no point in a university worrying about IPR or having concerns about the exploitability of its intellectual property in general unless it has a commercialization arm and procedures in place as well as an agreed policy towards the effective management of its intellectual property portfolio. If in doubt, review the university's current business processes and determine whether these are as effective as possible. To determine a policy towards the management of intellectual property, the university will require:

- a commercialization route (through the university, or its own company or via third-party agents);
- a clear revenue-sharing policy for inventors as an incentive;
- a concise statement of the university's contractual position

towards its employees and its students (undergraduate and postgraduate);
- an overall policy guidance document advising how intellectual property is to be handled;
- a strategy (or part of a strategy) for each school, department or research centre, indicating likely intellectual property generation;
- a position on intellectual property as part of the university's standard contract research terms and conditions;
- a systematic methodology towards regular technology audits, self-assessments and technology disclosures to ensure all intellectual property is recognized, identified and properly disclosed.

The best guide is that by AVRIL (AVRIL 2002).

4.22 Pricing negotiations

Negotiation on price depends upon the following prerequisite information being available to the university:

- Value of research in the marketplace (i.e. uniqueness, competitors, value to industry and users in terms of their business share of the global market, their competitors).
- Other unique selling points (USPs) in favour of the research.
- Estimation of the potential client's desire to undertake the work.
- Measure of quality which can be attached to the research (for example, the latest UK Research Assessment Exercise ratings).
- Previous client satisfaction.
- Confidence of the researchers in the strength of the business proposition which underlies the research proposed.

It is also important to have formed an impression of the strength, seriousness and capability of the likely client (for example, current share price, intellectual property portfolio, product and process range, competition, current news stories).

There are two basic approaches to fixed price negotiation:

- Set a high asking price with a range of negotiation steps in view and hold to that position.
- Begin by finding out what the potential client is aiming to pay and set out a research proposition tailored to the available sum but which meets the university's asking price.

Alternatively, the university can draw up a standard rate card, giving day rates, equipment charges and so on, and build up the price against the proposed research on a menu basis.

Any discounting arrangements, price reduction or price sharing must only be entered into knowingly and on the basis of prior agreement by the university.

4.23 Value

Value in research arises from the intellectual property it represents. Intellectual property should not be given up lightly because it represents the only 'product' the university has from its research. (See above section on intellectual property management.)

Price can be varied in accordance with the extent to which intellectual property is transferred through the research contract but, even then, only if the university stands to gain from the likely future commercial exploitation.

In general, price should be protected and defended so that the research pricing policy of the university is not undermined in the marketplace.

4.24 Summary

All accurate research costing begins by establishing the full economic cost for the specific proposed contract research, using principles associated with the transparent approach to costing (TRAC) guidance manual (JCPSG).

Price must be set to exceed full economic cost and should take account of market value. Price discounting must not erode the full economic cost.

Costs must not be regarded as negotiable (although they might be shared in the context of collaborative research). In cases of contract research costs must be recovered.

Universities should formulate policies towards an overall pricing strategy which should incorporate a clear statement against subsidizing contract work in accordance with public policy guidance (HEFCE, Universities UK, Treasury, JCPSG, or other national equivalents outside the UK).

Pricing strategy should be formally and frequently reviewed.

Value should be determined, as far as possible, by response to the likely generation of intellectual property.

The key to understanding the value of research is to ensure that the potential client understands fully the basis on which universities undertake research and are funded through public funds to undertake research and that the dual support relationship underpins the basis of the process of research grants-in-aid from the research councils and of research grants from the major national charities.

Research contracting must be undertaken without subsidy, partly in recognition that specific value is added to the client through the research contracted, giving commercial advantage. International competition regulations prevent 'hidden' public subsidy.

On the basis of the above, a negotiation can take place about the value of the research from which the price is determined. Contract research must not be confused with collaborative research or sponsored research, but, whatever classification applies, all research projects must be costed at the full economic cost and those costs must be fully recovered.

5

LEADING AND MANAGING RESEARCH

5.1 Introduction: doing research

Research is carried on by researchers, that is those staff and students who are directly engaged in the process of *doing research*, whether as part of one or more finite research projects, of an ongoing research programme, or simply in the context of a research career within a specific field consisting of different periods of research carried out in a centre, department or school in the university or beyond in other research organizations. Researchers might be:

- undergraduates (final-year project students);
- postgraduates (taught and research);
- contract research staff (whether postgraduate or postdoctoral);
- research fellows or other research staff in receipt of personal grants or scholarships;
- academic staff (full- or part-time employees of the university con-tracted to undertake teaching and research or research only);
- visiting researchers, attached scholars or partner representatives;
- support staff (non-academic or academic-related staff employed to enable research to be carried out).

Some researchers might argue that there is only the possibility of 'doing research', that ideas relating to notions of 'leading' or 'managing' are inimical to the research process itself and would not recognize what these terms meant in the context of their personal research. In essence, for some active researchers, research is about *acting* whereas leading and managing (and any other term for that matter) are about being *acted upon*. The subject is clearly a contentious one and can lead to confusion and misunderstanding unless explained with as much clarity as possible.

Being a researcher, as we have seen, is not the same as leading, managing, coordinating, planning or supporting research, although some researchers might also undertake one or more of those additional tasks. Doing research raises fundamental questions about the research environment and context, the nature of the particular academic discipline, the relationship between different research areas, the perception of research tasks and priorities, and their relevance to individuals and groups, and the appropriate structures by which to undertake, lead, manage, coordinate, plan and support research in an integrated way.

5.2 Some definitions

First, let us consider some working definitions as follows:

- *Research.* The process of undertaking or carrying out original investigation in all its forms: analysis, innovation, experiment, observation, intellectual enquiry, survey, scholarship, creativity, measurement, development, hypothesis, modelling and evaluating with a view to generating new knowledge or novel comprehension.
- *Research leadership.* The role of directing research, deciding upon its course, organizing tasks and priorities, setting goals and targets, identifying commercial potential, championing the research group or team, communicating findings, developing strategy, establishing the requisite research infrastructure and environment, managing and deploying resources, identifying opportunities and setting up links, collaborations and partnerships, operating the networks necessary for the continuation of the research area and the success of its projects and programmes.
- *Research management.* The duties and responsibilities commensurate with the successful implementation of the research strategy and its daily operational implications, the control and coordination of specific research projects, their quality and the related tasks of sponsor management.
- *Research coordination.* The process of balancing resources and matching them to priorities, projects and programmes which might involve accountability and responsibility for these resources at a particular level in the university.
- *Research planning.* The process of formulating a research strategy or of ensuring that specific local research strategies are formulated and integrated in accordance with the aims and objectives of the

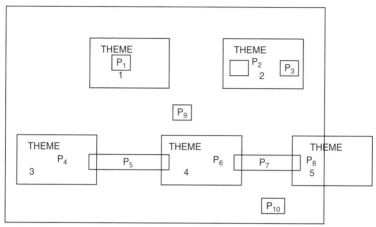

Themes 1–5
Projects P_1–P_{10}

Figure 5.1   The unit of research: organization and resources
© R. W. Bushaway and P. J. Waddell

university's overall research strategy taking account of available resources, aspirations, missions and targets.
- *Research support.* The tasks of enabling, facilitating and nurturing research, usually from a corporate perspective and, in particular, financial and human resources management, research information management, advice and guidance on research and funding opportunities, networking, coordination of policy and procedures and strategy-setting, as well as supporting the commercialization and exploitation of research results in the form of intellectual property.

5.3 The unit of research

In Figure 5.1, the outer box simply represents a designated envelope of resources formed into an integrated unit, and is equivalent to a group of researchers organized as a centre, department or school within which research is carried out. It does not necessarily represent the entirety of that unit's resources or activities which might also involve teaching and learning, as well as outreach or third task objectives (such as consultancy, technology transfer, exploitation of know-how, short courses and so on). The unit allocates its research resources across a number of distinct themes or priorities in order to define what research is to be carried out within the envelope and to assign resources which can be measured against targets and outputs in those themed or priority areas.

The 'shape' and scale of each theme or priority will vary according to its importance and the amount of resources allocated to it, and some themes or priorities will cross unit boundaries and involve other units in their development. Themes will be large or small and not necessarily correspond with one unit. Some units might not have any identical themes at all.

The smaller squares represent individual research projects, most often defined by being funded from *external* sources as discrete research grants or contracts. Many of these will closely be related to one or more themes; some will cross unit boundaries; some will stand distinct from existing themes; some will cross themes within units. Some projects might exceed the scale of some themes or even exceed the size of a single unit. Some will be unfunded in the sense of not receiving external research funds.

Resources allocated to themes might include:

- staff;
- accommodation;
- equipment and other facilities;
- other recurrent resources;
- other non-recurrent resources.

The total available resources allocated to a unit provides the absolute limit for the envelope of research undertaken by a particular unit or group of researchers. There is no ideal or perfect number for the researchers in the research group. Larger teams are necessary for some research areas; others depend on a critical mass of researchers to be effective; while in others the tradition of the independent and individual scholar persists. Whole units and individual themes might well be directed by research leaders or champions. Themes and projects might be the responsibility of one or more research manager(s).

Most research leaders have a clear idea of the size and composition of the research team necessary for success in their fields. Group dynamic theory tends to indicate that around ten individuals, bringing a balance of skills to the task, makes an effective team, but the university must be flexible enough to encourage groups to form, grow, change, interact, decline, transform and reform as fluidly as possible, on the basis of research performance measured against objective benchmarks. Perhaps the most difficult task for the university is to manage the process of closing down a particular unit of research or themes within it and switching resources to other units or research teams when a specific research area has ceased to be productive, and in particular being able to distinguish between temporary fallow periods in the research cycle and wholly moribund research fields.

The university must decide the method for allocating its resources for research and, therefore, the number, size and range of units which undertake research. The units themselves are most usually responsible for the number of research themes, based upon decisions about prioritization in the case of the research resources allocated to it by the university. The unit is also generally responsible for the number of discrete research projects undertaken, where these might be externally funded, on the basis of its efforts to submit successful research grant applications and to undertake contract research. The university sets the framework in which the processes applying to research grants and contracts operate and the university must, as a minimum, establish the financial rules by which research is costed, priced and valued.

Whether resources are allocated to units for research, commensurate with those responsible for teaching and learning or to separate cross-disciplinary units, the structure must be comparable with the establishment of a research environment conducive to the fostering of new research ideas and proposals and to developing research within the context of the field and its related disciplines, and the vision and aspirations of its most able researchers and most capable leaders.

The most important principle for the university is to ensure that, whatever resource allocation method or structure is adopted, resources for research are allocated directly to the research groups or units where successful research is carried out as measured by objective and externally referenced benchmarks and in accordance with the university's mission for research as well as the targets and objectives of its research strategy. Further or additional investment of resources for research should be based upon a business plan approach indicating where the most likely research successes will occur. Judgement on likely future research success should be based on the development of research strategies by units tasked and resourced to carry out research. In other words, those who actually research the best are best placed to draw up plans for future research and to deploy resources to undertake those plans. On the other hand, those who are responsible for supporting or managing the implementation of research plans do not necessarily have to be part of the team tasked with carrying forward the research programme or projects.

5.4 Leading research

Research leadership is perhaps the most difficult task to undertake in the structure of university-based research. Many qualities are required, so that a better description for the leadership function might be that of research champion. Research champions are individuals who head recognized research groups or teams, often at a professorial level, within units of university-based research. Such units make up the profile of research in science, engineering, medicine and some of the social sciences, but where research themes do not emerge, the role of individual scholarship remains fundamental to university-based research in arts and humanities and other parts of the social sciences. The research champion is also the linchpin of the research group, around whom the other members of the group are organized and on whom the performance of the team as a whole depends. The research champion provides the overall research vision and attracts to the team, either directly or indirectly as participants, the best researchers necessary to the success of the research group. The research champion identifies the techniques, methodologies and facilities necessary to carry through the proposed research programme and sets about identifying and securing the resources for these. Individuals who champion a particular research area or theme do so from a fundamental commitment to and enthusiasm for the field which cannot be provided by more managerial approaches.

In essence, the research champion is mission-orientated and is someone who has a proven track record for research in the requisite subject, has managed successful research programmes, including externally funded research projects, has taken part in all the processes of research related to the field with direct and demonstrable experience of advancing knowledge either incrementally or in innovative steps. The research champion also possesses an acknowledged external reputation by which their expertise is recognized widely by their national and international peer group. Reputation and experience will take the form of formal engagement in the research funding process at every level, from proposal referee through peer college membership to operational and programme direction and research policy setting. External recognition will also be evident in relevant and appropriate exploitation of research outputs in the particular field among users and beneficiaries.

The research champion will be familiar, in relevant subjects, with commerce and industry in the relevant market sectors or to policymakers in government and the public sector or in clinical fields of medicine and health, or in the wider world of knowledge. Research reputation can best be judged by considering the extent to which the research champion is known rather than by following the network of those the research champion knows. The successful research champion will take part in popular dissemination concerning their field by interaction with the research media, the news media, and in other forms of public engagement. The research champion will be an effective communicator of their ideas and will be able to explain, describe and justify the importance and significance of the particular research field in ways which are clear and comprehensive but also accessible to non-experts.

Within the university, the research champion will have developed over time a research group usually consisting of the following:

- external partners, collaborators, beneficiaries and users;
- senior research fellows and individual scholars;
- contract researchers;
- other academic colleagues;
- postgraduate research students;
- international partnerships and networks.

Such a group will vary in size according to the particular subject and may be more or less extended, involving other research groups and research champions as well as subgroups or related research teams.

In some fields of scholarship, especially in the arts and humanities, the position of the research champion is somewhat different as the tradition of scholarship favours the world of individual research. The individual scholar/research champion will be an acknowledged leader in the field and will advance knowledge individually or collectively with partners and collaborators outside the university. Nonetheless, such research champions will no doubt supervise postgraduate research students and work with collaborators and other scholars in partnership as appropriate throughout their careers.

In both the environment of the research group or the individual scholar, the international dimension is of fundamental importance. The research champion's group will involve international scholars and visitors, attachments from overseas and partnerships with laboratories and centres of research in other countries. There will be an *e-search* dimension to the work of the group, often involving a website and electronic networking. Effective leadership will be acknowledged on an international scale. The individual scholar/research champion will also engage in international research and will receive visits from leading researchers abroad in the relevant field.

Recognizing the pivotal role of the research champion and therefore the importance of the research group is an important and significant step for the university because of the recognition that research groups tend to operate on a basis and structure not equivalent to that which applies to the delivery of programmes of learning and teaching in academic disciplines. Some research champions operate across the boundaries provided by academic disciplines, interacting with one or more areas of research beyond the confines of their own subject boundary. Some research champions operate in the space between disciplines and some operate in wholly new fields which go beyond the current understanding of academic structures.

Research champions are able to establish their research interests in a particular university and build the components of a successful group around them during their period of tenure. They might pursue a career trajectory which is satisfied within one institution or they may require periods in several universities in order to progress. The trajectory for their careers is influenced and shaped by the research environment provided by the university and the extent to which research career goals can be achieved in harmony with the university's institutional or corporate goals.

5.5 Managing research

Research management requires the skills of project management to be combined with the ability to formulate a longer-term strategy and implement its objectives in terms of operational development. The research manager can combine with the role of research leadership if the individual research champion has the range of skills and the time, inclination and ability both to manage the research environment within which the research group operates and simultaneously to undertake research and direct its goals. In appropriate circumstances, this can be achieved if the research champion is supported by a research manager who will take on the daily responsibilities connected with the research programme such as:

- financial management;
- logistics;
- infrastructure;
- human resources issues;
- quality assurance;
- project management;
- networking;
- marketing and promotion;
- sponsor management;
- liaison with the university;

- liaison with research services;
- international and other collaborations;
- partnerships and links management;
- organization and administration;
- media relationships.

The research manager is responsible for managing the research environment, for ensuring that specific research projects are managed in accordance with their contract specifications, and also for supporting the research infrastructure necessary for the research group such that an efficient and effective environment is maintained, enabling successful research to be undertaken.

The research manager can be a member of the research team in that they would have responsibility for specific research tasks, or can be simply a part of the group with specific non-research duties and responsibilities. It is important that the research manager understands the research imperative, shares the mission orientation and also the direction and goals pursued by the research champion so that in interpreting the leadership role the research manager facilitates the work of the research group.

The research manager should be responsible for the maintenance of research networks, contacts, collaborations and partnerships necessary for the success of the group and will spend time in managing partners and sponsors as well as liaising at a corporate level with the university and its overall research strategy, operations and policies. The prime goal for the research manager is to relieve researchers of the distractions and diversions which are the inevitable consequence of sophisticated research environments.

5.6 Research coordination

The coordination of research is a collective responsibility within the university and involves the interaction of several management levels, from the corporate level to the unit of research, to the particular research group and its research champion, to individual researchers. In essence, effective research coordination requires the matching of appropriate resources with successful research groups and the alignment of research group priorities with those of the unit of research and the university as well as the personal goals of the research champion and members of the research group so that research tasks can be accomplished, results can be successfully exploited and promoted, external funding for research projects can be won and the sum of knowledge can be advanced.

Research coordination appears to be deceptively simple but is, in fact, a complex and difficult matter. To be accomplished, the university must:

- possess an effective mechanism for performance review which is based upon externally referenced objective criteria;
- develop a personal development planning mechanism where individual researchers can be encouraged to set personal goals and performance targets and be supported by the university at every level to attain them;
- understand the aspirations of its research champions and research groups and their strategies for the future;
- decide upon the overall priorities for research and support them through an efficient resource allocation model which rewards research success and penalizes indifferent research;
- decide upon the university's research strategy and the absolute envelope of research resources available for allocation;
- generate motivation and enthusiasm for the best research through recognition, reward, remuneration and retention schemes;
- ensure an environment for effective research with policies and procedures conducive to research;
- provide support for research both to maximize investment in the university's research and to exploit research outputs through dissemination and commercialization;
- attend to the needs of all researchers but especially the career development of contract researchers and postgraduate research students;
- be clear on its ethical, environmental, health and safety, contractual and financial requirements for research;
- provide decisive corporate research leadership.

Research coordination needs to be effective at each level so the unit of research – the school, centre or department responsible for a designated envelope of resources for research – needs to ensure that the requirements at university-level are replicated at unit level.

The research champion has a fundamental responsibility to produce a strategy for the group which can be subjected to objective measurement of research performance and research goal-setting. If the research champion undertakes the formal appraisal of the individual members of the research team, the process must involve constructive discussion of personal performance and goals. Equally, when the performance of research champions is considered, similar constructive discussions should take place with the unit head or other appropriate manager.

The whole process of research coordination must be based upon an honest, realistic and objective evaluation of progress, attainment and success and prioritization for the future.

5.7 Research planning

Research planning is a collective process carried out at every level in the university towards establishing an interlocking and integrated research strategy at corporate level. The strategy should be greater than the sum of its parts – the research strategies formulated by units, research groups and individual career development plans – but must also reflect its component research sub-strategies.

Research planning means regarding research as a process which can be described, measured and for which inputs and outputs can be identified. Through effective research planning, resources can be attributed, results can be attached and the contributions of individuals and the research team as a whole can be evaluated. Research planning cannot be undertaken in a vacuum and requires an understanding of the research market in which the university is operating. Measurable and comparable performance by research competitors must be made available and analysed on a systematic basis as well as new opportunities identified. The danger inherent in research planning is for the university to be guided by the current range of research undertaken and the available research outputs – in market terms, to be product-led – whereas, by considering new opportunities based upon information on new requirements, funding opportunities and likely future trends, the research planning process should become more attuned to new areas of research development – in the language of business, to be market-led. By this means, the university can avoid the pitfalls of being constrained by its existing research strengths – to be driven by *technology push* – but can develop new research strengths in accordance with research intelligence – to be driven by *market pull*. New research opportunities should be kept at the forefront of the research planning process and the tendency to depend on existing but waning research engines should be avoided.

Research planning should include the approach of mapping – drawing up a map of current research, indicating its axes, thematic priorities and cross-cutting themes, providing, in diagrammatic form, a ready summary of existing research strengths and their interrelatedness.

At the same time, researchers should note that most external research funders now produce maps indicating their future plans for research funding in terms of themes, interdisciplinary priorities and cross-cutting areas. By adopting a similar approach to the *knowledge market* as a whole and to those markets of central importance to the university, a series of maps can be overlaid which identify potential future directions as well as threats and opportunities for the university's research. This should be the basis for effective research planning.

5.8 Supporting research

The university should establish responsibilities at a corporate level for those support tasks which are necessary in helping research groups pursue research successfully. Supporting research at a university level involves:

- assisting the process of making research grant applications;
- supporting and enabling university research contracting;
- undertaking commercialization and exploitation;
- providing information on research opportunities and its dissemination;
- networking;
- managing sponsors (corporate level);
- marketing and promoting research;
- facilitating individual and group support in goal-setting;
- helping to set the corporate research strategy;
- developing policies and procedures conducive to the growth of research;
- assisting with research planning at every level;
- supporting research performance evaluation;
- encouraging cross-disciplinary research interaction;
- assisting with research costing and pricing;
- intellectual property management.

Most universities have established support services for research which bring together all or many of the above or which create structures working together for the purpose.

5.9 Information and intelligence

The research services office will be the central source within the university for information on all local, national and international research funding agencies, their schemes, initiatives and programmes. The service will regularly scan a wide range of information sources in paper form and via the internet as well as be the prime contact point in the university for many of the research funding agencies and organizations. The central task of research information management is to make relevant information available to as many staff as possible such that it effectively targets those whose interests are appropriate and relevant to the particular scheme or initiative. The dilemma to be resolved is not to circulate too widely by adopting a 'scattergun' approach nor to target so narrowly that interested individuals and groups are missed. The following approaches might be adopted:

- New research funding opportunities can be summarized in a publication circulated across the university on a frequent and regular basis. This information sheet, received by all members of research staff or academic staff with research responsibilities, will include brief details of all initiatives received with current timescales and can also be made available on line via the support services web pages as a central part of the university's website and a main point of information delivery for all academic staff. Current and back issues can be consulted via an archive and, by using a simple reference system, further details or expanded information on a particular opportunity can be made available on request.
- The research services office should be expected to hold relevant general information on all appropriate funders of university-based research, including application forms, guidelines, annual reports, contract information and other useful background guidance on the most frequently used research organizations, in particular, research councils, government departments, large research charities, the European Commission, international research organizations and industry and commerce. The service might also be expected to know something of the organization of research in other countries, for comparative reasons or in order to identify collaborations and partnerships.
- The research services office website should include links to the web pages of all relevant funders and should carry news on their thematic priorities or forthcoming programmes as well as provide a forum for the exchange of information between researchers in particular fields. The website might also contain reports on seminars and meetings with particular research funders or their representatives and might provide a gateway to commercially available sources such as external research databases, research fora or commercial research information, where researchers can search for information on funding opportunities and set up regular enquiries for automatic updating on relevant current research programmes

and opportunities. The website must also give a clear account of the university's own policy and procedures towards research and guidance on how to go about seeking support, being the cornerstone of the university's e-search environment.

• Information on priorities and themes in the form of research intelligence should be available through the research services office and its staff. Such intelligence should be the most recent and should be based upon as much 'inside information' as possible gathered from the research services office's own intelligence-gathering network which would consist of its own contacts with funders as well as information from those of the university staff engaged with particular funders in specific capacities.

5.10 Advice and guidance

After research information provision, the next most significant role for the research services office is that of advice and guidance. As highly experienced professionals, the research services office should be able to help prepare and assist with research proposals and contracts and in helping to target appropriate sponsors. Advice should be available to any member of research active staff or to research groups and research champions as necessary and should cover:

• finding the appropriate sponsor(s);
• making the best approach to potential external research funders;
• preparation of research proposals (particularly with regard to presentation, meeting the funder's objectives, management structure, resourcing and so on);
• completing application forms and negotiating research contracts;
• ensuring commercialization and exploitation of intellectual property;
• developing research strategies to broaden the net of research funding opportunities and identifying larger cross-disciplinary research initiatives involving one or more research groups.

5.11 Strategy and scrutiny

The most significant task for the university at the corporate level is the development of policies towards networking and research promotion such that the interface between the university research community and potential sponsors and collaborators of research is as efficient and effective as possible. The research services office will have a central role in national scrutiny exercises such as the UK Research Assessment Exercise and will take the lead in compiling and maintaining the university's annual research grants and contracts report and the database of publications and other outputs from research maintained centrally for the university as a whole. The research services office will be both a window into the university through which potential research sponsors can look and a gateway enabling not only research ideas to find appropriate sponsors but also potential sponsors to identify relevant research areas in as open and transparent a way as possible. One of the ways this can be achieved is by the research services office organizing regular seminars and visits from potential funders or policy-makers concerned with research so that the university has access to the latest information from the research funding agencies and other research organizations.

A particularly important role for the research services office is to connect research in different parts of the university in order to identify potential collaborations which, while consisting of component parts from individual research groups, will have a greater value as a whole. The research services office should be a key element in developing the university's research strategy and in the overall identification of research strengths and themes which might be exploited successfully as part of the university's research business. In particular, the research services office can help to coordinate interdisciplinary or multidisciplinary research groups which bring together expertise from various units in the university.

5.12 Commercialization

The university must develop services and functions which facilitate the commercialization and exploitation of the intellectual property arising from its research. Research services should embrace:

- the policy framework for intellectual property management;
- procedures to encourage commercial exploitation of research outputs from disclosure, to protection, to realization of their full commercial value;
- company formation (spin-outs and start-ups);
- licensing and other commercial routes to realizing intellectual property value;
- the exploitation of innovation and new ventures related to research;
- raising venture capital for investment;
- managing university consultancy;

- developing other business ventures relating to the university's know-how or inventions;
- forming partnerships and collaborations to aid the successful exploitation of the university's intellectual property.

The research services office should develop and improve its services to the academic community by striving for continuous improvement and through interacting with researchers and research groups, raising awareness of funding opportunities and extending the number of active researchers engaged in externally funded research, increasing the quality and quantity of research projects undertaken, and assisting the commercialization of research outputs in order to develop the university's research business. As such, the service must remain open to suggestions for improvement and to the feedback from the wider university academic research community on the range of its services currently provided. The research services office can also play a role in facilitating the university's overall business development and, in particular, its outreach or third task programme.

5.13 Research project management ■

5.13.1 Introduction

It is important for the university to insist upon the best possible research project management for three reasons:

- To ensure that all research projects carried out in the university's name, especially where funded by external agencies in the case of grant aid or by research contracts, are completed on time, to budget and in accordance with specification. Concerns for positive sponsor management and its own concerns for successful research should lead the university to foster effective project management to ensure that research is properly priced, is conducted in accordance with university policies and procedures, conforms to ethical principles, and complies with human resources, health and safety, contractual procurement and other legislation or regulation.
- To encourage the best research by insisting upon the adoption of quality assurance principles and practices through effective research project management or, at least, to support their adoption wherever possible.
- To protect the university in any dispute concerned with research performance where a record of sound project management can be referred to in its defence in cases involving:

- contractual disagreement;
- plagiarism;
- ethical concerns;
- complaint;
- liability;
- health and safety issues;
- insurance cases;
- misconduct or mismanagement;
- data protection;
- human resources;
- risk management.

In fact, the university's position on research project management should be to provide clear guidance and policy statements concerning the management of research, of which the most important is the proper maintenance of research records to which reference can be made.

5.13.2 Liability for research data

It is the responsibility of all researchers to ensure that proper records are maintained in the form of:

- laboratory notebooks;
- field notebooks;
- research notes;
- survey returns;
- experiment log books;
- research documentation;
- reports;
- financial documents;
- results information;
- research diaries and notebooks;
- quality assurance documentation;
- databases.

This responsibility extends to both data material in hard copy form and to electronic data and applies equally to the university's data as to those of third parties to whom the university is contracted or with whom the university is in collaboration. There are many good reasons for this, not least because good practice in managing research information leads to good research and is a general sign of a well-managed research project. Other reasons are:

- intellectual property issues (for example, copyright or patent issues);
- allegations of plagiarism or other misconduct;
- research contract liabilities for:
  - non-disclosure
  - protection of third party data
  - intellectual property matters
  - results;
- contractual obligations for research reports or other outcomes;
- accountability to research funders;
- ethical issues;
- quality assurance.

Particular attention should be given to the risks where research data are stored in electronic form. Back-up copies should be regularly taken and stored separately and securely. Reasonable levels of data security should be maintained to prevent unauthorized access or remote tampering (hacking), other breaches of confidentiality, loss or damage through accident or unforeseen circumstances. Systems which are installed should be regularly checked, especially where loss or damage to electronic data could lead to consequential contractual liabilities. Advice should be taken from the university's information services support or from commercial suppliers to ensure that research data are fully protected.

There are many sources of good practice available and the guide published by British Technology Group, entitled *Keeping a Laboratory Notebook* (BTG 1997) is useful. Copies of the guide can be obtained from BTG direct or via email byguk@btgplc.com or website at www.btgplc.com.

Attention should always be paid to the Data Protection Acts (1984 and 1998) and their requirements. Similar legislation operates in other countries and aims to protect human rights. Most UK universities will have appointed a data protection officer from whom guidance should be obtained as far as research practice is concerned.

5.13.3 Risk assessment and management

Risk management is a daily factor in all working environments and should be a continuous concern for vigilant researchers in universities. Risks will arise concerned with issues such as the health and safety, liability insurance, data protection and other regulatory matters. Researchers must always consult these policies or the services provided in their support for advice in assessing risk before undertaking research. Assessment is a continuous process which begins before and continues during and after the completion of the research project. The principle in most statutory requirements is that of a 'hierarchy of controls' for identified risks where such risks should be eliminated, substituted, enclosed, segregated, designed out, trained for, informed and protected against.

Risk also concerns areas which go beyond health and safety or conduct and ethics. Risk in research is also a matter for consideration in terms of business risk and attention should be given to aspects such as:

- business continuity plans, where contingency has been drawn up for continuing or safeguarding research despite unforeseen emergencies or accidents such as fire or computer viruses;
- research strategy exposure, where research business is affected by external threats or opportunities;
- contractual liabilities;
- commercialization and exploitation.

Risk alone should encourage the adoption of sound research project management techniques and methodologies.

5.13.4 Project or principal investigator

Effective research project management can be undertaken by the research champion or that person assigned to specific externally funded research projects generally identified as the nominated project investigator. The project or principal investigator is the principal researcher whose research proposal has been accepted for external funding in the form either of grant-in-aid or of contract. In many cases, the project or principal investigator will also take on the responsibilities of research project manager, ensuring that the project is undertaken in accordance with its specification and within budget. In some research groups the tasks of research project management are carried out by a specific post-holder appointed for the purpose and seen as a research manager for the group and all the projects for which the group is responsible, liaising with principal investigators as necessary. In either case, it is important for the university to designate an individual to carry out the functions of research project manager for each research project and to supervise the conduct of the research project, being responsible for the following:

- Ensuring that the specification requirements, as designated in the research grant proposal or research contract document are met within the contracted timescale, to the agreed budget and in accordance with the proposed requirements.
- The formulation of a research project plan which should include contract review points at predetermined staging posts during the research process itself.
- Consideration of the exploitation of potential intellectual property as opportunities arise and discussing them with the relevant university support service.
- Imposing budgetary controls and constraints on project expenditure within the overall control of the university's financial procedures and the requirements of the project.
- Ensuring that research undertaken outside the specification for the research project is supported by necessary variation agreements with the external agent responsible for funding the research project.
- Undertaking to coordinate the necessary resources and support for the research project and their management within the context of university procedures.
- Maintaining proper research data management control and document controls which should include information as follows:
  - project plan;
  - project schedule;
  - invoice schedule;
  - materials expenditure schedule;
  - project costs schedule:
    - budgetary/target costs;
    - actual spend to date;
  - the contract specification (where relevant):
    - tender specification (where relevant);
    - tender correspondence (where relevant);
    - grant proposal (where relevant);
    - correspondence (records of progress meetings, project-related internal memos and correspondence, other documentary material);
  - research data (including laboratory notebooks and so on).

5.13.5 The research project manager

The research project manager or the project or principal investigator should develop an overarching research plan to facilitate budget apportionment between the phases of the research project. Budgets should be set against each phase and each activity head. The over-arching research project plan will not include detailed analysis but will be modified as more accurate costs and timescale assessments are produced during the progress of the research project. These can be represented graphically in the form of a Gantt chart, which should be attached to the plan itself. Staging posts between discrete activities should be identified and should provide opportunities for research project review which should include consideration of research results and any potential intellectual property. Progress should be indicated on the research plan, which should be kept up-to-date on a systematic basis.

5.13.6 Budgetary controls

The project manager or project or principal investigator is responsible for the control of project costs, tracking costs against estimates and monitoring progress. This is a crucial aspect of successful research project management. Emerging costs should be closely monitored and should be based upon original estimates such that overspends in one area of the project will be considered in relation to the effect on other areas. Budget transfers may be necessary between some elements of the research project, but these should be carefully monitored and controlled to avoid cost overruns.

5.13.7 Internal progress review

The project manager or project or principal investigator is responsible for monitoring research progress against the research project plan. Internal progress review is best undertaken through informal meetings with the project team at which progress can be recorded on the basis of monthly management reports which can then be submitted to the research champion or the head of the particular unit or for consideration elsewhere in the university. Such meetings may be documented but it should be necessary to record only formal decisions or matters of concern arising from them.

At the relevant staging posts or milestones during the research project, further consideration can be given to matters such as commercialization and exploitation of arising intellectual property, and the appropriate support services in the university should be invited to discuss project developments where there may be concerns or where results justify consideration of any likely emerging intellectual property. Decisions reached at these meetings should be recorded. At the same time deviations from the research plan should be recorded and the research project manager or the project or principal investigator, together with other members of the research group as relevant, should endeavour to find ways of recovering any lost time or making up shortfalls in the expected research progress. Such actions should be recorded in a similar way.

5.13.8 External progress review

The research project manager or project or principal investigator must be compliant with the review requirements of the external funding agency. Wherever the research funding agency or research contract sponsor requires progress review, the research project manager or principal investigator is responsible for coordinating such meetings and complying with their requirements. In most cases, external progress review meetings will concentrate on examining all aspects of the research project to ensure that progress is being made in accordance with expectations, the specification and the schedule for the research, and as a result of such meetings any modifications to existing requirements which have been mutually agreed prior to their implementation should be recorded. A full record of the meeting should be distributed to all parties concerned and a copy retained on the research project file.

Where variations to the research project are agreed, it must be ensured that these meet with the university's acceptance where there are implications for resources or for other aspects of the university's research strategy.

5.13.9 Post research project review

A post project review meeting should be called by the project manager or project or principal investigator at the conclusion of each research project. The meeting should include the relevant research champion or unit head as well as representatives of the support services from the university and a record of the review should be circulated.

A typical post project review should cover several items in order to establish that the research project was managed in accordance with the original specification and where progress was achieved as well as any variations and their justification. Issues for consideration should include the specification or contract and, in particular, budget, timescales and outcomes. The review should also consider the nature of the project management and its success or otherwise, together with final budgets and reports.

One of the most important aspects of the post project review is to ensure that any consequent intellectual property has been effectively identified for potential commercialization or exploitation in accordance with the terms of any grant aid or the requirements of the research contract. At the same time, it is necessary to review likely dissemination routes to publication or other forms of disclosure and to make sure that, if these arise alongside exploitable intellectual property, the appropriate steps have been taken to cover disclosure and protection before such dissemination has occurred.

Finally, the post project review should include an element of reflection and consideration on any generic issues concerning the research or its management, lessons to be learned, matters to be followed up.

Successful research project management will lead to further research projects being identified and attracting external research funding support or taking the form of future research contracts. By ensuring efficient management of its research, the university signals to those with which it has engaged – external funders, contractors or partners and collaborators – that its research is assured at the highest possible levels of quality.

It is recognized that such careful research project management requires a considerable amount of time and effort in order to be carried through as a process. Time engaged in meetings, writing up, review and reflection is not time which can be devoted to the research task itself. Increasingly, professional research managers are being engaged by universities to work with research groups or in units to take on these responsibilities so that researchers themselves are freed to undertake more research. This is a trend, first observable in the United States, which is certain to continue as the world of university-based research becomes more complex and involves more parties in order to carry out research projects. The university should make sure, however, that professional research managers remain in constant contact with principal investigators and researchers involved with their projects so that the aspirations set in the original research plan are not lost within the details of project management. Research project management is a tool to the end of successful research rather than an end in itself.

5.14 Managing contract research staff

In the UK, the number of research staff employed on fixed-term contracts to work on specific research projects, based in universities and supported by external funds (typically, research council or charity grants or industrial contracts), has increased rapidly, on an annual basis, over the past ten years or so. It has become one of the most striking aspects of university research, particularly at a time when universities have been constraining the growth in number of their academic staff on open contracts.

Universities have always employed research staff on short-term contracts and, indeed, it has often been seen as the next step in a successful career following postgraduate research. The postdoc, as this type of appointment is known colloquially, has been seen as an important part in the training and experience of future academic staff, professional industrial researchers or those following other research careers. Yet the proportion of staff who will actually become academic staff or professional researchers has decreased dramatically. The danger in the UK is that contract research staff become a crucial part of the university research process and, at the same time, are its human waste product. More and more attention needs to be paid to their well-being, career development and to their employment terms and conditions.

In 1996, a concordat on contract research staff was drawn up by the UK research councils and the universities which aimed to promote the active management of the careers of contract research staff and to recognize the need for review and guidance to be undertaken on a regular basis by the university employer. The concordat set objectives which were more aspirational and concerned with:

- obtaining employment terms and conditions in line with those of open contract staff;
- improving the provision of career guidance and personal development planning for contract research staff;
- developing career opportunities for future research leaders/ champions from contract research staff;
- securing better career progression, pay and conditions.

The overall thrust of the concordat was to improve the lot of contract research staff and to provide them with a greater sense of their worth, at the heart of the research unit and the wider research community in universities.

Most universities have accepted the concordat and have produced and implemented local plans for the support of contract research staff. In 1997 the Research Careers Initiative was introduced and in 1998 the guide *Employing Contract Researchers: A Guide to Best Practice* (OST/Universities UK 1998) was drawn up.

The impetus has been maintained by regular national meetings and seminars and by follow-up statements, yet the position of contract research staff remains a concern for universities, facing the likely impact of European human rights legislation.

It is within the research unit that the most significant action can be taken. Universities should encourage the research unit to ensure that contract research staff are supported by:

- a full induction programme;
- regular career reviews and information and guidance;
- full participation in the academic life of the unit (for example, seminar programmes, involvement with postgraduate students, teaching and learning – where appropriate);
- social programme;
- access to wider research environment of the university (for example, cross-developing initiatives between research units);
- access to the university's facilities and support services for research;
- regular news and information;
- full involvement with the research project to which they are appointed (for example, access to the full research proposal which is the basis of the grant or contract supporting the work);
- regular appraisal and review;
- full access to the university's pay and promotion review system;
- involvement in decisions and general policy-making in the unit and the university (school committees, senate and so on);
- access to mentoring;
- access to staff development training and experience;
- access to information on future career opportunities and personal grants.

Contract research staff are the engines of most research projects, driving forward the basic research plan, undertaking much of the research itself, and feeding into the work of the research group and to the ideas of the research leader/champion. In some cases, contract research staff will produce the core ideas for future research proposals, will be 'named' on future grant applications or contracts and might even have written those proposals under the aegis of the research leader/champion or principal investigator.

Universities will need to consider further the position of contract research staff, perhaps moving towards the idea of an experienced pool of such staff who can be sustained on open contracts moving from one research project to another or the creation of new kinds of appointment with terms and conditions which relate to sustained careers as researchers, commensurate with the career path of academic staff.

The external funding agencies remain convinced of the need for universities to improve their record on contract research staff. Both the research councils and the Wellcome Trust appear to want to establish a full career ladder for contract researchers, and universities remain motivated to improve their lot if only to secure the best researchers and to carry out research projects of the highest quality.

The Research Careers Initiative, originally convened by Professor Gareth Roberts, continues to monitor progress in the UK and produced its third (interim) report in September 2001 seeking to monitor university progress towards attaining the standards set in the original concordat in the following areas:

- Recruitment:
  - provision of research training and continuing development;
  - planned career development;
  - re-entry routes.
- Performance management arrangements:
  - provision of effective research environments;
  - supervision and regular review.
- Terms and conditions of employment including rewards and remuneration:
  - access to terms and conditions;
  - equal opportunities.
- In-service training.
- Career guidance and development.

Further information and copies of the above documents can be consulted at www.universitiesuk.co.uk.

The UK Office of Science and Technology also maintains a researchers' forum which is open to all researchers based in companies, universities and other research-based organizations. This can be consulted at www.researchforum.gov.uk. Participation is based upon a registration process for individuals who wish to:

- seek solutions and advice on managing collaborative projects;
- post information about new research opportunities and calls for proposals;
- make new contacts and seek potential partners; or
- leave basic details in the briefing section.

Although open to all researchers, the forum is of particular help to UK contract research staff. The *Contract Research Staff: Good Management Practice* (OST/Universities UK 1997) source of information was made available in 2002 at www.staff.ac.uk/~gmpcrs. This collaborative venture is based on ongoing development and is led by the

University of Sheffield. The website represents a further step in the Research Careers Initiative and is organized in four sections:

- Personal development – continuing professional development and research management skills.
- Staff review and development – appraisal, focus group events, questionnaires.
- Career tracking – career progression, career experience and employment, career tracking.
- Employment skills – skills awareness and experience.

The project will carry forward the Research Careers Initiative in a significant way, with different strands of work being undertaken by different UK universities or consortia, producing a variety of outputs, including handbooks, for use by research leaders/champions or principal investigators and contract research staff.

Training modules are also being piloted, including a programme on writing for publication which is aimed to run for six to nine months and will consist of three three-part units covering aspects from personal writing goals to abstracts and drafts, engendering in contract research staff both the motivation and confidence to write for publication.

Scotland has a separate but similar initiative promoted by the Scottish Higher Education Funding Council as the SHEFC Contract Research Staff Initiative. The document *Academic Research Careers in Scotland* was published in 2001 (IER/SHEFC 2001) and a series of funded projects has begun. Further information is available at www.shefc.ac.uk.

The issue, first raised in the White Paper *Realising our Potential* (1993) at the beginning of the 1990s, is an intractable one. The Association of University Teachers has long campaigned against fixed contracts and yet universities will inevitably wish to minimize financial uncertainty by employing research staff only for the lifetime of specific research projects.

Contract research staff themselves are concerned to monitor the national position, and information and links are maintained on an unofficial website entitled 'Contract Research Staff (CRS) in UK HE – Online resources' which can be found at www.mailbase.ac.uk/lists/contract-research-staff/files/crslinks.html~top.

Another relevant web publication is 'Science's Next Wave – Resources for the Next Generation of Scientists', which can be accessed at http://nextwave-uk.sciencemag.org.

Many universities in the UK now run relevant web pages as part of their intranet presence, aimed at contract research staff or providing a general forum for discussion of issues of concern which are often promoted through university staff development units or career services.

5.15 Managing research performance

Personal development planning in the context of performance appraisal and review within the framework of effective reward and remuneration policies, allied to research planning at each level in the university in an integrated manner, is the basis for successful management of researchers and research performance. As a managed process, success depends upon considering performance against agreed targets, on the basis of robust information indicating the value of research undertaken as measured by externally referenced and objective benchmarks. These might include a mix of measures of both quality and quantity such as:

• research publications or other forms of public output;
• research income in the form of research grants or contracts;
• other contributions in terms of research outputs such as official or commercial reports, consultancy or similar research-based activity;
• intellectual property-related outputs (patents, licences, companies, partnerships and so on);
• postgraduate supervision;
• connections to research environment;
• involvement with partners and collaborators;
• participation in national and international companies (for example, convenor, chair, paper delivery, participant);
• prizes and awards or other forms of recognition;
• citation analysis (when appropriate).

Individual appraisal and review is best carried out by the research leader or champion, as closely as possible to the research group itself, and should be formed on objective comparison with like areas of research on a confidential but open basis. The university's corporate research leader (normally a pro-vice-chancellor with specific responsibility for research) should manage a systematic process of annual visits so that the unit's research performance can be discussed and individuals and issues can be identified and reviewed.

There is probably no more controversial or sensitive topic than research performance in universities, but unless open, honest, realistic and regular reviews are a feature of the university's research policy, the university's research will not prosper. Research is undertaken in the climate of peer review in which knowledge is advanced by the open discussion and debate of objective research findings attributed to groups and individuals. The university should approach the management of research performance in the same spirit.

Researchers, making up a designated unit of research, research together and some evaluation of the unit's success, the deployment of resources against themes, the integration of research projects and their interaction with other research units inside and beyond the university, must be made as part of the corporate strategy-setting procedure.

Research units should be asked to produce annual research plans (or, if part of larger departments, alongside plans for learning, teaching and outreach activities) in the form of business plans. They should measure overall performance against the targets set the previous year, and consider strengths and opportunities for research while recognizing and dealing with threats and weaknesses. For universities, research is a core business, and only by adopting methodical business planning techniques can research be sustained, developed, expanded and retained as a commercially viable activity. Research groups are in the nature of operating businesses and their performance is crucial.

Adopting such an overtly commercial approach does not mean abandoning fundamental academic values concerning academic freedom, research ethics, the pursuit of knowledge for its own sake, intellectual stimulation and curiosity, and research choice. Why the university undertakes research is core to its ethos as well as to its business. To sustain the university's research ethos requires the sustaining of its research business, and the two aspects are mutually comparable and beneficial when moulded into a university-wide system of research performance management and organized with consideration and sensitivity.

It is usual to identify responsibilities with tasks for the corporate management of research in most universities. It is not possible to coordinate research without a structure for research planning. In some cases, deans might be responsible for research in their faculties or, in others, a pro-vice-chancellor will be nominated to deal with research in collaboration with unit research leaders. In many cases, a central research committee is a key component. Research committees clearly do not *do* research, nor can they directly engage in the pursuit of research in the relevant units let alone at the level of groups and individuals, but central research committees can coordinate research and be responsible for research planning. This requires more functionality than simply administering central research funds in the form of allocating grants for conferences, travel, start-up research and so on.

The research committee, supported by sub-committees as necessary representing perhaps cross-cutting research thematic priorities or areas of the university's research, should be linked into both the university's academic governance (reporting to senate or council) and its strategic planning (reporting to its finance or strategic planning committees). The research committee should support the pro-vice-chancellor for research in carrying out the university's agreed system of research performance review and should task the university's research services office.

The committee should oversee the research business planning process, produce the university's corporate strategy for research and be responsible for the university's research policy and procedures. The committee would normally be chaired by the pro-vice-chancellor for research who is responsible to the vice-chancellor, principal or rector.

6

SUPPORTING RESEARCH

6.1 Introduction: beginnings

The idea of supporting research has been more fully rooted in the United States and for a longer period of time than has been the case in Britain, probably because of the American experience of managing large-scale research projects which dates back to the Second World War and the practical, although controversial, lessons of the Manhattan Project, and especially its concentration at Los Alamos in March 1943 under the direction of J. Robert Oppenheimer and General Leslie R. Groves. In peacetime, the American commitment to high-prestige research projects such as the national space programme (NASA) and, in the private sector, those of international pharmaceutical companies and the aerospace industry, have underlined the importance of the provision of well-managed research support as much as research itself. In particular, the relationship between research and commercialization has been well understood such that applied research has been closely connected to the enterprise ethos and to the development of new markets: a relationship exploited successfully in the postwar world by nations such as Japan and Germany. Basic or pure research of the generic kind has also prospered in the United States with the professional assistance of research institutions or universities.

Within the US Department of Health and Human Sciences, the National Institute of Health (NIH) has a multifunctional role in supporting medical and health research by providing health information, grants and funding opportunities, an e-news service and other scientific sources as well as running its own research centres and institutes. The NIH provides support for research, and its mission, simply stated, is to valour and knowledge. Alongside the National Science Foundation, these two agencies provide US science with strong federal support and a systematic organizational framework for funding and for information. Eighty-two per cent of the NIH's funding is made in grants and contracts to more than 3000 research institutions over the United States, while simultaneously supporting over 3000 research projects in its own institutions.

The US federal government, identifying the need for new research programmes, creates funding opportunities targeting specific issues. An example of this process is the National Institute on Ageing (NIA). Established as one of the NIH's 25 institutes in 1974, NIA has the task of improving the health and well-being of older Americans through research.

The experience in the United States is of a federal approach to nurturing research, not just with funding, but also on the basis of information, networking and other scientific resources in an environment of supporting research as well as simply pursuing research.

Since the mid-1980s and the advent of national research scrutiny exercises across the world, universities in Europe, America and the Far East have begun to invest significantly in the provision of research support facilities to help increase both the quality and quantity of research undertaken and its profitability. This is especially so with respect to externally funded research grants and contracts where a more managed approach to corporate research strategy and to the relationship with key external research funders exists.

The external world of research funding has become progressively more complex since 1980 as, first, more sources of funding for university-based research have begun to appear, with more funds to deploy and with an ever greater number of schemes and programmes requiring detailed comprehension and prepared applications. Second, governments have been less inclined to leave universities to their own devices and, while resisting any frontal assault on university autonomy, have adopted an indirect approach in providing ringfenced or earmarked funding elements for research to encourage universities to adopt strategies favourable to government policies. Research leaders or champions are now obliged to maintain not only flourishing research programmes and individual research projects, but also a flow of funding from external sources for their support – sometimes producing as many as two or three research applications a month in order to guarantee, through the successful award of research grants and contracts, the stability and security of their research group.

Third, the expansion of research in universities has created a requirement for training and development programmes in support of research to assist those starting out on research careers or those wishing to shape their future research at whatever stage in their careers. Professional support has become a necessity in universities with a stated research mission and serious research ambitions, and few, if any, universities now operate without some form of corporate research services office or range of research support.

As more attention is paid to the notion of the knowledge-based economy, and as researchers are placed under more and more pressure to perform in a way which produces increased visible inputs and outputs, the help of such services is often required even by the most experienced researchers to enable them to fulfil the non-research tasks necessary for their success such as: research administration; information on research opportunities; grant application drafting and research contracting; commercialization; promotion and publicity; research scrutiny returns; research staffing and development; and the myriad of other functions which are not directly concerned with undertaking research itself. Some cynics might dismiss these functions as bureaucratic time-wasting or as an unwelcome part of the hyperbole surrounding modern-day research in a global society in which research itself is relegated to the status of a second-order task behind the need to establish a reputation and to be visible with the 'story-makers' of press and other media or with the policy-makers seeking to defend and extend their budgets. An ethos of 'research and survive' might be deemed to be the priority from the perspective of a cynical observer and, whether accurate or not as a description, it is nonetheless true that the researcher in the twenty-first century university has to pay attention to many more aspects than simply the research programme or project itself. The role of the research services office can be to undertake these additional tasks, leaving researchers to research.

At the same time, governments have begun to take a close interest in the outputs from publicly funded research in universities in order to ensure not only that the quality of funded research is high but also that commercial exploitation and the path to market for university research and development is fully exploited. Governments wish to see a good return on the public investment made in university research. Industry and commerce have also begun to increase their interest in university intellectual property as a source of potential added value for their products, processes and services at the same time as their investment in their own R&D facilities has been progressively cut back or outsourced since the 1980s.

At the beginning of the 1990s, universities in the UK expanded in number, size and range, endeavouring to meet new growth targets for student numbers and to develop the research base after many years of financial retrenchment. Research, always a significant factor in building successful individual and personal academic careers, began to have much greater importance at the corporate level as a source of reputation and revenues. In the UK, the world of external research funding became more complex. The UK research councils were reviewed, the White Paper *Realising our Potential* was produced, through commercial opportunity the Wellcome Trust became the largest funder of medical research in the UK, and regional policy as a driver for university research became even more important.

In the UK, universities began to explore unitary administration and new resource allocation models with devolved funding to academic departments or the university's business organizations. Some began to establish professional units or offices whose job was to support research in all its facets, enabling individuals and groups to pursue research through conducive university policies and procedures and to promote their research strengths with potential external funders as opportunities arose. The research support and industrial liaison office was an example of these new university support units which reflected the recognition by the research-led universities of these trends.

As a new approach, the tendency towards specialist research services units laid new foundations on earlier ones in the 1980s whereby some research-led universities or those whose research was generally closer to industry or was of a more applied nature had begun to set up commercialization and exploitation agencies through university companies and science parks. It was clear that the previous monopoly arrangements insisted upon by the UK government that exploitation should take place only through a national body, the forerunner of the British Technology Group, had been set aside by the general move towards the deregulation and privatization common to the 1980s. This is not the place for a detailed exposition of Britain's experience of intellectual property exploitation through government agencies or government-stimulated initiatives, but briefly, the National Research Development Corporation (NRDC) had been established in 1948 to commercialize British research, followed by the setting up of a mandatory 'first referral' in 1950. In 1975, the government set up the National Enterprise Board (NEB) to help existing British companies. In 1981, NRDC and NEB were merged and the British Technology Group (BTG) was formed. In 1985, the government relaxed the monopoly to allow universities to make their own exploitation arrangements. In 1992, British Technology Group was privatized and became BTG in a management buyout, and in 2000 BTG made a rights issue, raising £120 million for future investment.

University commercialization of research, through the management of intellectual property, had been under way across the world and particularly in the United States where the examples of Stanford, MIT, and other institutions with a considerable track record for the exploitation of research offered tempting models. This began to be matched in the UK by a band of universities including Imperial College, UCL, UMIST, Cranfield, Cambridge and Warwick.

In the main, in the UK, supporting research at this early stage came to mean bolting on some additional units both inside and outside the university to offer services or to operate exploitation monopolies with a few, more business-minded, research champions from among their academic communities. University policies rarely placed these units at the centre of corporate life in the first days of developing research support. Many had to struggle to command attention, find a niche and develop a role but, through the 1980s, most serious research-led universities had established pioneer structures of some kind to support their research.

Although there were common generic themes between them, each structure differed to meet the particular needs of the individual university and the principle was established that the preferred structure had to suit the university concerned. Universities evolved structures from their early versions and organized and reorganized services until finding the most appropriate and suitable structures for their particular academic research communities.

There were few models for the skills sets necessary for the professional research services and commercialization staff concerned, and many universities chose to 'grow their own', finding it difficult initially to recruit the right people. Indeed, finding staff with the best university–business interface skills remains a matter of national concern especially as a similar arrangement is being extended to the NHS and the market for such individuals will expand while the available pool will reduce. Many and varied backgrounds were possessed by those first staff such as:

- former industrial and commercial careers in R&D;
- entrepreneurial backgrounds in high-tech companies and early spin outs;
- science or research park experience;
- academic research careers;
- venture capital, commercial or banking backgrounds;
- university administrative generalists.

Rudimentary policies and procedures were developed, often on the basis of US models, or disseminated by the early professional bodies which appeared such as the Association of University Research and Industrial Links (AURIL) or its predecessor organization, University Directors of Industrial Liaison (UDIL), or the UK University Companies Association (UNICO) founded to encourage professional standards and best practice among their member universities. (A full list of relevant organizations is given in Appendix 2.)

6.2 Supporting research: towards a definition

What does 'supporting research' mean? What tasks are encompassed by the term? At its foundation, the term always involved administering research, that is:

- Costing, pricing and financial administration of research grants and contracts.
- Authorization of research grant and contract applications, proposals and tenders.
- Administering the human resources functions arising from research grants and contracts:
  - research contract staff;
  - terms and conditions of employment;
  - appointment, review and promotion.
- Health and safety aspects.
- Estates issues:
  - laboratory accommodation;
  - equipment and facilities.
- Academic administration:
  - postgraduate affairs;
  - research degrees and regulations.
- Legal issues.

These, largely passive, tasks were carried out by a small number of staff, usually spread throughout the central administration or the university's faculties and departments.

In the UK, in the 1980s, government policy began to favour an increasing separation of public resources for teaching and research in universities, insisting on their separate accounting while, at the same time, requiring an ever greater emphasis upon selectivity of research funding based upon research performance. The national spotlight focused on university-based research in a way it had not previously done and the former passive administration of research was no longer found to be sufficient. Universities began to move from *administering* research to *supporting* research, a trend which appeared at about the same time throughout the world, as could be seen by the interest taken in the subject by university administrative conferences and training seminars.

6.3 Supporting research as a business process

No two universities are identical, nor are any two university research services structures, and nor should they be. There is neither single model nor blueprint, and each university is best advised to develop a service which is suited to its own mission, structure, circumstances and ethos. If the service is to be of optimum use and is to find acceptance with the academic community, its form must be appropriate to the university and its research strategy.

The most basic decision for the university to make is whether to place the organization wholly within the university's other central corporate services or to set up a company outside the university or to outsource the whole operation through an external agent. In fact, these positions represent different points on the same continuum and the university can choose to form a research services structure which combines different approaches. There are two important considerations:

- The extent to which the research services office understands the university research community (strengths, areas of special expertise, particular facilities and so on).
- The extent to which the research services office accesses a 'proper' business ethos and can operate on a commercial basis.

Some universities prefer to have their research services operate at arm's length from the university in order to permit fully objective business decisions to be made and commercial judgements to be exercised. Other universities seek the confidence of knowing that their research services are fully familiar with their research community and that their academic and research staff find that its operations are complementary to their research strategies and fully conversant with them.

Few universities opt for a fully contracted out service, although many will contract specialist services on the basis of need such as legal services, patent services, venture capital support, marketing and promotional services or other specialist services, drawing in such support around a core of university-based research services staff.

The size and number of staff making up the service should reflect the size and range of the university's research programme and ambition, but it is necessary to have a scale commensurate with the scale of research undertaken, otherwise work bottlenecks will occur and the service will become a barrier to the flow of research undertaken (grant processing, contracting, commercialization and so on) rather than a gateway through which research work will flow unimpeded.

There is no particular standard unit for the research service: each customer will require more or less time dependent upon the nature of the enquiry, so it is difficult to assess or calculate the rate or volume of flow of research work. The only measurable data will be the amount carried out in the previous period of time. Demand is therefore unpredictable, whether a voluntary or compulsory service is offered.

The range of functions to be carried out will also depend upon the individual university whose decision will need to be made on whether to adopt a single point of contact – a one-stop shop – or to distribute functions across a number of corporate service providers. For example, whether the research services office is to undertake costing and pricing, using its own accountants, or whether the finance function is to remain with the finance office, is a decision which must be made at the outset as it determines a fundamental aspect of the initial structure for the research services office and the flow of business.

The university, in deciding upon the most appropriate research services structure, should begin by identifying and mapping its particular research business process. How do researchers pursue research and at what point does this process interact with the corporate policies and procedures and touch the university's operational requirements? How far does the university's research strategy map on the plans of researchers and research groups, and when does the research services office ensure that researchers are helped to deliver the corporate research strategy? For example, if the university aims to develop its EU research funding, it must enable researchers to be aware of funding opportunities, understand EU regulations, have access to an EU expert and be provided with full assistance to produce successful applications. This cannot be achieved without coordinating and focusing support for European research so that help is available to facilitate the business process of fostering successful European research grant and contract applications.

The business process for research begins with the research context in which groups and individuals are located:

- Research environment
  - Ongoing research programmes and projects within the research unit.

- Research plans and goals
  - Targets for future research within identified research strategy agreed as part of the university's corporate research strategy.
- Research ideas
  - Generation of research ideas (large and small scale, and short and long term).
  - Feasibility of research ideas (discussion with research colleagues).
- Fundable proposals
  - Conversion of some feasible research ideas into proposals for external funding in the form of grants and contracts.
  - Discussion of fundable ideas with research colleagues.
  - Discussion of fundable ideas with research support services.
- Commercialization
  - Does the fundable idea have commercial potential?
  - Is it a fruitful service of research publications or other outputs?
- Targeting the potential funder
  - Identifying the potential funder and considering the approach.
  - Information of potential programmes and thematic priorities.
  - Matching fundable idea to funder's programmes.
- Approaching the potential funder
  - Attending the potential funder's briefing.
  - Interacting with potential funder on proposal.
- Submitting the proposal
  - Completing applications or preparing proposals for possible submission.
  - Ensuring proposals are fully complementary with the funder's requirements.
  - Ensuring the proposal meets the university's requirements on price, statutory undertakings, strategy, operational procedures and is fully authorized.
- Receiving the outcome
  - Following up rejection to obtain full information.
  - Ensuring successful awards are properly managed in accordance with university procedures.
  - Setting up the funded project.
- Managing the research
  - Carrying out the research project or programme in accordance with sound project management techniques and the funder's requirements.
  - Checking for ethical and safety issues.
  - Exploring other risk factors.
  - Reviewing for commercial outcomes in the form of intellectual property and ensuring their protection and exploitation.

- Completing research
  - Reviewing the research project on completion and taking appropriate measures.
- Post project review
  - Outcomes.
  - Repeat business.

At every step the research services office should interact with the individual researcher and research group in as pro-active a manner as possible in support of the university's research business process.

6.4 Model structures for supporting research

In the research-led university, conducting research of the highest quality is central to the mission statement. Expanding and improving both the quality and quantity of research undertaken, and in particular seeking collaborative partnerships, contracts or external funding in the form of research grants, becomes a central business process both to support the university's research ambition and to provide a benchmark of its research excellence. As the research funding environment changes and becomes increasingly competitive, it is important to establish support mechanisms to help the academic community to secure its market share of research funding from a balanced range of funders and to secure fully priced, high-value research as a premium for the university's reputation on both the national and international research stages.

However the research services office is organized, it should focus on the following priorities:

- The requirement for researchers to be more aware of the policies and objectives which drive research funding and which underpin national research and its organization.
- The need for researchers to think in more comprehensive terms about potential sources of research funding and the actions necessary to expand funded research and the university's research-related businesses.
- The growing significance of collaborative research developed from networks and partnerships on a national, European and global basis.
- The significance of accessibility of information available on the internet through the *e-search* environment.
- The importance of ensuring research productivity and profitability.

In effect, the research services offered by the research-led university are as much concerned with underpinning the university's research business as about providing operational mechanisms for the conducting of research and its management together with targeting potential funding opportunities.

Research-related business – that is, those products and processes which can be produced from the university's research in the form of knowledge-related commercialization – should be deemed to include not only straightforward intellectual property exploitation (company spin-outs, licence agreements, revenue-earning agreements and so on) but the newly prominent priority attached to third task or outreach programmes and activities. These include continuing professional development courses, vocational and other short courses, top-up courses together with consultancy, and commercial services arising from the exploitation of both knowledge and facilities in the university research laboratories.

Most universities will have created the following functional areas to accomplish some or all of the above:

- Research services office;
- Continuing professional development and short-course service;
- Consultancy company;
- Science or research park;
- Commercialization company;
- Spin-out companies;
- Venture capital provision;
- Financial services;
- Health and safety;
- Ethics and conduct committee or service;
- Shared facilities/services and collaborative units;
- Legal services.

These represent other points on the continuum previously described and it is unlikely that any university will have organized all of the above into a single integrated support structure. The decision as to what functions to include in a single office or what to leave as part of a wider, more generalized function within a traditional service such as the academic affairs office or the finance office is a matter for each university to determine.

What follows is based upon personal experience of a single office for the provision of research and enterprise services alongside a university commercialization company and a research park development. In many ways, this structure provides an ideal solution to the problem of how best to provide services to the academic community and the external world in that it combines the advantages of a core service with those of an independent commercial company when these are required.

The structure, however, raises concerns about identification of the task and ease of access which need to be overcome by close working relationships, communication and detailed liaison on general operational procedures and policies, formation of the university's corporate strategy for research and the day-to-day working on specific cases.

In the previous chapter the goals for the research service were set out as:

- business intelligence on funding opportunities for research;
- advice and guidance on targeting funders and making successful research grant applications or completing successful research contracts;
- links and networks for research (identifying partners, marketing the university's research strengths, developing fruitful links); and
- coordination (policies and procedures concerned with undertaking research in the university, operational practice, assisting with the formation of research strategies, maintenance of performance information and coordination of national scrutiny exercises).

These generic functions remain central to the service and, in partnership, commercialization services are offered through the university's company, again as set out in the previous chapter.

For this partnership to be effective, both the research service and the university company must operate closely as two sides of a single coin in that they must both possess a close understanding of the university's research environment, research strengths, policies and procedures, and operate harmoniously in pursuit of the same goals and objectives. It might be said that there is a tension between the commercial exploitation of research and the generation of new knowledge in the form of publications and other published output, and that these tensions apply not only to the academic community but also to the goals of the university's research service and its exploitation company. In fact, any such tension can be resolved in the operation of the two and can even be combined within a single organization, as many universities demonstrate effectively. For the tension to be fully resolved it is vital that there is full communication and coordination between both parties. For the academic community, it must appear a seamless service and the point at which either is involved in the research business process should be clear to members of the academic community, as should the specific roles and tasks which each carries out.

Drawing up specific plans and strategies for both organizations can be helpful in providing a clear picture of the university's overall service. Such plans should be published widely and made available for consultation through the university's web pages along with information on the range of services provided by both the research support service and the company.

In order to meet the requirement for research support, the university, in considering research as a business process, should ascertain the workflow and the quantity of research which would need support. From there it is possible to arrive at an estimate of the number of staff and the range of functions which the university will need. The following suggested structure is based upon the experience of a large British university with a broad and extensive research portfolio. In summary, support is offered in six areas to encourage the development of research and the university's outreach programme by:

- enabling effective 'grantmanship';
- promotion of the university's diverse research strengths and increasing the university's research income;
- development and exploitation of the university–business interface, including harnessing business intelligence on the future for research and research funding opportunities;
- responding to funding opportunities for research and for third task funding, including adopting a pro-active stance to anticipate future developments;
- shaping effective university policies, procedures and structures for research;
- assisting with processes and structures to encourage and enable full business interaction.

Such a plan requires the research services office and university company to work to the university's strategic targets and assist research units in achieving goals which make up those targets. This means seeking to achieve success by:

- continuing to develop the university's strategic approach to research;
- broadening the base of the research activity so that more members of the academic community are involved with successful research grant applications or profitable research contracts;
- extending the range of research and, in particular, increasing the volume of externally funded research from all categories available;

- encouraging research units to set challenging targets for research and to help their distribution across the units as well as assist in the measurement of research performance;
- developing the related programme of outreach to business and industry, thereby enabling additional revenue streams to be generated to support further research and the formation of substantial research collaboration, thereby in turn contributing to the university's core business of research.

It is clear from the description above that there is a complex interaction between goal-setting, the systematic measurement of research performance, the university's research environment and the assistance provided by the research services office so that the interactions across the university's business process for research is a complicated one in which several iterations occur in both directions. This emphasizes the reality that it is not a linear business process.

6.4.1 Model structure: the university company

Establishing a commercialization company is of no value unless the university has a clearly stated policy, enshrined in the conditions of service of staff, regarding the management of intellectual property. Following the decision to end the British Technology Group (BTG) monopoly, university companies were established to take over responsibility for the development and management of commercial routes for the universities' intellectual property.

Intellectual property rights can exist in many forms and can be protected in many ways; novel inventions may be protected by patent; computer software, creative work and literary texts can be protected by copyright; designs may be protected by design right. All knowledge, even knowledge in the form of know-how which cannot be legally protected, can still have a commercial value which the university is able to exploit.

Exploitation by the university company can usually be undertaken in one of four approaches and the company should be able to recommend the most effective route:

- *Licensing.* Exploitation can take the form of licences to the intellectual property granted to an industrial or other commercial licensee in return for the payment of a royalty sum or other lump sum. It is usual to arrange for option fees and advance payments as well as percentage royalty payments which the university company can be responsible for during negotiation for licence arrangements.

- *Manufacture.* The university company will be able to explore the possibility of manufacturing and selling products directly, perhaps through a separate company, particularly in the case where an invention is not able to be protected legally or if the market is not sufficient to attract industrial licensees. In such cases the new manufacturing entity would receive a licence from the university and in return pay royalties.
- *Joint venture.* It is possible that the university company might establish a joint venture with an industrial or commercial partner to exploit intellectual property directly.
- *Agent.* Where the intellectual property position is difficult to enforce or where an international profile is required, the university company might partner with a technology agent such as BTG to arrange for the exploitation of intellectual property. In all cases, approaches to such technology agents should be left to the university company and should not be made directly by members of academic staff.

Confidentiality

In all cases, it is important to observe confidentiality in relation to intellectual property. Any unintended disclosure will invalidate patent protection and can prejudice future successful commercialization. In the interests of both the university and the inventor, it is important to exercise at an early stage a mutually binding confidentiality agreement in any discussions about commercialization.

Revenue-sharing policy

All universities which are serious about exploiting commercial opportunity in the form of intellectual property must develop a policy for sharing revenues with inventors or authors on terms which are attractive and where, through the apportionment of revenue, both the university and the inventor will benefit. Such revenue-sharing agreements will vary from university to university but it is usual to take, as a first charge on the income arising from inventions, all direct costs, including the fees of the university's exploitation company, before any further disbursement of revenues takes place. A typical apportionment might be as follows:

- Fifty per cent accrues as personal income to the inventor, author or designer, where there is more than one person involved the money should be apportioned equally among them;
- Twenty-five per cent would be allocated for disposal on the recommendation of the head of the unit in which the member of

staff resides, assuming that all direct costs have been covered already;

• Twenty-five per cent would be allocated to the university.

It is usual for such policies to include a sliding scale approach, with a reduced apportionment for revenues in excess of the first £100,000 per annum. In those cases it is usual to reduce the revenues accruing to the inventor in favour of the unit and the university.

University companies should also consider operating university consultancy services or consultancy companies developed to exploit know-how from the academic community. To attract consultancy work of this kind it is usual for the company to offer a reward scheme whereby the consultancy fee is retained in part by the consultant and in part by the university and the university company. Again, apportionment varies from university to university but it is usual to offer an attractive package of access to the university's liability insurance, help with promotion of consultancy services and subsequent billing, and use of the university's name, reputation and brand image. The income from university consultancy companies can be considerable if the right balance is struck in the sharing of income.

6.4.2 Model structure: the research services office

The ideal structure for the research support service will match the scale and ambition of research undertaken by the university. However, it should consist of a director with overall responsibility for coordinating both research support and enterprise development activities in the university, including outreach programmes, enterprise strategies, links to commercialization and research policy together with the remit for the university's response to national scrutiny exercises such as the Research Assessment Exercise and for sponsor management, providing the framework for management training and advice on research funding and the overall direction of the service. Other posts might be determined as follows:

• *Research contracts officer.* This person should be responsible for coordinating all university research contracts, consultancy, research tenders and provide advice and guidance on research contracting and the nature of agreements. The post will require additional support commensurate with the flow of contracts increases, and in large universities would consist of a research contracts sub-office of a number of posts.

- *Outreach programme coordinator.* This person will coordinate and support the delivery of a range of services from the university's research units and other specialist centres and enhance the interfaces between the university, business and the community.
- *Enterprise officer.* This person is responsible for the development of the university's enterprise strategy in liaison with the support service and the university's commercial company together with the remit for developing student enterprise and operating within the region and at a national level on enterprise policies. (This post might oversee a range of business development officers who are organized on a sector-wide basis to develop particular interface relationships with sectors of commerce and industry or for particular clusters of academic disciplines.)
- *Information development officer.* This person is responsible for the development and maintenance of the service's dissemination of information on funding opportunities, including the e-search environment.
- *National research programmes officer.* This person has the remit for all national funding programmes and sponsors relevant to the university's research, and organizes the interface to these sponsors, advising on proposals and providing funding information on policies and procedures.
- *European and regional officer.* This post-holder focuses on the European community and regional developments, disseminating information on funding opportunities and advising on proposals as relevant.
- *Training officer.* This is the post concerned with staff development programmes for research which are provided to research units or researchers as individuals, and with maintaining and updating the university's approach to personal development planning in the research community.

It is increasingly difficult in the UK to identify and recruit key staff to operate at the business–university interface, as more and more institutions and organizations appear to wish to recruit such staff (the NHS, regional development agencies, local government and so on), but one important factor is to ensure that staff have some *direct* experience of *doing research* and so can understand and share with researachers their enthusiasm and commitment.

It is possible to consider the establishment of other posts in support of the research support function, but the above provides a minimum structure for a large research university bearing in mind the initial comments made in introduction to this chapter.

6.5 Service-level statements

In order to ensure the quality of the service provided by the research support function it is necessary to develop a policy of service-level statements in which the mission for the university is set out together with an itemized list of services available to the research community. If the mission of the service office is to increase research and enterprise at the university by providing core services supporting the achievement of the university's central aims of excellence in research and constructive partnerships with business and the community, it is important to identify how the provision of services helps to shape research, business and community strategies at both the university and the unit level and the operational policies and procedures whereby assistance is provided to all researchers, as well as to forge and maintain research relationships with external sponsors and partners.

The service-level statement operates at three levels:

- corporate and strategic services;
- unit and operational services; and
- individual support services.

If the service-level statement is structured in this way and is based upon discussion and consultation with the research community, it is possible to produce a realistic and reasonable document which will form the basis of the relationship between the research support service, the university company and the research community as a whole. This is particularly important when it comes to understanding research community expectation and managing the allocation of resources to different sets of tasks, as well as providing a framework for interaction and dispute resolution alongside a complaints procedure. The service-level statement provides the minimum level of service but should be constantly reviewed and refreshed as new requirements and developments arise. This might be done by occasional systematic review involving external commentators and practitioners to ensure that the research support service and university company retain their position at the leading edge of such university-based services.

In a similar fashion, it is important to extend a review process to maintain the professional standards of research managers and administrators operating in research units so that there is a common standard or benchmark which they attain in delivering their own services as part of research programme and project management.

6.6 Ethics and conduct

It is important for the university to have a fully developed and well-publicized code of ethics and conduct and procedures applying generally to university business but covering in specific detail research and the provision of knowledge-based services. For research in the medical and biomedical fields, it will be standard practice for the university to have established an ethics committee under the arrangements referred by the Home Secretary for a local ethical review process (LERP). This became mandatory in the UK with effect from 1 April 1999 in respect of the use of all animals regulated under the Animals (Scientific Procedures) Act 1986.

The purposes are threefold:

1 To give independent ethical advice to the university's nominated certificate holder on project licence applications and the statements on animal welfare.
2 To issue advice and guidance on ethical issues to those undertaking research where such issues might arise.
3 To develop and promote awareness of ethical issues concerning animal welfare and to initiate the development of applications which meet the principles of reduction, replacement and refinement as far as the use of animals is concerned.

Most universities have placed these responsibilities under the appropriate unit concerned with biomedical and medical services and the already established research advisory committee which advises on issues of medical ethics as far as clinical research is concerned. This is an aspect of research support where clear professional advice, guidance and monitoring of the university's ethical practice are a statutory requirement.

Beyond issues of animal welfare, it is valuable and appropriate for the university to consider establishing a sub-committee of its governing body able to advise on issues of ethics and conduct with regard to students and staff at the university. The remit of this body should embrace the following:

- Personal conduct in teaching and research in terms of behaviour, propriety, integrity, plagiarism, professional conduct, practice and misconduct and so on.
- Procedures for handling in a confidential manner complaints and accusations of misconduct.
- The maintenance of the university's code of conduct.

- The promotion and awareness of the university's procedures regarding cases concerned with ethics and conduct.

There are many reasons for the university to be concerned about ethical practice:

1 Legislation (such as that concerned with conduct in public life or animal welfare) requires the university, as a public institution, to have policies and arrangements in the fields of professional conduct.
2 Many external funders now require evidence of 'scientific integrity' in the form of a published code of conduct.
3 Such an approach provides a route for individuals to bring forward cases of misconduct in confidence ('whistle-blowing') and gives the university a detailed and published procedure for handling such cases.
4 If the university is serious about its research provision, it should also be serious about its scientific integrity and should do all it can to demonstrate that it is.
5 It is a source for guidance and support of researchers engaged in research programmes and projects when doubtful issues arise so that difficulties can be avoided by preventing unintentional misconduct.
6 In times of risk, the university can demonstrate in cases of legal challenge and for purposes of insurance that it has taken steps to safeguard itself from the accusation that, at an institutional level, no advice or guidance was available or procedures in place to deal with ethics and misconduct issues.

A statement of guiding principles should inform the process of setting up a procedure. This might cover:

- truth and integrity;
- openness (subject to appropriate commercial or other confidentiality);
- fairness and equity;
- professionalism;
- avoidance of conflict of interest;
- statutory compliance (especially in areas such as health and safety); and
- the observance of regulation, legal requirement, professional standards and university regulation.

It should be a requirement that all staff and students, in whatever academic or other activity they engage in the university, accept and agree to abide by the code on registration or employment. The code should clearly state that breaches of the code may lead to disciplinary action, but it should also point to the sources of support and advice on conduct when in doubt.

Specific terms of reference should be drawn up as to the remit of any ethics and conduct committee and attention should be drawn to data protection and to the importance of maintaining research data in a durable and auditable form (for at least five years for scrutiny purposes), and that such data are available for discussion with other researchers as necessary.

The code of conduct should also refer to publications, in particular issues of plagiarism, supervision conduct, conflict of interest and any other issues the university wishes to include, while recognizing the principle of academic freedom and individual conscience.

In cases of development funds or external funds, provision should be made for considering these where particular sources of funding are deemed necessary for scrutiny, with an implication that in unsuitable cases such sources might be declined.

Misconduct, in the context of the code, must be clearly defined and should include:

- falsification and fabrication;
- misappropriation of the ideas of others or their research data without acknowledgement or permission; and
- misleading ascription of authorship or ownership.

Members of staff have a duty to report misconduct and should be encouraged to do so within the terms of the code of conduct.

More than a policy or code, the University should be able to promote standards are to highest order and should support responsible research at all levels. This task involves active management, staff development programmes, spot checks and quality assurance, promotional campaigns and guidance.

THE MAKING OF A UNIVERSITY STRATEGY FOR RESEARCH

7.1 Personal development planning and support

Research is dynamic, and research performance is measurable only against the most recent research results. For researchers and for the university alike, it should be understood that research requires development as a continuous process measured against new challenges and stated objectives which should be set, reviewed, renewed and resourced in a given period of time.

The university's research reputation is made up of the collective achievements of many researchers and research groups across time, but must continue to be built upon by the next generation of researchers, otherwise the institution will start to decline, being remembered only for past achievements. Each individual researcher or group has a stake in the university's research and has a different perspective on current and future research plans and programmes, requiring to be motivated and developed in different ways. Their different contributions need to be integrated into a single institutional plan or corporate strategy for research such that their differing perspectives are drawn together and are united in the pursuit of research excellence, thereby building the university's research reputation in the present and for the future. The university must continue investment in the development of the best researchers, facilities, equipment, networks and partnerships. The process is mutually reinforcing as the best researchers will always migrate to the best research universities with the best facilities where they are able to undertake the best research.

The process, however, should begin with a fundamental reappraisal of research and why it is pursued by the university in the first place, alongside a thoroughgoing revision of personal or collective incentives, rewards, motivations on the framework of regular appraisals for the researcher and the research group against international benchmarks. It is important to remember that universities do not themselves undertake research. It is their academic and research staff, research groups and postgraduate research students who actually *do* research. These groups, no matter how much corporate loyalty they have, are only temporarily a part of the institutions employing them or to whom they are registered as postgraduate research students. Like professionals in all organizations, they must be carefully nurtured and developed, encouraged and rewarded, motivated and incentivized, supported and serviced. Their selection, conditions of appointment, terms of service, working environments, appraisal, reward and remuneration are crucial areas for operational policies which are as conducive as possible to undertaking research.

The basic ingredient of the successful university research strategy is an operational policy in which researchers are motivated to develop their personal research contributions through their own personal development plans and to ensure that these are mapped on to those for the research group which are in turn incorporated into the university's corporate research strategy rather than to attempt to design a high-level strategy of which all researchers are invited to become a part. This is not an easy task and requires that a full appraisal system for research is in operation, usually under the aegis of the pro-vice-chancellor for research and head or directors of units, centres or departments, to identify personal research goals and to see how these are integrated into research planning at every level in the university. Personal development plans represent the career aspirations of those who make up the university as a research community, and therefore their personal goals are directly relevant to the corporate research strategy and are drawn from the perspectives of different research groups and units in the university.

The importance of developing researchers so that they can achieve their personal research goals as part of their career trajectories should not be lost on the university as its research strategy is entirely dependent on these. An objective for the university's staff development provision for researchers should be the development of both their research and non-research skills.

Research skills include:

Familiarization and awareness
- The laboratory environment and practice.
- Computing and information technology (C&IT) for research.

- *E-search* – the world of electronic communication and access to research resources on the web.
- Induction into the unit and the wider university.
- Working with information services.
- Marketing and promotions.

Research
- The world of external research funding and the organization of science and technology in the UK and elsewhere.
- Pricing research – a guide.
- Research standards and ethics.
- Working in a research group.
- Experimentation: best practice.
- The management of intellectual property.
- Setting research goals and measuring attainment.
- The laboratory notebook.
- Writing successful research grant applications.
- Research results.
- Writing up.
- Research contracting.

Skills (non-research)
- Presentation.
- Writing for publication.
- Setting deadlines and working to time schedules.
- Project management.
- Team-playing in research.
- Personal initiative-taking.
- PC packages and C&IT skills.
- Communication and interpersonal skills.

Training for experienced researchers or those in mid-career may seem to be unnecessary or even unhelpful but, even in those cases, there is a place for the availability of upskilling or updating modules. All training provision should be tailored to the needs of the particular research area concerned, should take into account the local environment, and should be based upon experiences and case studies relevant to the field. All training provision should be regularly reviewed and refreshed to ensure that information is up to date and remains accurate.

7.2 Mapping on to personal motivation

Personal motivation and individual career advancement are, for researchers, the most important aspects in pursuing university-based research and should be the basis of any corporate research strategy. The university should be aware at the significance of individual imperatives and aim to create a research environment in which personal research ambitions can be fulfilled and career enhancement can be encouraged so that achieving personal research goals is recognized, rewarded and celebrated within the university community.

'News' stories about research achievements should be regularly and frequently circulated in the university's internal and external publications. Press releases about research should be a regular factor of the university's relationship with the media. Celebrating research success should be a regular part of life on the campus. The university's reward and remuneration scheme should place a significant emphasis on research success as measured by output criteria. Such schemes should be fair, open, equable, well-publicized and transparent. Staff who succeed in research should be the basis for case studies or examples of best practice and should be featured in staff development programmes and training modules. The benefits of their research experiences and knowledge, aspects such as research contracting, knowledge transfer or grant applications should be disseminated throughout the university research community so that their expertise can become a beacon to guide others setting out on the research path.

Among the university's stakeholders, news items on research can have an important impact, and a flow of research stories should be maintained to influence the external world of 'policy-makers and opinion formers' either through the media or in the form of the university's own public relations campaign or regular circulation. Alumni relations should also be a focus for research news and can have a positive effect on the university's development campaign or fund-raising projects as well as influencing individual alumni to have a positive image of their former university which can lead directly to collaborations with the organizations and companies in which they are now well placed as members of staff. Remember, however, that fund-raising and external support for research in the form of grants and contracts are not the same things and should *never* be confused either in the university's central services organization or in the minds of stakeholders.

The university should not only organize programmes of staff development support for researchers but also create a positive climate in which researchers willingly engage in personal development planning. This planning should be carried out so that their goals and targets are well known and can be embedded in research group plans and drawn down into the university's corporate research strategy.

The university should make clear the reasons why the institution is engaged in research and its centrality to the university's way and purpose. At the same time, its operational policies and requirements for research should be well known, for example its costing and pricing, intellectual property management, contract issues.

Why do universities engage in research?

- The ethos of the university should be to encourage the advancement of knowledge through original research which is a core value of higher education and an essential component of academic freedom.
- It is often part of the university's stated role as enshrined in its original charter or other foundation instrument. Most such documents refer to the advancement or pursuit of knowledge or to original research, thereby providing a strong legitimization of the university's research focus.
- Most universities with serious research aspirations have ensured that the requirement to conduct research is embedded in their more recent mission or vision statements. Such statements, usually communicated widely to the external world, are important assertions of identity and purpose, and therefore place research at the heart of the university's self-identity and role.
- Most governments have produced policies or have instituted investigative reports which define the purpose of higher education. Such policy statements feature the advancement of knowledge and the conduct of research as essential to the nation's global economic success and the quality of life of its citizens. Government policy underwrites the research mission.
- Most universities would strongly support the notion of the link between teaching and research and would claim the positive reinforcement of the one by the other, suggesting that a high-quality research environment in which its staff operate informs the standards of their teaching and the learning experience for students. This should not be confused with the idea of scholarship. Scholarship concerns active personal engagement with the subject or disciplinary area and a continuing commitment to develop the subject or disciplinary area.
- Individual researchers pursue their own career trajectories, and research goals should feature in their personal development plans. The task for the university is to support those plans and, by helping the individual researcher achieve their goals, support the

university to deliver its overall research strategy of which it is composed.

The report of the *Joint EPSRC/University Exploitation Audit Pilot Exercise: People, Partnerships and Programmes* (EPSRC 1997) underlines the centrality of the idea of intellectual satisfaction through research as a key personal motivation for academic staff in universities: 'Findings showed that intellectual curiosity was the primary motive for university researchers but that external drivers were well understood and were integrated in the process of conducting university-based research.' (see also Chapter 1)

- Individual researchers are enthusiastic about their research and should be encouraged by all around them, not least the university, which should celebrate research successess and remain committed to research as an enjoyable activity in which researchers and research teams engage in order to achieve life ambitions.

- The university's terms and conditions of employment, and its reward and remuneration policies, place university research as a core requirement for its academic and research staff. Phrases such as 'contributing to the advancement and diffusion of knowledge through advanced study and research' are common in employment terms and conditions for many research-led university.

These basic human and institutional drivers need to be understood, encouraged and supported in setting the university's policies and procedures for research and in drawing up a corporate research strategy. Such an approach should not be adopted to the detriment of teaching and learning or outreach activities, and equal stress should be given to all these activities.

A further fundamental issue might, however, be explored as to why researchers try to win external funds to support their research? Universities should point out the following facts to all its researchers:

- All research is a cost to the university and, as a business activity, research must not be loss-making.

- In the UK, the element of the funding allocation from the funding councils for research – the R stream – is not and never has been adequate to support all the research which universities wish to undertake. It is one part of the dual support system to which other research funds must be added by competitive application to other funding bodies.

- The university does far more research than it is able to fund directly from its own sources of income. The extent of its research ambitions can be met only by research, funds won from external sources.

- Certain types of funding for research enable the university to engage in certain kinds of research for example:
  - capital grants for equipment and facilities;
  - capital grants for new buildings and refurbishment;
  - other equipment grants;
  - grants to facilitate collaborations and partnerships with industry and others;
  - grants to foster interdisciplinarity or to develop new areas or research themes;
  - grants to support able researchers;
  - grants to enable knowledge transfer or support the commercialization of intellectual property;
  - grants to recognize research excellence or researchers of international quality;
  - grants to enable the development of research.
- External funding from industry and the private sector can be used to lever public grants as matched or contributory funding or in the form of in-kind support.
- External funding for research is held to be a performance measure in individuals, groups and departments, as well as for the university as a whole.

The perspective which researchers have about the importance of these and other motivations may vary in accordance with their responsibilities for research and the stage they have reached in their research careers.

7.3 Perspectives on research

So far, the perspectives on managing research reflected in this book have been largely those of the director of the university research services office. This section turns to the perspectives of researchers and those responsible for research across and beyond the university.

7.3.1 The postgraduate research student

The postgraduate research student remains the building block of any successful university strategy by:

- undertaking research;
- contributing to the research ethos and environment;

- promoting the university's research through papers, posters and presentations at national and international conferences;
- providing 'research news' stories for use with the media or inclusion in the university's own publications or promotions;
- publishing original research either as individual researchers or jointly with research collaborators, therefore increasing the university's research output;
- linking to potential clients through their activities either as externally funded students or through their own endeavours in pursuit of career advancement;
- providing, in themselves, a performance measure for the university's research success as part of scrutiny exercises such as, in the UK, the Research Assessment Exercise;
- remaining in touch with their research colleagues at the university when they have moved to other employers, thereby becoming a potential source for university research partnerships;
- helping generally in the unit, centre or department by assisting in the teaching of undergraduates, supporting research activities, contributing to the life of the unit, centre or department.

The unique role of both customer and colleague gives postgraduate research students a unique perspective on the university's research. As postgraduates, their research is both a contributory part to and a product of the university's corporate research strategy. Their relationship with the university is defined in several ways:

- through the graduate school;
- with their research supervisor;
- with their contemporary research postgraduates;
- with their academic colleagues;
- through their interactions with the university's support services (including the careers service, staff development and the research services office).

The university, in considering its corporate research strategy, should be careful to consider whether these interfaces are operating effectively for the postgraduate research student not only to ensure the quality of their experience as customers of the university but also to strengthen the quality of their university research contribution.

Postgraduate research students are starting out on their careers and the university should support their first hesitant steps and recognize that their career aspirations are the most important driver for their ambitions at that stage. Many will wish to see themselves in later life pursuing academic careers, although, in reality, only a tiny percentage will do so. Research, for the postgraduate, is a means to an end whereas to the university it can seem an end in itself. Postgraduates are the barometer of a successful university research climate and their development should be central to the university's corporate research strategy.

7.3.2 The postgraduate research supervisor

The supervisor can be any member of academic staff whose experience and willingness qualify them to supervise postgraduate research and whose chosen field and interests have some relation to the topic of research proposed by the postgraduate research student. Becoming a supervisor presupposes not only the willingness of the individual member of staff but also that they have the time and resources to supervise successfully. The supervisor contributes to the university research strategy by:

- facilitating successful postgraduate research;
- coordinating the postgraduate research project and through the development of the individual;
- contributing to the research ethos and environment;
- helping the individual to prepare posters, presentations and publications for conferences and other output;
- assisting in the presentation of original research and its dissemination as publications or other outputs;
- providing opportunities to the individual for experiential learning, career advancement, networking, making links to potential partners or other beneficiaries;
- ensuring that the research project is well managed and completed on time and to the best of the individual's ability;
- creating the framework in which the individual will be able to prosper in the unit, centre or department through regular and systematic supervisory meetings, reviews and reports;
- assisting, in general, the university's graduate school to succeed;
- identifying potential outcomes from the individual's research in the form of intellectual property, or further opportunities for grant-aided or contract research.

The supervisor has a difficult task to ensure that postgraduate research is completed successfully, as a measure of the unit, centre or department's success, but at the same time to make sure that the process of research assessment is fair, objective and impartial.

The supervisor's relationship to the university is defined in several ways:

- Through the postgraduate research experienced by the individual research postgraduate student for whom the supervisor is responsible.
- Through the graduate school whether operating at the university level or at departmental level.
- With their academic colleagues (many of whom will also be fulfilling the role of supervisor).
- With the head of the unit, centre or department.
- With the relevant university support services (including the careers service, the academic registrar's office and staff development).
- With the external world of research funders, collaborators, partners and beneficiaries who will be interested in the research being pursued by the postgraduate research student.

Supervisors repeat the experience many times if they are effective at the role, yet each time is the first time for the individual postgraduate. It is, therefore, essential that their supervisor remains fresh, up to date, at the forefront of the field of study, engaged, enthusiastic and committed. It is essential for the university to motivate supervisors in this respect, reward the most successful, support supervisors in becoming as effective as possible, and giving them guidance and assistance through the postgraduate research agreement.

Research, for the supervisor, means a project undertaken by an individual with whom they collaborate which might or might not relate directly to their own fields of enquiry. In most cases, supervisors will also have begun their research careers as postgraduate research students and, therefore, supervisors need to sharpen one particular faculty: their memories of what the postgraduate experience was like for them. If it was a successful one, the supervisor might model their practice upon it. If it was a difficult one, the supervisor should learn from it and not repeat the same mistakes.

7.3.3 Member of contract research staff

Contract researchers are the key members of staff who deliver to the university the ability to carry out more research than its permanent academic staff can accomplish, and at a faster rate. The availability of contract researchers, therefore, enhances the university's research capacity and capability, bringing to the research group's programme the possibility of additionality and acceleration. Both these aspects mean that more research can be completed and in a shorter time than would have been the case for the research group otherwise.

Often, contract research staff are associated with specific research projects, appointed to and supported by funding from a single research grant or contract. Sometimes, contract research staff are part of a pool of support, drawn on in connection with more than one project and assigned for part of their time to different research projects. Some universities recruit contract research staff into a collective resource and maintain them in research employment on a rolling contract basis, reviewing their appointments as funding permits. Such practice, in Europe, will be affected by the legal regulations regarding part-time employment. Contract research staff can be at a variety of different career points, from first-time appointments to experienced and mature researchers. The norm is to regard contract research staff as either postdoctoral, that is having completed their period of doctoral research and going on to an appointment of contract researcher to deepen their experience of university-based research, or as more junior researchers at postgraduate level either pursuing postgraduate research at the same time or as a first step towards deciding whether to pursue further research as a career move following graduation.

More mature researchers will have completed one or more periods of appointment of typically three years or more. The implications of European legislation for such staff are being considered by most UK university personnel departments.

In any event, the conditions of service of research contract staff has become a matter of national and international importance and concern. In the UK steps have been taken to improve their lot through the research staffs code of conduct or practice (see Chapter 5, section 5.14 for details).

The relationship with the principal investigator whose grant or contract funds them is crucial not only to their well-being but also to delivering the university's research successfully.

Research contract staff often complain about the uncertainty and instability of their circumstances while recognizing their importance to universities in delivering their corporate research strategies. At the same time, they often regard themselves as forgotten or overlooked, not given the full status of permanent academic staff, not able to initiate research or research proposals for external funding, often having great expertise but not always receiving the credit for their contribution.

Contract research staff contribute to the university's research strategy by:

- undertaking research;
- enabling the principal investigator to deliver their research grant or contract commitments;
- contributing to the research ethos and environment;
- providing the aspects of additionality and acceleration to university research programmes;
- promoting the university's research through posters, presentations and publications, attendance at conferences and, in some cases, being regarded as independent researchers in their own right;
- publishing original research either individually or jointly with their academic colleagues;
- linking to clients, partners, funders and beneficiaries in the wider research framework;
- providing a measure of research performance through their own research outputs and in themselves as the indication of successful research grants and contracts;
- helping generally in the unit, centre or department, with undergraduates, postgraduate research students, and with research groups and contributing to the life of the unit, centre or department.

Contract research staff are the research workhorses in most universities and contribute directly to carrying out the university's research programme, thereby adding to its research reputation. Their relationship with the university is defined in several ways:

- through the unit, centre or department;
- with the research group and the research group leader or champion;
- with the principal investigator to whom they are responsible;
- with other academic colleagues;
- with other contract research staff in and beyond the unit, centre or department;
- with the external research network;
- through their interactions with university support services (for example, careers centre, personnel, staff development, research services office).

Contract research staff are, in many cases, the 'front of house' representatives for the university's research programme, being in frequent and direct contact with many of the university's key partners, external funders, beneficiaries and collaborators. They often play an ambassadorial role and yet most universities fail to cultivate them in this respect, and have only recently begun to provide services in training and supporting them in their career goals and aspirations, enabling them to achieve their full career potential. Wise universities not only support the concordat in the UK or similar codes of conduct or practice but also regard them as a key resource to be carefully developed and deployed.

7.3.4 The principal investigator

In the research-led university, most permanent academic staff members are expected to be fully active and engaged in research and are appointed to posts governed by specific terms and conditions of employment requiring both teaching and research to be pursued. Research active members of staff, unless beginning their careers as junior members of staff, would expect to have operated in the capacity of principal investigator on an externally funded research grant and contract. In the humanities and in some areas of the social sciences where the idea of obtaining research grants and contracts is relatively unfamiliar and new, it is nonetheless likely that staff will take on the responsibilities of principal investigator at some stage in their careers as more funding from external sources becomes available for research in their fields of enquiry.

Principal investigators can be at various points on their career trajectories, from starting out with little experience to achieving national and international renown with extensive experience of having run several major grants and contract-funded research projects. Principal investigators need to manage their research aspirations in accordance with the research context of the university, unit, centre or department as set out in Chapter 1, balancing between short- and long-term research ideas, current and proposed research projects, practical and aspirational research proposals. The university should support principal investigators as their main priority in its corporate research strategy as these are the key 'business operatives' for research as a core activity. They are the skilled researchers, generating the flow of innovative ideas and concepts, responsible for the piloting of research proposals for external funding or making up the bulk of the research groups in units, centres and departments. They are the networks for research, operating in an *e-search* environment, in contact with the world of researchers, partners, external funders, potential users and beneficiaries, clients and the media. Principal investigators operate at the forefront of research and are the key components of the university's corporate research strategy. They are the real drivers of the research cycle, completing research projects and, at the same time, generating the bulk of new research grant applications or ideas for research contracts. They are the researchers whose intellectual efforts produce employment for contract researchers and topics for study by postgraduate research students. It is the principal investigator who produces the visible outputs from the university's research in terms of academic publications and intellectual property, or as research news stories for the media. Principal investigators make their contribution by:

- leading specific research projects, usually funded by external sources, and taking responsibility for their project management;
- undertaking research;
- organizing the programme of work of contract researchers and others related to the specific research project;
- acting as supervisors of postgraduate research;
- producing new research ideas as the basis of future research grant applications or proposals for research contracts;
- identifying potential outputs from research and producing academic publications and intellectual property therefrom;
- contributing to the research ethos and environment;
- promoting the university's research strengths in various ways and through attendance at national and international conferences;
- contributing to the research news flow from the university to the media and in order to influence policy-makers and opinion formers and raise potential 'friends' for the university's research programme as well as funds to support it;
- networking with potential collaborators and clients;
- delivering the research goals set by the university and the unit, centre or department.

The principal investigator, at whatever stage on their career journey, is the university's deliverer of research whose responsibility for the advancement of knowledge is the core of their employment.

Whether starting out on their careers or as more senior researchers, their relationship with the university is defined in various ways:

- Through the terms and conditions of their contract of employment.
- Through their responsibility for research to their immediate research group leader or champion or to their head of unit, centre or department.
- With their contract research staff, employed on funding sources managed by the principal investigator.
- To their academic colleagues.
- With external clients and collaborators.

- With postgraduate research students whom they supervise.
- Through their interaction with the university's support services including the finance, research services, public relations, and personnel offices.

The most important factor of the university's corporate research strategy should be to aim to develop fully this valuable staff resource, supporting principal investigators as necessary but ensuring that they are able to fulfil their research aspirations and goals which, in turn, make up the university's corporate research ambition. Success should be fully rewarded and celebrated in the university and their achievements should be the basis of research news items to the media.

7.3.5 The research group leader or research champion

Research leadership is an essential ingredient for a successful corporate research strategy. It is set by senior management in providing the vision for the development of research for their university and by ensuring that there is sufficient investment in facilities, equipment and human resources to support the ambition of the research vision. It is also exercised through the increasing selectivity of resources by deciding in which areas to invest and whom to appoint. The judgement exercised on staff appointment or promotion especially the professorial or research champion posts and research group leaders is a key determinant for the future development of the university's research programme and the delivery of its existing research goals embodied in its corporate research strategy. Too many bad senior research appointments can lead to the faltering of the university's research.

Research leadership is also exercised by research group leaders and research champions themselves in their own decisions about which research direction to pursue, staff to appoint, facilities for equipment to procure, and the day-to-day operation of the research team for which they are responsible. It is important for the university to identify research groups, where these have been formed, and the role played by specific research champions, enabling them to develop their research, achieve their goals and move forward in their careers, while simultaneously recognizing that their success will determine the success of the teams around them. Even in the world of the individual scholar-researcher, eminence in the field is recognized as their careers advance and they achieve a recognized position as research champions for their areas of research both within and beyond the university.

Their contribution to the successful university research strategy is made by:

- undertaking research;
- coordinating and leading specific research areas and research groups;
- supporting and developing the researchers who make up the research group for which they are responsible (including post-graduate research students);
- selecting and planning the research direction being taken by the research group and providing judgement on equipment and facilities to procure and researches to select;
- supervising postgraduate research;
- promoting the research group and the research field to the external world of clients, funders, partners and beneficiaries;
- contributing to the research ethos and environment;
- ensuring a regular flow of visible outputs for the work of the research group in the form of academic publications and intellectual property (where relevant);
- measuring the research group's performance against other research teams across the world pursuing equivalent objectives;
- understanding the markets for the research group's findings in order to recruit able postgraduate research students, enlist the support of partners and collaborators, secure their market share of research grants and contracts from external funders, raise the profile for their research with the media;
- ensuring the standard of ethics and integrity in the research group;
- networking more widely in the *e-search* environment;
- ensuring the financial viability and integrity of the research group;
- assisting in general the work of the unit, centre or department in which the research group is located;
- underpinning the research quality of the research group's work;
- contributing to the university's corporate research strategy.

The research group leader or research champion is a seasoned professional, well versed and playing an active role in the world of external research funding, understanding government policies for research and aware of current research trends, themes and priorities. At the same time, the research champion accepts the role of supporting the research groups and bringing on the best researchers.

The research group leader's relationship with the university is defined in several ways:

- Through the other members of the research group for which they are responsible.
- With the head of unit, centre or department.
- With the university's senior management.
- With the university's support services for research (especially the research services, planning, personnel and finance offices).
- With their academic colleagues.
- With the external world of clients, partners, funders and beneficiaries.

The university appoints its research group leaders and research champions and thereby defines the directions to be taken. The relationship is reciprocal and the university should also ensure that the research group leader or research champion is fully supported and empowered to fulfil their research goals, thereby delivering the university's own corporate research strategy.

7.3.6 The research manager or administrator

The research manager coordinates the daily operational tasks for a single research project, a group of research projects, the research programme of a specific research group or groups, or the entire research undertaken by a unit, centre or department, so designated by the university. In some cases, the management of research will form part of the duties and responsibilities of a manager or administrator with a broader range of tasks, perhaps embracing learning and teaching, computing and information technology, for groups of staff or units, centres and departments as determined by the university. In other cases, the tasks are prepared by a full-time professional, recruited for the purpose rather than by an academic member of staff simultaneously combining management duties with the research.

In general, the research manager is not likely to be actively engaged in undertaking research, although this may be the case in some instances. More likely are the circumstances in which the research manager is dedicated to the tasks associated with managing and/or support research, dealing with the practical challenges of carrying out a programme of research and coordinating the interactions between the researcher or research group and the external world, as well as with the university's management structure and corporate services.

Such posts are the key mechanism for the *delivery* of the research goals specified in the project, programme, group or unit's research plan, and research managers contribute by:

- coordinating the project management aspects of successful research in accordance with a stated operational schedule which identifies the key stages and milestones to be attained and the research outputs or deliverables to be met;
- ensuring the financial viability and integrity of research through efficient and effective management of resources;
- maintaining best practice and standards to underpin the quality of research;
- maintaining the research infrastructure (equipment, facilities, human resources, management and so on);
- identifying potential and exploitable research outputs in the form of intellectual property or other deliverables;
- overseeing good laboratory practice and ensuring compliance with relevant statutory legislation;
- overseeing the ethical standards and integrity of research;
- coordinating the external networks of clients, funders, partners and beneficiaries and organizing the interaction with these groups;
- ensuring good media relations and a flow of research news stories;
- contributing to the research ethos and environment;
- working with others in the unit, centre or department;
- working with the principal investigator, research group leader or champion and head of unit relevant to their research management;
- contributing to the research planning process as part of the university's corporate research strategy.

Research managers are common in the research laboratories and universities of the United States but are becoming more apparent in the UK and Europe as well. They are the linchpins of research, ensuring its smooth running, monitoring progress, supporting the financial and other requirements laid down by the university and coordinating the operational progress of the research and its compliance to statutory requirements or contract specification. Many research managers become highly skilled at representing the interests of their researchers and promoting them to the external world, acting in practice as business development managers, helping with research applications and proposals and securing both 'repeat business' and new business for the research group or unit.

The research manager's relationship is defined in many ways:

- Through the research group and research group leader or champion.

- Through the principal investigator on research projects.
- With individual researchers and postgraduate research students in a research group.
- With other academic staff.
- With the director or head of a unit, centre or department designated to carry out programmes of related research.
- With the external world of clients, partners, funders and beneficiaries (as business development managers).
- With the university's research services office, finance office, and other parts of the corporate administration.

Many will have career aspirations in their own right which take them into active research as they will have, in many cases, completed postgraduate and postdoctoral research or have worked in industrial or commercial research environments. Many more will have identified careers as research management professionals, moving between universities and other employers to develop their experience and skills, enabling them to take on more significant posts as their careers mature. Some will seek to return to research careers.

7.3.7 Unit, centre or department director or head

Unless the designated unit has been set up exclusively as a research centre, the head or director will have responsibilities for other functions as well as research, including learning and teaching and third task or outreach tasks. The head or director will therefore usually balance a range of objectives and manage a series of income streams to deliver an integrated portfolio of learning and teaching, research, and outreach activities which are in budget and, it is to be hoped, making healthy surpluses for the university. To do so, the head or director maintains an environment consisting of a physical infrastructure (space, equipment, facilities, communications, computing and information technology), a staff resource (teachers, researchers, managers, support, technicians, IT specialists), a student community (undergraduates, taught postgraduates, together with a range of non-traditional students or those engaged on short or continuing professional development (CPD) courses), a collegiate entity (cooperating and collaborating with others in the university or the external world), an international reputation (as evidenced by the media, by academic peers and by opinion-formers and policy-makers), and a reservoir of knowledge in the field or discipline represented by the academic interests of the unit.

This is multitasking on a grand scale and, put simply, the head of the unit is the head of one of the university's operating businesses – the equivalent to a chief executive officer of a small company (in some cases directly responsible for an annual turnover much larger than that of many small companies). The action plan for the operation as a whole is multilayered, interactive, complex and must be integrated with the plans of several other operating businesses which make up the corporate business of the parent company which is the university.

In most cases, individuals are appointed solely in accordance with academic criteria, usually led by their research reputation, are given no particular special training in the post and are not, at least in their view, usually adequately supported with staff to help them run the affairs of the unit for which they are responsible. On the whole, in the UK, this is changing and a growing recognition that the success of the university's research depends in large measure on the success of these individuals is being translated into more supportive action by universities concerned to develop this scarce and valuable human resource.

The head or director of the unit contributes to the university's corporate research strategy directly by:

- planning research in the unit, centre or department, taking into account the plans of research groups, and the aspirations of researchers and postgraduate research students for whom they are responsible;
- undertaking research (often as a research group leader or champion in their own right) or, at least, participating in their research;
- developing the research ethos and environment;
- maintaining the viability and integrity of the research programme within the unit, centre or department;
- ensuring compliance with statutory legislation and the ethos and integrity of research undertaken;
- monitoring the quality of research undertaken and insisting upon its objective comparison with absolute standards and measures of performance;
- promoting the *e-search* environment and links to the external world of clients, partners, funders and beneficiaries;
- liaising with opinion-formers and policy-makers, the media and the general public in fulfilment of the task of assisting the public awareness of research;
- promoting and marketing the unit's research strengths;
- encouraging academic publication and the generation and

commercialization of intellectual property and overcoming any perceived tension between the two;
• securing the financial stability of the unit, centre or department;
• helping to develop researchers and postgraduate research students so that they can attain their career goals (including specific responsibility for the graduate school agreement and the contract research staff concordat together with compliance with statutory legislation);
• identifying, forming and sustaining long-term strategic collaborations and partnerships appropriate to the research themes and priorities of the unit;
• liaising with the university's research support and other corporate services;
• cooperating with the university's senior management.

There are many metaphors which might be used to describe the role of head or director of a unit, centre or department from the world of industry and business but, perhaps, the model of the football manager is the closest, in that the manager has to run a viable football club and all that is necessary for success together with coaxing performances from players to give the club success in the league and to continue to do so from one season to the next. The relationship with researchers is a similar one as the best research performances cannot be coerced but only encouraged. What quality standard is achieved by researchers will be judged by their academic peers or measured by performance comparison. Research quality cannot be attained through simple instruction or through normal line management techniques associated with business and industry.

The relationship of the unit, centre or department director or head with the university is defined in many ways:

• through the success of the unit, centre or department;
• through the integration of the unit's research plans into the university's corporate research strategy;
• with research group leaders and champions;
• with researchers;
• with contract research staff and postgraduate research students for whom they are responsible;
• with the university's senior management;
• with the university's research and enterprise services office and other corporate services;
• with the external world;
• with the markets and external business drivers vital for the unit, centre or department.

These are increasingly complex roles requiring great professional skill, and universities are beginning to develop such people as a key human resource without which the university's research would simply collapse.

7.3.8 University senior manager

For the university's corporate management, research is but a single arm of the university's core business (alongside learning and teaching and other services related to third task activities or out-reach). For the research-led university, success in research partly defines the identity and mission of the institution and describes accurately and succinctly what the institution does. It also forms a major part of its history and development record which, for some institutions, will be extensive, historic and of great repute. The record of its research will be dotted with great advances, discoveries, inventions or innovations, 'milestoned' by the careers of illustrious researchers of the past and defined by moments of great significance. Even in small institutions with more modest reputations, research will be seen as a major component of business activity, capable of attracting and retaining the best staff and producing new advances for the future.

At the same time, research is expected to drive forward the university's future, and, in part, secure its financial viability and stability. The realization that, in the UK at least, research, whether financed from public or from private sources, has essentially lost money and, far from being a profit centre, has been a consistent loss-maker, has been not so much a shock as confirmation that the nettle of underfunding of research by government, of not fully costing research by universities and other external funders and of operating in a low-price culture with research clients, has simply not been grasped.

University senior managers will glance enviously elsewhere in the world, and in particular to America, where the research culture is different and high value is attached to research in universities, attracting a high price for its products from industry and government, and where, in some cases, universities have become wealthy as a result. Even the largest UK universities, with substantial research histories and reputations and incomes to match, will have managed their research portfolios at an overall financial loss. Yet research simply cannot be abandoned by research-led universities in favour of more lucrative ventures. It is the seedcorn for all growth in commercial activities. Universities can turn to premium-priced degrees and short courses, the recruitment of international students, other more profitable services, but *research* is quite simply what universities do and what university academic staff seek to pursue for their own intellectual stimulation and satisfaction.

Universities cannot turn to the manufacture of washing machines or other goods. They are quite simply in the 'knowledge business' and research is the production method utilized for the generation of advanced knowledge. University senior managers seek to make research pay in the future, insisting on increased cost recovery, a proper research pricing policy, business planning for research in units, centres and departments, accountability through research target-setting and systematic review of research performance, together with full commercial exploitation of its intellectual property and realization of its knowledge assets.

The problem is that by 'sweating the assets', driving down costs, insisting upon tight financial policies, maximizing income and pressing researchers for ever improved research performance in the form of productivity and profitability, the research environment can be adversely affected, researchers can be demotivated and the best ones move on to more congenial institutions leaving the less successful behind them. Stress levels increase, a fatal separation between 'them' and 'us' divides managers from academic researchers, fracturing the university's collegiality, and internal relationships become a significant distraction. For senior managers, the goal must be to increase research productivity and profitability, to continue to invest in new research capability and capacity, to improve the conduciveness of the research environment and to maximize the commercial return from research outputs while minimizing loss-making research within an overall balanced portfolio of external research funding.

Senior managers make substantial contributions by:

- planning and implementing successful research strategies and operational policies;
- maintaining and enhancing the research infrastructure and environment;
- removing obstacles and barriers to successful research;
- providing support services which facilitate research;
- insisting on absolute standards of ethical integrity in research;
- ensuring the maintenance of quality in research;
- raising 'friends' through corporate networking at regional, national and international levels;
- through its staffing policies, ensuring equitable reward and remuneration and developing terms and conditions of service

which encourage the best research and the attainment of career goals through personal development planning;
- ensuring that postgraduate research students enjoy the best possible research experience and can achieve their career goals through supportive structures such as the graduate school;
- managing intellectual property policies to maximize income from the commercialization of research;
- maximizing research income by effective costing and pricing;
- managing the university in the context of the external world of research funding, the policies of research funders and the volatility of research markets;
- ensuring compliance with statutory requirements;
- making effective appointments to senior positions such as those of research group leader or champion and head of unit, centre or department;
- insisting upon the regular review of research performance against external benchmarks at every level;
- leading the institution's research effectively and shaping relevant national and international policies where these have an impact on research by influencing policy-makers and opinion-formers.

To operate effectively, senior managers must have a firm grasp on the range and quality of research undertaken in the institution, its best practitioners and its corresponding areas of weakness. Senior managers must understand market trends and policy themes affecting research and have a comprehensive understanding of and challenging vision for the development of research, enabling timely and appropriate investment in research facilities, equipment and personnel to secure the university's future.

Senior managers relate to the university in many ways:

- By their relationship to staff and students through terms and conditions of service agreements.
- Through their responsibility for corporate strategy and operational policies.
- Through the structures by which research is organized and resourced.
- Through the corporate services provided in support of research.
- Through the appointments made to senior positions.
- By the standards set for research ethics and integrity, quality and excellence, performance and measurement, productivity and profitability.

Senior managers are ultimately responsible for the success or failure of the corporate research strategy without being able to direct research on a command economy model. Rather senior managers set the environment in which research can flourish and academic choice can be exercised as to the direction of research to maximize the available opportunities for external funding and to meet the intellectual challenges faced.

7.3.9 The external funder (public)

The tasks of those responsible for funding research in universities through the use of public finances or private donations are considerable. At one level their duties concern a fundamental requirement for accountability both for the funds themselves and for the research supported by them. This, in part, explains the need for audit, scrutiny, regulation, review and monitoring which seem to many university researchers an unnecessary bureaucratic overhead and intrusion. Many researchers will complain of an overburden of administrative requirements associated with many forms of public grant in which, in their view, accountability is taken to extremes. Of all the research funders, the European Community is seen universally by university researchers as being the most excessive in this respect. In reality, most audit requirements are easily comprehended and managed, assuming that researchers are prepared to put in a little effort over project management and the maintenance of clear records.

Public funders of research are rarely concerned with the outputs of research projects funded by them and are more interested in allocating research funds as efficiently as possible in the context of fixed, annual, cash-limited budgets, which are usually heavily oversubscribed, rather than assessing the long-term effectiveness of the research undertaken. Their only role is to administer research funds in accordance with the terms and conditions which apply to the various schemes and initiatives for which they are responsible. Research council programme managers, for example, are responsible for the research programmes they oversee and are accountable to their boards and councils. Charities pursue the aims and objectives of their charitable trusts and foundations and are accountable to their trustees and, ultimately, the general public from whom their funds are raised in the form of donations or to their corporate or individual benefactors whose beneficence is laid down by the terms of the relevant will or trust. In the case of public authorities making grant awards, the objectives of policy determine the role of managers and administrators whose chief concern remains the distribution of funds as smoothly as possible. The pattern in each case is to encourage a sufficiency of compliant and eligible applications, an open and fair system of assessment using stated methods (peer review, panel judgement and so on), and conformity with guidance and deadlines. Oversubscription means that administrators are looking for non-compliance and ineligibility as the first way to sift out and reject applications while, at the same time, encouraging the maximum number of applications in order to meet resource allocation targets.

In the case of public funds being used for contracting university research, similar motives drive the public administrator only within the framework of contract law or in accordance with the memorandum of agreement. Nevertheless, a sufficiency of eligible tenders is still required and consideration of legal compliance is the major factor conditioning the management of the contract process.

Peer review is often used to assess applications and the perspective of the peer reviewer differs from that of the programme manager in that the process is based upon academic criteria and research excellence. Peer reviewers, at other times, are applicants, and applicants also act as peer reviewers, so perspectives can often range from detailed knowledge of the field and the circumstance of the research programme to more generalized understanding. Peer reviewers can be thorough or cursory depending on the magnitude of the task, the nature of the critical feedback required, the form of assessment – whether qualitative or quantitative – and the overall funding available. In every case, however, clarity and objectivity should apply. The applicant needs to understand what is happening in the desk holder's world and why the programme has been initiated and explain concisely what their proposal or tender does to achieve the programme's objectives.

The external funder has the role of:

- arbiter as to the nature of the terms and conditions which apply to the particular research funding programme and the compliance or otherwise of all applications received;
- auditor on all matters relating to the proper use of public funds by the successful applicants;
- desk holder as the custodian of the programme's mission and purpose and related contexts;
- guide when assisting applicants in making applications;
- promoter for the particular research programme in order to ensure a sufficiency of eligible applications;
- administrator of the system of review and assessment of applications;
- manager for the research programme, ensuring its integrity and success in meeting its objectives.

This multiplicity of roles can be confusing for the university applicant or grant or contract holder and it is essential to understand the different tasks and functions carried out by the programme manager or administrator so that the maximum usefulness can be gained from contact with them.

As custodians of public funds, the probity of the administrative system used to allocate resources is vital to the confidence which the research programme inspires in the academic world. Far from being pointless bureaucracy, the administration of research grants or contracts by external funders is designed to ensure fairness and integrity and to avoid abuse, corruption, bias, prejudice or other forms of maladministration.

7.3.10 The external funder (private)

In the UK, companies, businesses, industrial organizations and other private sector agencies interested in university research usually proceed from the viewpoint either of research contracting or collaboration in connection with a public research grant scheme such as Link or Teaching Company. Sometimes companies are interested in the fruits of university research in the form of the resulting intellectual property. In whatever circumstances interest arises, however, the essence of the relationship is commercial. Business means business when related to university research, and those responsible for university research contracts or links are usually seeking a commercial outcome, through problem-solving or the applicability of research findings to their business needs.

Such organizations are rarely interested in university research for its own sake, even less abstract concepts such as the advancement of knowledge. Equally, their agents show little concern for academic problems which affect research. What is required by them is that work is undertaken in accordance with a specific schedule and is completed successfully, on time and in budget. They are not interested in the underlying issues of research environment and infrastructure or equipment and facilities available at the university, except in so far as they facilitate the work in hand. Some commercial organizations are interested in acquiring knowledge to inform the business products, processes and services central to their economic well-being, and, in some cases, such knowledge is acquired through people in the form of postgraduate research students or researchers becoming employees or working in the company with the existing workforce on a short-term secondment. For companies, university research is simply the means to an end rather than the end itself.

Contractual obligations are binding, and commitments will need to be honoured in both the spirit and the letter of the contract or agreement covering the research to be undertaken. Accountability is a prerequisite of contract, both for the financial aspects and for the overall success of the project and its efficient management.

Reviews are necessary to monitor progress. Review meetings take place to explore potential difficulties and to overcome problems. Such progress monitoring is familiar to the private sector and should not be regarded as unwelcome bureaucracy by the university researchers undertaking the research.

Confidentiality requirements are also common and are not usually designed to silence academic freedom but simply to allow commercial exploitation. In most cases, the limiting factors of confidentiality agreements delay publication which can then take place after patent protection has been obtained. Universities should, however, be suspicious of and refuse all illegitimate blocks on freedom to publish results where more sinister purposes are involved such as attempts at 'gagging'. The university must maintain the objectivity of its research at arm's length from commercial concerns, and attempts to prevent academic researchers from discussing or disseminating their results are generally to be deplored and resisted.

External funders in the private sector are:

- legal custodians protecting the company from financial irregularities, liabilities and risks in its contracting;
- customers or clients of the university's research business, interested only in their specific problems or contractual commitments;
- strategic partners or collaborators seeking to develop long-standing relationships from which research of mutual interest can be pursued;
- managers or administrators of contracts who must ensure value for money and cost-effective research outcomes of benefit to the company or business whose interests they represent;
- gatekeepers presiding over access to the company or business, often performing the role, in larger organizations, of university liaison officers;
- researchers in their own right carrying out similar duties to academic researchers in the environment of a private research laboratory or industrial research centre;
- operations or production managers concerned only with the immediate problems of the production process.

Private sector agents can be all or some of these and it is as well to understand which brief is held by the agent with whom the university is in contact.

It is important in dealing with external funders in the private sector to be clear and concise in dealings, to avoid confusion and to be prepared for the requirement of full project management.

7.4 Strategic partnerships

The most successful university research strategies are founded on an understanding of the unique strengths of the particular university's research, the nature of the competition and the markets available in which its research can be promoted. Research developments are improved by market intelligence, an understanding of market need and a clear perspective of the value of the university's research to those markets. One important component of the university's research strategy should be the identification and development of long-term strategic partnerships or collaborations. Such partnerships, especially those which endure for more than two to three years, are founded on people and needs. Contacts at every level should be established with organizations or companies where the university identifies itself as a key partner with or supplier of:

- graduates;
- postgraduates;
- intellectual property;
- research;
- training and continuing professional development;
- other short courses;
- other services (conference facilities, business support, consultancy and so on);
- investment support (especially with potential investment partners);
- access to specialist facilities or equipment.

An audit of the university's customer base should quickly reveal where these potential strategic relationships can be formed. Most universities have only a sporadic view of their strategic relationships, relying on researchers to develop contacts or, occasionally, at corporate level, engaging their senior managers in the life of the university (development campaigns, degree congregation celebrations, annual events and so on). Some relationships are highly focused, such as those with public institutions like the NHS trust hospitals or more generally with the NHS.

The university must manage its corporate strategic partnerships positively and effectively, cultivating and developing them as operating areas and through regular and frequent exchanges of information, shared intelligence, common approaches to similar challenges, discussions and events. Such partnerships will embrace public bodies, funding agencies, policy-making institutions and the wider world of industry. This is not simply a matter of the supply–demand equation of purchasers and providers – know your customers – but concerns the fundamental link between generic research in science, technology, social sciences and humanities and the nation's future culture, well-being, products, processes and services. This link concerns both research and learning because value can only be added permanently to culture, well-being, products, processes and services through a highly skilled workforce and a high-quality advanced research base. Each of these should influence the other in a virtuous circle which spirals upwards, increasing added value as it goes. The university can form successful strategic partnerships if it bears in mind the following:

- Know the markets, users, beneficiaries, potential businesses and industries that the university's research and learning are underpinning through their products, processes and services, and understand their needs and requirements better.
- Identify potential partners by identifying where the university's graduates, postgraduates and postdoctoral researchers are already being recruited or where research or other services are used.
- Implement a clear strategy towards cultivating these key partners, identifying who will take responsibility for such activities in the strategy, and review regularly.
- Where written agreements are to be instituted, make these clear, simple and precise (especially in areas such as the ownership of intellectual property) to avoid misunderstanding or misinterpretation.
- Build up trust and confidence through regular communication and exchanges of information and appoint someone to manage the relationship and be responsible as a point of contact.
- Take the longer view and share ideas and approaches by building on small-scale collaborations from which larger shared projects can emerge over time.
- Build for quality by looking at benchmarks for performance and developing mutual best practice.
- Establish a reciprocal relationship in which knowledge and support pass both ways.
- Make use of the interface and support services existing on each side to provide a window on each other's operations.

- Be prepared to share and exchange approaches and perspectives on relevant issues.

Large, medium and small companies can be engaged in this process, although it is often best to establish local networks of small and medium enterprises as a collaborating group rather than try to develop a multitude of one-to-one relationships.

7.5 Making a corporate research strategy

Operating businesses are usually best placed to understand business needs and opportunities and to have a clear vision of how to succeed in a marketplace within the framework of corporate policy and operational procedures. Together they offer choices and options for business prioritization or direction to be decided upon at the corporate level, but they have the most detailed knowledge on both the supply and demand sides for the business they undertake. Therefore university corporate strategy for research should also include a process of action planning in which research targets can be identified and set out and in which options can be appraised for incorporation in the making of the university's corporate strategy. This goal cannot be advanced in isolation and should involve researchers themselves, research group leaders and heads of units, together with support professionals who can provide business intelligence on the external world of research funding, new opportunities, new policy themes, changed priorities and on the competition in the marketplace. It is, therefore, a *collective process* directed by corporate management, but it is also a *managed process* in which the framework of policy and procedure has been set down prior to the beginning of the process and the prerequisites (see Chapter 1) have been defined and prepared.

The resulting strategy is a matrix of vertically linked action plans for the operational units and horizontally linked research themes and priorities in which the aspirations of individuals, groups, units and the university itself are woven together to produce an integrated, realistic, feasible and challenging strategic plan for research.

By building an environment in which research can grow and increase, in which goals from personal development planning or operational targets are located in the context of competitive threats and market opportunities, universities can build a positive framework of operational policies and procedures in which research will increase and become both more profitable and productive and provide intellectual satisfaction while achieving the highest standards of quality and ethical probity and the advancement of knowledge. At the same time, visible outputs will be produced in the form of intellectual property, and commercially applicable know-how and information whenever possible. Research success is not only an outcome. University research is both a process and an outcome. For university researchers, enquiry is both an end and a beginning, a state of being and of doing, a departure and an arrival and the journey in between. In managing research in higher education, the research journey for researchers and postgraduate research students alike should be the main focus for the university, as the quality of the journey will be indicative of the arrival.

APPENDIX 1: GOVERNMENT DEPARTMENTS

Cabinet departments

Cabinet Office: http://www.cabinet-office.gov.uk
Department for Culture, Media and Sport (DCMS): http://www.culture.gov.uk

Agencies

The Royal Parks: http://www.royalparks.gov.uk

Department for Education and Skills (DfES)

http://www.dfes.gov.uk/index.htm

Agencies

British Educational Communications and Technology Agency:
    http://www.becta.org.uk
Employment Service: http://www.employmentagencyservice.gov.uk/English/
    Home/default.asp
Sector Skills Development Agency: http://www.ssda.org.uk
Teacher Training Agency: http://www.canteach.gov.uk
Higher Education Funding Council for England: http://www.hefce.gov.uk

Department for Transport (DT)

http://www.dtir.gDov.uk

Agencies

Driver and Vehicle Licensing Agency (DVLA): http://www.dvla.gov.uk
Driving Standards Agency (DSA): http://www.dsa.gov.uk
Highways Agency (HA): http://www.highways.gov.uk
Maritime and Coastguard Agency: http://www/mcagency.org.uk
Planning Inspectorate: http://www.planning-inspectorate.gov.uk
Vehicle Certification Agency (VCA): http://www.vca.gov.uk.gov.uk
Vehicle Inspectorate (VI): http://w ww.via.gov.uk

Department of Health (DOH)

http://www.doh.gov.uk

Agencies

Medical Devices Agency: http://www.medical-devices.gov.uk
Medicines Control Agency: http://www.mca.gov.uk
National Patient Safety Agency: http://www.npsa.org.uk
NHS Estates: http://www.nhsestates.gov.uk/home.asp
NHS Modernization Agency: http://www.modernnhs.nhs.uk/scripts/
    default.asp?site_id=10
NHS Pensions Agency: http://www.nhspa.gov.uk
NHS Purchasing and Supply Agency: http://www.pasa.doh.gov.uk

Department for International Development (DFID)

http://www.dfid.gov.uk

Department of Work and Pensions (DWP)

http://www.dwp.gov.uk

Agencies

Benefits Agency – merged with the Department for Work and Pensions Child
    Support Agency: http://www.csa.gov.uk

Department of Trade and Industry (DTI)

http://www.dti.gov.uk

Agencies

Companies House: http://www.companies-house.gov.uk
Employment Tribunals Service: http://www.employmenttribunals.gov.uk
Radiocommunications Agency: http://www.radio.gov.uk

10 Downing Street

Cabinet Office: http://www.cabinet-office.gov.uk

Agencies

CCTA – The Government Centre for Information Systems; as from 1
   April 2001, CCTA became an integral part of the Office of Government
   Commerce: http://www.ogc.gov.uk
Central Office of Information: http://www.coi.gov.uk
Centre for Management and Policy Studies: http://www.cmps.gov.uk
Charity Commission for England and Wales: http://www/charity-
   commission.gov.uk
Crown Prosecution Service: http://cps.gov.uk
Government Car and Despatch Agency: http://www.gcda.gov.uk
OGC Buying Solutions – formerly The Buying Agency (TBA):
   http://www.ogc.buyingsolutions.gov.uk
Property Advisors to the Civil Estate (PACE): http.//www.property.gov.uk

Office of Deputy Prime Minister

http://www.odpm.gov.uk

The Foreign and Commonwealth Office (FCO)

http://www.fco.gov.uk

Her Majesty's Treasury

http://www.hm-treasury.gov.uk

Agencies

National Savings: http://www.nationalsavings.co.uk
National Statistics: http://www.statistics.gov.uk

Treasury Solicitor's Department: http://www.treasury-solicitor.gov.uk/
   tsdhome.htm
Bona Vacantia Division: http://www.bonavacantia.gov.uk

Home Office

http://www.homeoffice.gov.uk

Agencies

Fire Service College: http://www.fireservicecollege.ac.uk
Forensic Science Service: http:/www.forensic.gov.uk/forensic/entry.htm
HM Prison Service Agency: http://www.hm-prisonservice.gov.uk
UK Passport Service: http://www.passports.gov.uk

Lord Chancellor's Department

http://www.lcd.gov.uk

Agencies

Court Service: http://www.courtservice.gov.uk
Public Guardianship Office: http://www.guardianship.gov.uk

Department of Environment, Food and Rural Affairs (DEFRA)

http://www.defra.gov.uk

Agencies

Centre for Environment, Fisheries and Aquaculture Science:
   http://www.cefas.co.uk/homepage.htm
Central Science Laboratory: http://www.csl.gov.uk
Food Standards Agency: http://www.food.gov.uk
The Intervention Board – replaced by Rural Payments Agency
Pesticides Safety Directorate: http://www.pesticides.gov.uk
Rural Payments Agency: http://www.rpa.gov.uk
Veterinary Laboratories Agency: http://www.defra.gov.uk/corporate/vla/
   default.htm
Veterinary Medicines Directorate: http://www.vmd.gov.uk

Ministry of Defence (MoD)

http://www.mod.uk

Agencies

Army Training and Recruiting Agency: http://www.atr.mod.uk
British Forces Post Office Agency: http://www.bfpo.org.uk
Defence Analytical Services Agency (DASA): http://www.dasa.mod.uk
Defence Aviation Repair Agency: http://www.dara.mod.uk
Defence Bills Agency: http://www.defencebills.gov.uk
Defence Storage and Distribution Agency: http://www.dsda.org.uk
Defence Estates: http://www.defence-estates.mod.uk
Defence Diversification Agency: http://www.dda.gov.uk
Defence Evaluation and Research Agency – from 2 July 2001, DERA has
    separated into two organizations:
        Defence Vetting Agency, QinwriQ – launched on 1 July 2001 following its
            official vesting as a public limited company from the larger part of the
            government's Defence Evaluation Agency.
        Defence Science and Technology Laboratory (DSTL) – an agency of the UK
            MoD: http://www.dsti.gov.uk/index.htm
Defence Procurement Agency (DPA): http://www.mod.uk/dpa
United Kingdom Hydrographic Office: http://www.ukhs.gov.uk
Warship Support Agency: http://www.mod.uk/wsa/
Veterans Agency: http://www.veteransagency.mod.uk
Northern Ireland Office: http://www.nio.gov.uk
The Scotland Office: http://www.scottishsecretary.gov.uk

Other government departments

Board of Inland Revenue: http://www.inlandrevenue.gov.uk

Agencies

The Valuation Office: http://www.vao.gov.uk

Central Office of Information (COI): http://www.coi.gov.uk
Export Credit Guarantee Department: http://www.ecgd.gov.uk
Forestry Commission: http://www.forestry.gov.uk
Government Actuary's Department: http://gad.gov.uk
HM Customs and Excise: http://www.hmce.gov.uk
HM Land Registry: http://www.landreg.gov.uk
Office of the E-Envoy: http://www.e-envoy.gov.uk
Office of Fair Trading: http://www.oft.gov.uk
Office of Gas and Electricity Markers (OFGEM): http://www.ofgem.gov.uk

Office for National Statistics (ONS): http://www.statistics.gov.uk
Office for Standards in Education (Ofsted): http://www.ofsted.gov.uk
Office of Telecommunications (Oftel): http://www.oftel.gov.uk
Office of Water Services (Ofwat): http://www.ofwat.gov.uk/index.htm
Ordnance Survey: http://www.ordsvy.gov.uk
Serious Fraud Office: http://www.sfo.gov.uk
Treasury Solicitor's Department: http://www.treasury-solicitor.gov.uk/
    tsdhome.htm

Parliamentary

House of Commons: http://www.parliament.uk/about/_commons/
    about_commons.ctm
Hansard – House of Commons: http://www.parliament.the-stationery-
    office.co.uk/pa/ld/hansard.htm
House of Lords: http://www.parliament.uk/about_lords/about_lords.ctm
Hansard – House of Lords: http://www.parliament.the-stationery-office.co.uk/
    pa/ld/hansard/htm

APPENDIX 2: SOME ORGANIZATIONS CONCERNED WITH RESEARCH IN UNIVERSITIES

Academic–Industry Network
http://www.acindus.net
AIRTO
Applied Industrial Research Trading Organization
http://www.airto.org
(formerly the Association of Independent Research and Technology
  Organizations)
AMRC
Association of Medical Research Charities
http://www.amrc.org.uk
AUA
Association of University Administrators
http://www.aua.ac.uk
AURIL
Association for University Research and Industry Links
http://www.auril.org.uk
AUTM (US)
Association of University Technology Managers
http://www.autm.net/index_n4.html
CBI
Confederation of British Industry
http://www.ebi.org.uk
CEST
Centre for Science and Technology Studies
(Berne, Switzerland)
http://www.cest.ch
CIPA
Chartered Institute of Patent Agents
http://www.cipa.org.uk

EARMA
European Association of Research Managers and Administrators
http://www.cineca.it/earma
FORESIGHT
http://www.foresight.gov.uk
Funding for Young European Researchers
http://www.cordis.lu/improving/opportunities
House of Commons Select Committee on Science and Technology
http://www.parliament.the-stationery-office.co.uk
House of Lords Committee on Science and Technology
http://www.parliament.the-stationery-office.co.uk
ICARG
Inter-company Academic Relations Group (A working group of the CBI's
    Technology & Innovation Committee)
http://www.cbi.org.uk
IP
Intellectual Property
http://www.intellectual-property.gov.uk
IPLA
Intellectual Property Lawyers Association
http://www.ipla.org.uk
LES (Britain and Ireland)
Licensing Executives Society
http://les-europe.org
LESI
Licensing Executives Society International
http://www.les:-org
NCURA (US)
National Council of University Research Administrators
http://www.ncura.edu
OECD
Organization for Economic Cooperation and Development
http://www.oecd.org
(see particularly IMHE – the Management in Higher Education programme)
OST
Office of Science and Technology
http://www.ost.gov.uk
POST
Parliamentary Office of Science and Technology
http://www.parliament.uk/post
PREST
Policy Research in Engineering Science and Technology,
University of Manchester
http://lcs.man.ac.uk/PREST
PSC
The Parliamentary and Scientific Committee
http://www.pandsctte.demon.co.uk

RAGnet
Research Administrators' Group Network
http://www.ragnet.ac.uk
The R&D Society
http://www.rdsoc.org
Researchers Forum Website (UK government)
http://www.researchersforum.gov.uk
RS
The Royal Society
http://www.royalsociety.ac.uk
SPRU
Science Policy/Technology Management
(University of Sussex)
http://www.sussex.ac.uk/spru
TTI
Technology Innovation Information
http://www.tii-org
UACE
Universities Association for Continuing Education
http://www.uace.org.uk
UKBI
UK Business Incubations
http://www.ukbi.com
UKSPA
UK Science Park Association
http://www.ukspa.org.uk
UNICO
The UK University Companies Association
http://www.unico.org.uk

BIBLIOGRAPHY

Allen, M. (1988) *The Goals of Universities*. Buckingham: Open University Press.

Association for University Research and Industry Links (AURIL) Confederation of British Industry (CBI) (1997) *Research Partnerships Between Industry and Universities: A Guide to Better Practice*. London: AURIL/CBI.

Association for University Research and Industry Links (AURIL) Confederation of British Industry (CBI) (2001) *Working in Partnership Guide to Better Practice*. London: AURIL.

Association for University Research and Industry Links (AURIL) Universities UK (UUK) Patent Office (2002) *Managing Intellectual Property: A Guide to Strategic Decision Making in Universities*. London: AURIL.

Atkinson, H., Bond, R. and Mullins, P. (1992) *An Anatomy of Research Personnel in UK Universities*. London: Science and Engineering Research Council.

Bacon, F. ([1597] 1962) *The Advancement of Learning* (G.W. Kitchin ed.). London: Dent.

Bacon, F. ([1597] 1884) *The Essays*. London: George Routledge and Sons.

Becher, T. (1989) *Academic Tribes and Territories: Intellectual Enquiry and the Cultures of Disciplines*. Buckingham: Open University Press.

British Council (1996) *A Guide to the Organisation of Science and Technology in Britain*, 4th edn (prepared by Dr Paul Cunningham and Sue Hinder, Policy Research in Engineering, Science and Technology). Middlesbrough: ICI.

BTG (British Technology Group) (1997) *Keeping a Laboratory Notebook*. London: BTG Marketing Group. www.btgplc.com

Cheese, J. (1990) *Attitudes to the Exploitation of Science and Technology Final Report – Centre for Exploitation of Science and Technology (CEST)*. Manchester: CEST.

Clark, R.W. (1962) *The Rise of the Boffins*. London: Phoenix House.

Clark, R.W. (1971) *Sir Edward Appleton*. Oxford: Pergamon Press.

CVCP (Committee of Vice-Chancellors and Principals) (1988) *Costing of Research and Projects in the UK Universities* (Hanham Report). London: CVCP.

CVCP (Committee of Vice-Chancellors and Principals) (1992) *Sponsored University Research: Recommendations and Guidance on Contract Issues*. London: CVCP.

Crowther, J.G. and Whiddington, R. (1947) *Science at War*. London: HMSO.

Davidson, Ann (1989) *Grants from Europe*, 5th edn. London: Bedford Square Press.

Dearing, Sir Ron (1997) *Higher Education in the Learning Society*. London: The Stationery Office.

DfES (Department for Education and Skills) (2000) *Opportunity for All in a World of Change*. London: The Stationery Office.

DTI (Department of Trade and Industry) (1989a) *Policy and Strategy for Higher Education*. London: HMSO.

DTI (Department of Trade and Industry) (1989b) *Organisation and Management in Higher Education*. London: HMSO.

DTI (Department of Trade and Industry) (1989c) *Research and Development*. London: HMSO.

DTI (Department of Trade and Industry) (1996) *Industry–University Co-operation Survey 1996*. London: DTI.

DTI (Department of Trade and Industry) (1999) *Our Competitive Future – Building the Knowledge Driven Economy*. London: DTI.

DTI (Department of Trade and Industry) (2000) *Working with Foresight*. London: DTI.

DTI (Department of Trade and Industry) (2001a) *Science and Innovation Strategy 2001*. London: The Stationery Office.

DTI (Department of Trade and Industry) (2001b) *Excellence and Opportunity: A Science and Innovation Policy for the 21st Century*. London: DTI.

Drucker, P.F. (1985) *Innovation and Entrepreneurship: Practice and Principles*. New York: Harper & Row.

EPSRC (Engineering and Physical Sciences Research Council) (1997) *Joint EPSRC/University Exploitation Audit Pilot Exercise: Research Exploitation Audit Process (REAP) Report – People, Partnership and Programmes*, February 1997. London: EPSRC.

Harris, M. (1996) *Report on the Review of Postgraduate Education*. London: HEFCE.

HEFCE (Higher Education Funding Council for England) (1996) *Review of Postgraduate Education*. London: HEFCE.

HEFCE (Higher Education Funding Council for England) (2001) *HEFCE Review of Research Policy and Funding*. London: HEFCE.

HEFCE (Higher Education Funding Council for England) (2002) *Research Relationships Between Higher Education Institutes and the Charitable Sector: Policy Report*. London: HEFCE.

HEFCE/CVCP/SCOP (Higher Education Funding Council for England/Committee of Vice-Chancellors and Principals/Standing Conference of Principals) (1996) *Review of Postgraduate Education*. London: HEFCE.

HEFCE (Higher Education Funding Council for England) (1999) *RAE 2001: Assessment Panel's Criteria and Marking Methods*. London: HEFCE.

HESA (Higher Education Statistics Agency) (2000) *Resources for Higher Education Institutions 1998/99*. London: HESA.

Hill, C. ([1965] 1972) *Intellectual Origins of the English Revolution*. London: Panther.

Institute of Economic Affairs Education Unit (IEA) (1989) *The Funding of Research*. London: IEA.

IER/SHEFC (Institute for Employment Research/Scottish Higher Education Funding Council) (2001) *Academic Research Careers in Scotland: A Longitudinal Study of Academic Contract Research Staff, their Jobs and Career Patterns*. Scotland: IER/SHEFC.

Ives, E., Drummond, D. and Schwarz, L. (2000) *The First Civic University: Birmingham 1880–1980: An Introductory History*. Birmingham: University of Birmingham Press.

JCPSG (Joint Costing and Pricing Steering Group) (1998) *Costing, Pricing and Valuing Research and Other Projects: Report and Recommendations to Universities*, March 1998. London: CVCP.

JCPSG (Joint Costing and Pricing Steering Group) (1999) *Transparency Review of Research: Proposals for a New Uniform Approach to Costing of Research and Other Activities in Universities and Colleges in Higher Education*. Report to the Science and Engineering Board Co-ordinating Committee. www.jcpsg.ac.uk

Jones, G.R. (1998) *Cyber Schools: An Education Renaissance*. Englewood, CO: Jones Digital Century.

Juran, J.M. and Gryna, F.M. (1993) *Quality Planning and Analysis*. New York: McGraw-Hill.

Konecny, E., Quinn, C.P., Sachs, K. and Thompson, O.T. (1995) *Universities and Industrial Research*. London: Royal Society of Chemistry.

KPMG (1996) *Management Information for Decision Making: Costing Guidelines for Higher Education Institutions*. London: HEFCE.

McClintock, M. (1993) *Supporting Research*, General Practice Series no. 14. Manchester: Association of University Administrators.

Melville, Sir Harry (1962) *The Department of Scientific and Industrial Research*, The New Whitehall Series no. 9. London: George Allen & Unwin.

Musson, A.E. (ed) (1972) *Science, Technology and Economic Growth in the Eighteenth Century*. London: Methuen.

National Commission on Education (1994) *Universities in the Twenty-first Century: A Lecture Series*. London: Paul Hamlyn Foundation/Council for Industry and Higher Education.

OECD (Organization of Economic Co-operation and Development) (1998) *STI: University Research in Transition*. Paris: OECD.

OST (Office of Science and Technology) (1993) *Realising our Potential: A Strategy for Science, Engineering and Technology*, Cm 2250, May 1993. London: HMSO.

OST (Office of Science and Technology) (1995) *Technology Foresight: Progress Through Partnerships: Reports 1 to 15*. London: HMSO.

OST (Office of Science and Technology) (2000) *Excellence and Opportunity – A Science and Innovation Policy for the 21st Century*. London: DTI.

OST (Office of Science and Technology) (2001a) *Science Research Priorities 2001–02 to 2002–04*. London: DTI.

OST (Office of Science and Technology) (2001b) *The Forward Look*, Cm 5338, December 2001 (published annually since 1994). London: The Stationery Office.

OST/DTI (Office of Science and Technology/Department of Trade and Industry) (2001) *Quinquennial Review of the Grant Awarding Research Councils*. Report by the Review Team, Stage One and Two. London: The Stationery Office.

OST (Office of Science and Technology)/Universities UK (1997) *Contract Research Staff: Good Management Practice*. Sheffield: University of Sheffield. www.staff.ac.uk/~gmpcrs

OST (Office of Science and Technology)/Universities UK (1998) *Employing Contract Researchers: A Guide to Best Practice*. London: The Stationery Office.

Peters, T. (1987) *Thriving on Chaos: Handbook for a Management Revolution*. London: Pan.

Peters, T. and Austin, N. (1986) *A Passion for Excellence: The Leadership Difference*. London: Fontana.

Policy Research in Engineering Science and Technology (PREST) (1998) *Industry–Academic Links in the UK*. Manchester: PREST.

Roberts, M. (2001) *Adding Advantage: The Regional Contribution of Higher Education in the West Midlands*, April 2001. Birmingham: West Midlands Higher Education Association.

United States Congress (1994) *Unlocking our Future: Towards a New National Scientific Policy*, September 1994. Washington.

Universities United Kingdom (UUK)/Higher Education Funding Council for England (HEFCE) (2001) *The Regional Mission: The Regional Contribution of Higher Education – The National Report*. London: UUK.

Wellcome Trust (2000) *Guidelines on Good Research Practice*. London: Wellcome Trust.

Whiston, T.G. and Geiger, R.L. (eds) (1992) *Research and Higher Education: The United Kingdom and the United States*. Buckingham: Open University Press.

Whitchurch, C. and Mackie, D. (eds) (1994) *Planning for Performance: Research Contexts and Directions for Universities in the 1990s*. Manchester: Association of University Administrators.

Wright, P.W.G. (1990) *Industry and Higher Education*. Buckingham: Open University Press.

Ziman, J. (1989) *Restructuring Academic Science: A New Framework for UK Policy*, Paper No. 8. London: Science Policy Support Group.

INDEX